Semiotics and the Analysis of Film

JEAN MITRY

Translated by CHRISTOPHER KING

THE ATHLONE PRESS
LONDON

First published in the United Kingdom 2000 by
THE ATHLONE PRESS
1 Park Drive, London NW11 7SG

This English Translation © 2000 The Athlone Press

Originally published as *La Sémiologie en Question*
© 1987 Les Editions du Cerf

Publishers' note:
The publishers wish to record their thanks to the
French Ministry of Culture for a grant towards the cost
of translation.

British Library Cataloguing-in-Publication Data
*A catalogue record for this book is available from The
British Library*

ISBN 0 485 11532 8 HB
0 485 12151 4 PB

Typeset by Acorn Bookwork, Salisbury, Wiltshire
Printed and bound in Great Britain by
Cambridge University Press

Contents

List of Illustrations

Preface

From the moment critics started to theorise about the cinema, they were concerned not just with a new means of expression, but with a kind of language capable of signifying ideas and feelings where the meaning depended on editing, the types of shot and their relationships, as much as on the objects represented in them. Yet they were using the term language in a purely metaphorical sense. It was during the 1950s, however, following some socio-psychological work and research at the Institut de Filmologie that the idea of language was considered in an objective and concrete fashion – only to be refuted immediately by certain theoreticians, notably Gilbert Cohen-Séat[1].

In responding to his objections, I believe I was one of the first to argue that the cinema is effectively a *language*. I wrote at the time:

It will perhaps be argued that film is a form of writing rather than a language, since the image which shows things without naming them has no phonetic equivalent. Clearly, the cinema could never be a *language* if language is meant in the sense of a means by which exchanges of conversation take place. Yet, if the images are used not as a simple photographic reproduction but as a means of expressing ideas through an association of logical and meaningful relationships, then clearly it is a *language*. A *language* in which the image fulfils the roles equally of verb and subject, noun and predicate through its symbol structure and potential qualities as a sign. A *language* through which the equivalent of the data of the perceptible world is provided, not via more or less standard abstract forms but through the *reproduction of concrete reality*. Thus reality is not being "represented" by some graphic or symbolic substitute. It is *presented as an image* and this image is what is used to signify. Trapped in a new dialectic for which it provides the actual form, it serves as an element of its own *narration*[2].

In 1963, when I was writing the above, I had not previously considered the relationship between the cinema and linguistics for the simple reason that I believed them to be separate from each other. The following year, however, a young semiologist Christian Metz gave me a manuscript entitled "Le cinéma, langue ou langage?" [The cinema: language or language system][3]. I was impressed by the seriousness and depth of this work basing itself on linguistics in order to study in detail the signifying structures of film and applying a much more precise terminology than usual, film criticism deriving mostly from theatre and stage convention.

However, it seemed to me that Christian Metz had a tendency in his research to take linguistics as a model rather than a simple reference, assuming that verbal and film expressions were comparable, capable at the very least of being associated in an all-encompassing structuralism.

This considerable work – which it subsequently became – seemed to me to be on the wrong track. However great my admiration, I had no hesitation in telling him so, his error being based, it seemed to me, on irrelevant linguistic considerations.

The fact remains that, from 1966 onwards, the theories of Christian Metz and his imitators enjoyed a success which cannot be adequately explained merely by the scientific nature of semiology. Also, in response to the unexpected proliferation of courses in this discipline in universities recently devoted to cinema studies, I had intended to write a book entitled "Le mot et l'image" [The word and the image] (already announced in the press), in order to point out how and why this type of research was unproductive and to give a warning to the many teachers who, better qualified in linguistics than the cinema, were wandering blindly through the minefield of structuralism as they applied it to motion pictures.

However, I had already undertaken a history of the cinema and even with the five volumes so far published I could see no end in sight. Which is why I started to publish a series of articles in *Cinématographe* which scratch the surface of these questions. Reworked in greater detail, these articles form the basis of the present book, which is not intended to be exhaustive, merely a simple adumbration of my position and my caution with regard to film semiology – such as it is interpreted by linguists.

Now that the excitement about semiology has died down, it has become less a question of putting up a defence against it (certain aspects of it have been particularly rewarding) than of explaining why it has generally fallen short of the mark.

It was not my intention to direct my remarks to a small coterie of linguistic or semiological specialists or exclusively to film critics, but as far as possible to the maximum number of lovers of the cinema interested in film theory. At the same time, although the teaching of cinema studies is becoming more widespread, as much in secondary schools as in universities, it may be that many students will find themselves ill-prepared to read a book like this.

This is why, following the suggestion of my editors and seeing the value of their argument, I have prefaced the main body of this book with some preliminary thoughts intended to put the newcomer in the picture. There is no need to explain words which have passed into common usage such as *shot, sequence, angle, reverse-angle* and others. The emphasis is less on techniques than on their application and their consequent meaning, and, in particular, certain ideas relating to "film language", to linguistic structures and semiology. The reader familiar with this terminology will be able to "skip" directly to the first chapter without missing anything.

(n.b. Because this book is a digest of a series of articles, it should come as no surprise to find certain repetitions, which I have chosen to leave as they are, since occasionally the same subjects are considered from different angles.)

I

Preliminaries

No one could have imagined at the start of the cinema that it could become an art, or an industry. Or, indeed, a kind of language, a "visual event" loaded with meaning.

Before we move on to the first theories or principles, we should first of all remind ourselves briefly how the cinema became the art-form we are pleased to recognise in it.

Before 1908

As we all know, the first public showing of the "Lumière Cinematograph" took place in the Indian room under the Grand Café on the 28th of December 1895.

At that time, the cinema was just a machine for recording and reproducing movement – remarkable in itself, since it was the first time this had been achieved. A spectacle equally novel in being projected on a screen instead of in a theatre.

However, it is worthy of note that *L'Arrivée d'un train en gare de la Ciotat, La sortie du port, Le goûter de bébé* are already instinctively "cinematic". Not only are the scenes shot "from life", but the train which first appears in the background thunders straight into the lens; the embarkation is seen from the top of the pier; and Mme Lumière feeding her baby is framed from waist up in a shot similar to what would be called later on the "American shot" [translator's note: a term coined by French critics to describe a mid-shot wide enough to include cowboys' holsters in American Westerns]. The view-point is that of an observer seeing things from the best angle and on an appropriate axis. *From the word go, the narrow confines of stage representation were broken.* Space took the place of the stage. The only limits were those of the edges of the image – which appeared as a kind of window on the world.

Indeed, the direct possibilities of the camera, and the advantages of being able to move it, were discovered very quickly. The first film-makers were not men of the theatre deferring to preestablished aesthetic dogma, but simple photographers using the tool as any amateur might use his box Brownie.

From 1896 onwards, Alexander Promio, Felix Mesguich and Francis Doublier, who made many long foreign trips to show off the Lumière Cinematograph, brought back "views" from all four corners of the globe. It was then that Promio on holiday in Italy had the idea of putting his camera in a gondola. The camera set-up was "fixed" (as it always was up until 1909), but the movement of the gondola allowed him to film wide panoramic views such that *The Grand Canal in Venice* (1897) was the first ever "tracking-shot". Inspired by his discovery, Promio subsequently attached his camera to several different moving platforms, such as a railway wagon, the bridge of a transatlantic boat and the MontBlanc cable-car.

In his own way the illusionist Georges Méliès, thinking that the Lumière brothers' camera gave him the opportunity to record and broadcast the magic shows which until then he had put on at the Robert-Houdin theatre, was the first to conceive of the cinema as a show, the first therefore to introduce the idea of "mise-en-scène" [translator's note: directing or, literally, putting on stage].

Whereas Lumière, capturing "nature in the raw" and preserving its authenticity, was content to record it literally, Méliès was the first to create an original spectacle with the aid of the cinema. Though he was filming scenes prerehearsed with theatrical technique, he introduced new illusions with which camera technique supplemented the deficiencies of the stage. And these techniques, though they may be seen as those of an illusionist rather than the elements of a language still to be developed, were discovered and exploited by Méliès with matchless control.

What makes his art fundamentally theatrical is less the arrangement of the sets or painted backings and the quality of acting than the *constant unity of the point of view*: the camera, rigidly set before a uniform theatrical space, presents, always in the same way, the spectacle occurring in front of it, rather than revealing it or finding it wherever it should be occurring.

As André Malraux observed:

as long as the cinema was used merely as a means of reproducing movement, it was no more art than photographic repro-

duction. In a circumscribed space – generally an actual or imaginary stage – the actors played out a dramatic or comical scene
which the camera did no more than record. The birth of the
cinema as a means of expression (rather than reproduction)
coincides with the destruction of this *circumscribed space*); from
the moment the film-maker imagined his story divided into
separate shots, he had in mind, not the photographic reproduction of a play, but the recording of a sequence of individual
moments, the movement of the camera to and from the characters on the screen (thereby making them bigger or smaller
when required), but more particularly of replacing the theatrical
stage with a "field of view", a space limited by the screen – an
area where the actor comes in and goes out which the film-
maker chooses, instead of being a prisoner of it[1].

In the meantime, Méliès' "field of view" was that of the theatrical space and his limits of the screen those of the wings of the
stage. His various locations may be different, but one by one they
become overlapped in the same container, presented as a series of
theatrical "tableaux" for a spectator sitting in his seat seeing
events from the same point of view.

Clearly, there is a narrative continuity, a chronology between
each of these tableaux, but as these follow on from each other
there is always an "interruption", just as there is between one act
and another on the stage – except that, because the scenes are
joined end to end, the curtain or "scene change" is replaced with
an instant transition from one tableau to the next. Yet this instan-
taneousness is not applied to the continuity of the movement, or
the action – or indeed the time. Time, movement and action are
presented in small *discontinuous* bits, like successive jumps.

Filmed from an unchanging point of view, these are identical
spaces (however different their content may be) following each
other in identical time sequences. The discontinuity of the
tableaux is emphasised by the *absence of any movement in their
space and time*, more than by an absence of any linking mechanism.

The absence of linking mechanism – in itself the consequence of
an absence of space-time mobility – produces "repetitions" or
distortions when the intention (as sometimes happens) is to
present – consistently from the same view-point, in the same axis
and at the same distance – different aspects of the same action.

Thus, in *Le voyage à travers l'impossible*, Professor Mabouloff's car travels across (a model of) the mountains of Switzerland. Suddenly it starts down a very steep slope. Right at the bottom, Mabouloff misses a corner and crashes into an inn, knocking down its walls. End of the tableau.

In the next tableau, we are inside the same inn. Naturally, none of the above has happened yet. Diners are sat at their tables, merrily chatting away. Suddenly, to everyone's great alarm, the car smashes through the walls of the dining-room and knocks over the serving-table.

Later on, editing will enable the event to be seen from two different points of view, but within the same unity of movement, since the possibility of seeing events simultaneously is limited by the universality of the view-point. Here the discontinuity is more marked because the same time is divided up by having to be split into successive tableaux.

As for the set design, any props which do not actually "feature" are painted on canvas and depth is created by a forced perspective. The vanishing-points all relate to a single point of view, which is that of the camera placed just outside and in the centre of the set – the same as that of a spectator sitting in the front row of the stalls, immediately behind the orchestra pit.

This unity of place of observation is what Sadoul and I termed the "point of view of someone sitting in the stalls", any change of view-point requiring the *observer to move relative to the observed object* rather than the set to change in front of the stationary spectator.

The recent discovery of a collection of short films made before 1906 has given rise to arguments about the origins of editing and shot variation, along the lines that what was discovered between 1901 and 1903 ought to have put an end to film-making in "discontinuous tableaux", which in fact continued nearly to the end of 1906. This is how Pierre Jenn claims to prove the "variety of points of view in Méliès' films" with the explanation that, from one tableau to the next, the sets reveal different aspects of the same objects. Now the camera in Méliès' films – as in Zecca's and many others beside – remained static. And yet we must be careful not to confuse the "world changing in front of the camera"[2] with the camera moving in the world (change of point of view and shot).

On the other hand, the description of these films as "filmed theatre" is completely wrong, since neither Méliès nor Zecca, when they were shooting their little fairy-tales or comic sketches, were adapting from the theatre – especially since the theatre is the art of speech and their films were silent. Méliès would never have been able to produce on stage what he created with the camera. At the level of the image his films were already pure cinema, but his direction or mise-en-scène (and that of others) was as though for the stage. Instead of "filmed theatre" we should refer to it as stage directing, in contrast to film directing whose beginnings were marked in 1903 in a rather remarkable way by Edwin Porter's *The Great Train Robbery*.

It is no exaggeration to say that, if the first directors were limited by the confines of the painted set, it is because they were ignorant of the capabilities of the cinema. Even the earliest films of some of them – notably the Englishman George Albert Smith and the American Edwin Porter – show evidence of the art of editing, indeed almost of the seventh art. Smith's 1902 film *Mary Jane's Mishap* contains some very precise action cuts outstanding for its time.

As unlikely as this may seem, between 1901 and 1902, when Edwin Porter was filming his documentaries – his "panoramic views" – he included panning shots over the natural settings and even the odd reverse-angle. However, when he came to shoot his "fictions", like *Uncle Tom's Cabin*, he returned to the conventions of the stage with the painted back-cloth and trompe-l'oeil sets.

This tug-of-war between reality and the stage is characteristic of the earliest days of the cinema. The reason for it was not technical but, curiously, psychological. It was not the film-makers who insisted on remaining on the theatrical treadmill, but the public who imposed it. Used to stage representation, the public found it hard to understand – or accept – that a fictional story or drama could be represented in any other way. The directors were therefore forced back to "tableaux". Not only were the actor's movements not continued from one tableau to the next, but the unity of view-point meant that the set had to be shot *head-on*, involving inevitable repetitions and constant overlaps. The strangest of all was that it was perfectly acceptable to have a variety of images – or *shots* as they soon became called – when it came to documentary "views" – doubtless because it was a "real" world being represented where it was possible to move about. It then became quite natural to create an impression of reality by having various different points of view recorded by the camera. Yet, when it came to "drama", the public took a long time to accept that the representation of a fictional world could conform to the data of "true" reality. Something which certain critics even nowadays find it hard to understand, if we take as an example Alain Masson's thesis on the subject in the review *Positif* (April 1985–July 1986). He writes:

> Audiences at the beginning of the century were no more stupid than they are today.[...] Suddenly confronted by horses with invisible legs, the audience of *The Adventures of Dollie* (Griffith, 1908) must have thought that, rather than legless monsters, what they were seeing were horses whose legs had not been filmed.

Obviously they understood they were seeing horses, but they did not understand *why* the horses were being shown like that, nor why the action had been divided up into successive fragments.

An artificially composed world: *Great Expectations*, by David Lean, 1946.

Expressionism, reborn in 1943 in Carl Dreyer's *Day of Wrath.*

Particularly since in 1908 it was exactly as it had been between 1900 and 1908. Yet it must not be forgotten that the fact of telling a story with moving pictures did not exist before the cinema. Therefore known values had to be employed as reference, with the resulting application of theatrical forms to cinematic representations, since any new invention always creates scandal – and shock – upsetting habits, conventions and traditions.

1908–1918

While editing was being discovered in the U.S.A., European cinema, freed from the shackles of theatrical representation, developed under the heavy influence of painting. Because the theatre is verbal and the cinema silent, inspiration would be drawn from painting and not from the theatre. For the images to be meaningful, all that was needed was to ensure that they express everything the painting might express, any movement providing an added value.

Composing with images – that is, composing the *image* – with its internal structures, exploiting its surfaces, its lines and volumes, light and shade, with the symbolism of shapes and objects, this was the direction of the experimentation conducted by Danish film-makers heavily influenced by pictorial expressionism. Composing the image in fact consisted of composing artificially the world being presented.

Of course, it would have been perfectly possible to *organise* reality without recomposing it. The simple effect of placing a character or object relative to another, of structuring the content *relative to a frame* would have emphasised the objects shown by giving them a temporary meaning. It would have been possible to consider the world from a particular angle without necessarily altering it.

However, this would have required the use of lenses not developed at the time, providing the opportunity to play with perspective, introducing a greater variety of shot, a dependence on editing – considerations which were practically unknown in Europe.

An interpretation or stylisation of the world could only occur if it were recreated using the techniques of *design*. The camera recorded a pre-prepared, aesthetically developed universe full of *meaning*. A meaning, moreover, acquired from values outside those of the cinema.

Stage representation had been abandoned and replaced by the application, in a quite different but nonetheless definite sense, of the principles of stage-craft.

Given the intentions of the Danes, these aesthetic principles were justified. They allowed the surface values of direct reality to be transcended, to display a quasi-dream world, revealing "from within" its deepest meaning. A symbolic world whose meanings, assuming an exclusive importance, provided value for simple, intentionally melodramatic stories but through which the grossly magnified, "fantastical" reflection of genuine anxieties, real social problems or underlying truths could appear as though in miniature.

Developed during the period 1912–1915, these aesthetic principles gave rise to *German Expressionism* (1918–1925), which was one of the great strands of the cinematic art.

More symbolic than discursive, the signifying values of expressionism nevertheless had more to do with the expectations of psychoanalysis than with communication structures for which editing seemed to be the necessary basic principle.

Editing

In the primary sense of the word, editing consists of joining shots (or takes) end to end in the order required by the logic of the drama (story or narration). In this sense, editing is as old as cinema itself. It can also be used in the sense of joining together a series of cuts made to abbreviate a movement, change an action or link various sequences. But this sort of editing, practised mainly by Méliès at the beginning of the cinema in order to extract the maximum dynamism from within his "tableaux", derives from the area of trick effects of which he was the past master, rather than the foundation of *signifying relationships*. Meant in this sense – the only appropriate aesthetic meaning possible – editing consists in the *joining together of two or more shots such that their relationship determines a meaning belonging to neither of them separately*. But let us first examine how this came about.

As more and more importance was placed on films and a greater variety of shots and framings developed, it became clear that, while building the drama, the simple linkage of shots created arbitrary relationships between the represented objects by giving them an allusive or symbolic meaning. Among the directors who became involved in the research and experimentation developed from this discovery, the most influential was the American David Wark Griffith, whose universally appreciated work is analysed in every historical study of the cinema. It was he specifically who used editing to involve the spatial, rhythmic and discursive forms of the narrative.

1. By showing events, actions, characters, sometimes in close-up, sometimes from a distance, face on or in profile, from the back or in three-quarter profile, from below or above, film placed the audience *among* the characters of the drama, *within* the space of the drama. By seeing objects from different, interrelated points of view, the audience was observing those objects *as though actually moving around them*. In this way the impression of spatial reality was established.

2. By creating – through the intensity of the drama, through the various different points of view and framing – relationships of *duration* between the shots, editing imposed a *rhythm* specific to each film. Moreover, by manipulating time and the interrelated spaces, it allowed for all kinds of ellipses and abbreviations.

3. The association of shots implied, suggested an idea which, in linguistic terminology, might be called the "connoted signified" or *connotation*, the meaning of the objects shown being referred to as the *denoted* meaning.

Long before semiology ever entered the arena, it was said simply that "what matters is not the images but what exists *between* the images" (Abel Gance), or else that "the images signify less through what they show – whatever the signification of the objects represented – than by their ordering and less by that ordering than by their rhythmic and semantic relationships" (Jean Epstein).

Rhythm and signification

Refined, developed and extended by Griffith in *The Birth of a Nation*, the first master-piece of the world's cinema (1914), then in *Intolerance* (1916) – films which were not known in Europe until after the First World War – visual rhythm burst onto the screen with Abel Gance's *La Roue* in 1922.

Contrast cutting – the rich and the poor – in David W. Griffith's *The Speculators*, 1909.

Replacing painting, music then became the only valid reference, so much so that for several years all people could talk about was "visual music": "Would that film could be for the eye what music is for the ear", wrote one critic at the time, forgetting that these two organs have quite distinct sensory ranges. Which did not prevent a certain "avant-garde" from recognising the eventual possibilities of an entirely rhythmic cinema, dubbed, rightly or wrongly, "pure cinema"...

Over the same period, having also discovered rhythmic structures and cadences via Griffith's films, Soviet film-makers undertook research based on rhythm but, more particularly, on *relationships* for which they leaned heavily on dialectics and Marxism. The most outstanding discovery – purely accidental – derives from Kuleshov's experiments into acting: the arbitrary relationships between a subject "observing" and various different "observed" characters (supposed observing and observed) induced in the audience's mind various expected meanings. In other words, the audience bestowed on the "observer" ideas or feelings which it might or should have expressed about the observed facts consistent with an established socio-cultural logic. The quasi-linguistic nature of the cinema was thereby partly established.

First theories

Apart from any aesthetic considerations, more literary based
than scientific, such as those of Canudo, Delluc, L'Herbier and
the shrewd analyses of a previously unknown American psycholo-
gist Hugo Munsterberg, who associated film understanding with
the formal structures of Gestalt psychology, i.e. direct perceptual
understanding, the first genuinely scientific studies (at the level of
regular science) took shape with Kuleshov's experiments.

Jean Epstein was the first to emphasise the importance and
significance of the *close-up*, particularly the close-up of objects; the
meaning and conditions of rhythmic editing; the symbolism of
objects, signifying values still generally considered and designated
– following the lead of Delluc and Canudo – by the vague term
photogenics:

> I describe as photogenic any aspect of objects, beings or souls
> which increases its moral quality through its cinematic repro-
> duction. [...] The photogenic aspect of an object is the effect of
> its variations in space and time[3].

Though not exactly a code, Eisenstein had in mind a kind of
cine-dialectic in which editing played a vital part. He writes:

> The shot is by no means an *element* of montage [translator's
> note: the French term montage covers the general principle of
> editing, and Eisenstein's more specific application]. The shot is
> a montage *cell*. Just as cells in their division form a phenomenon
> of another order, the organism or embryo, so, on the other side
> of the dialectical leap from the shot, there is montage. [Pudov-
> kin] loudly defends an understanding of montage as a *linkage* of
> pieces. Into a chain. Again "bricks". Bricks, arranged in series
> to *expound* an idea. I confronted him with my viewpoint on
> montage as a *collision*. A view that from the collision of two
> factors *arises* a concept.

From my point of view linkage is merely a possible *special* case.
Eisenstein goes on:

> If montage is to be compared with anything, then a phalanx of

montage pieces, of shots should be compared to the series of explosions in an internal combustion engine, driving forward its automobile or tractor: for, similarly, the dynamics of montage serves impulses driving forward the total film[4].

For Eisenstein, then, meaning depends on the conflict between associated elements rather than an idea initiated by a narrative sequence. However, the signified becomes a signifier within a continuity which, like any other, is a *development* (ideological, factual, dramatic, etc.), but a development which, instead of being *continuous*, based on the linearity of the narrative, is *discontinuous*, based on the collision of *almost simultaneous* elements creating ideas in the same way as a harmonic development. Yet apart from *real* simultaneity as in "depth of field" (which developed after Eisenstein's cinema), this simultaneity is inevitably altered in continuity, *signified* rather than represented. What follows – from the effect of the non-linearity of the development – is a broken, fragmented continuity, i.e. one in which fragmentation is *relied on* to produce the meaning.

In other words, in Pudovkin, the narrative continuity lends itself to montage and controls its effects, whereas in Eisenstein it is montage which constructs, controls a continuity which is both descriptive and discursive.

Believing in his turn that "montage only becomes constructive when it allows to be revealed what the images themselves do not show", Béla Balázs nevertheless endorsed the "intellectual montage" advocated by Eisenstein, which "resulted in hieroglyphs or ideograms needing to be decoded like a puzzle". He laid great store on the powers of the *close-up* and especially on the fact that *framing* effected a change to the relationship between the audience and the represented world. He wrote: The image is an interpretation, not a carbon copy. Nothing is more subjective that a lens[5]...

Rudolf Arnheim, a disciple of Köhler and Wertheimer (the founders of Gestalt and the "psychology of form" in 1912–14) was the first theoretician of the cinema to establish the connections between film perception and gestalt structures. More conventionally than Béla Balázs, he underlined the differences brought out by film between reality and its image. However, his ideas, which were essentially based on the conditions of the silent cinema, eventually caused him to neglect and reject the talkies. As he wrote:

A mixture and not a synthesis of fundamental methods, the talkie will ultimately fail. It will then return the silent cinema to its former perfect purity[6].

An assertion yet to be proved and one which doubtless will never be proved.

For a whole decade, critics avoided any theorising, on the assumption that the first talkies precluded it. It was not until after the war that theoretical essays with any degree of consistency started to reappear, starting with Gilbert Cohen-Séat's *Essai sur les principles d'une philosophie du cinéma*. Making a distinction between the filmic (aesthetic expression) and the cinematic (technical process), in particular studying the forms of "film discourse", Cohen-Séat highlighted what was for him the basic difference between the verbal code and visual expression. Packed with interesting insights, his work is unfortunately rather neglected by modern critics, as is Albert Laffay's *Logique du cinéma* (1964), a collection of articles on reality, fantasy and the great themes of the silver screen, seen from a rather existentialist angle[7].

André Bazin on the other hand enjoys a universal reputation. Doubtless because he was the greatest critic of his generation and because, in that sense, his writings are of the greatest interest. Yet at the level of pure theory, his ideas are questionable. What is strange is that the critics whose ideology is the antithesis of Bazin's are those who praised him most vociferously.

Bazin adopts the exact opposite position to everything which was advanced, proposed and demonstrated before him and, again, after him. He accepts montage in the sense of means of construction but rejects the "arbitrary association of shots" as an inevitable "distortion of reality". Which is true. But art consists in transforming the world, not imitating it. And it is upon this reproduction – or reproductive faculty – in the cinema which Bazin concentrates in the name of transcendental realism which, associated with his theological convictions, brings him nearer the existential spiritualism of Gabriel Marcel or Emmanuel Mounier than the bergsonian idealism with which he has sometimes been associated.

With the rationale that the camera captures reality and avoids imbuing it with any *previous* ideological or cultural values, Bazin deduces that the "film image, the objective reproduction of objects, is the surest means of knowing true reality, reality before knowledge, "before perception", reality "in-itself"... For Bazin, the basis of cinematic expression is and could only be this "objective" reproduction of the world and its objects...

Bazin, admitting that the cinema is a language, refused to accept that the image may be reduced to a linguistic sign, i.e. through purely arbitrary symbols, to be merely the vehicle for concepts detached from concrete reality, whereas Christian Metz laid the foundations for "film semiology" by applying to the cinema the great building blocks of structural linguistics.

But what is semiology? What do these terms used in linguistics mean? After this short description of the steps by which film developed into a code, it is obviously time to explain this terminology for the benefit of the newcomer.

Word and image

Signification derives from psychology in that it associates an object, being or idea with a *sign* capable of evoking them. The notion of sign presupposes two different interpretations which often lead to confusion = *natural* signs and *artificial* signs. The latter are divided still further into *representation* signs, which reproduce the natural qualities of things, and *conventional* or arbitrary signs, which belong to a code.

Semiology (from the Greek *sêma*: sign) is the science devoted to the study of all sign systems – gestures, signals, symbols, etc. All signs include two values = a *signifier* (the sign itself) and a *signified*[8] (whatever this relates to). Natural signs are based on the relationship between a phenomenon and a common meaning generally justified by the qualities or inferences of that phenomenon. Thus dark clouds are the sign of rain, smoke the sign of fire, near or far.

The image reproducing a given reality – landscape, object or human-being – is the *direct sign* of what it shows, or a *formal* sign in that it is identical in form to what it reproduces. It may have a specific quality, but generally it signifies no more than is signified by what is represented. In these circumstances it is said to be "coextensive with the signified".

By contrast the *linguistic* sign is not a *duplicate*. It is fundamentally conventional, its own nature having nothing naturally in common with what it describes or signifies: "the word dog does not bite", as William James put it.

According to Saussure's definition, the linguistic sign – or word – is an arbitrary and unmotivated unit[9]. A double-headed unit in which the *signifier* is the oral statement and the *signified* a concept relating back to the concrete reference (the object being described). There is however an *inevitable* association between the sign and the signified (the *word* chair and the *idea* chair). It is the case that modern linguistics has tended to reject Saussure's bipolarity in favour of seeing the word as a global signifier relating both to a concrete (the object) and/or abstract (the concept) signified, the context making the distinction obvious during reading.

Though the word – or *moneme* – is indivisible as a unit of verbal signification, it is still made up of *phonemes*, sound units devoid of meaning, which may be loosely compared with syllables (except for phonological analysis). One of the essential qualities of language therefore is that it should have a *double articulation* = connecting the verbal units and connecting the phonetic components of the word inside it.

Semantics (from the Greek *sêmainô*: to signify) is the study of linguistic signification, i.e. the meaning of words, their *practically unchangeable lexical meaning and especially the associative relationships* between the signifier and signified. Signification at the level of semantics is created by speech. The word *dog* may conjure up faithfulness, the word *orient* the opulence of Babylon. As J.-A. Greimas points out, "the minimal structure of any signification is defined by the presentation of two terms and by the relationship uniting them". It is easy to see that this definition is applicable to montage.

The *syntagma* is a group of words with a single meaning placed between the word and the sentence. A short sentence such as *Peter is walking* is a syntagma. A slightly longer sentence may involve several syntagmas. In the cinema where a shot is the equivalent of one or more sentences, the syntagma is generally understood as a series of shots involving a global signification, or structure.

The fragmentation induced by semiology is of benefit in the study of film which until then had been divided into very short, indivisible segments – *shots* – and into parts – or *sequences*. However, it is of use only at the level of analysis. *Synecdoche* is a stylistic form which (in general) presents a part for the whole = a *sail* for a *ship*. In the cinema, it is the equivalent of a detailed close-up.

The image

When we refer to the *film image*, we mean a *moving image* and therefore a series of individual frames constituting a *shot*. Consequently, a shot or a film image means exactly the same thing, with this qualification that a shot may have a particular description (medium shot, close-up, long shot, etc.), whereas the image has a more general, more flexible meaning. There may be a shot of a particular kind, but always a *moving image*.

Not only is the *image* a complex signifier, it is always individualised, personalised, differentiated. The image is always of *that specific* dog, seen in *that specific* place, from *that specific* angle, never a dog *in general*. Any other image would show it in a different place or from a different angle, yet always within a space where certain elements would be included in the frame: the cinema contains no separate unit, no unitary, isolated signifier other than the close-up.

Christian Metz pointed out quite rightly that it is not possible to compare the form/content relationship with the signifier/signified relationship, and associate or identify form with signifier, content with signified[10]:

> In the inherent proposition that there is a kind of privileged kinship between, on the one hand, the effects of the signifier and the effects of the form and, on the other, the effects of the signified and the effects of the substance, there is the potential notion that the signifier has a form – or is a form? – where the signified could not have one; also that the signified has a substance – or is a substance? – where the signifier could not have one.

It is possible in fact to define the form and substance of signifier and signified by reducing them to the simple definitions below:

Form of the signifier: a series of perceptual patterns specific to a film; global structure of image and sound; organisation of their signifying relationships.

Substance of the signifier: "content-matter" of the image as the representation of concrete values; sound-track (speech, sounds, music).

Form of the signified: thematic structure; structure of the relationships of ideas or feelings; combination of the semantic elements of the film.

Substance of the signified: social content of the theme of the film; all the problems raised by the film, except for the specific form which the particular film gives these problems, i.e.:

Form of the content: style, expression, way in which the "story" (dramatic action, events described) is expressed, signified, formalised using the more or less "specific" techniques which distinguish this story from what it might have been had it been the subject of a novel or a play.

To study the form of a film is in fact to study the whole of the film by assuming as relevant an examination of its organisation, its structure: it is a structural analysis of the film, the structure being as much a structure of images and sounds (form of the signifier) as one of feelings and ideas (form of the signified).

On the other hand, when the "content" of a film is being studied, most frequently it is a study essentially concerned with the substance of the content alone: a more or less shapeless listing or description of the human or social problems raised by the film, as well as their intrinsic importance, with no serious study made of the specific form which the film under consideration gives to the problems. A genuine study of the content of a film would in fact be a study of the form of its content: unless the film is not what is being considered, but rather various more general problems for which the film is a point of departure, without its real content being in any way confused with them since this would be contained in the transformation coefficient imposed on these contents[11].

Film semiology: its reasons

For Ferdinand de Saussure, the study of linguistics was merely one area of semiology. Now, in the rearguard of the structuralists, most linguists came to regard semiology as nothing more than a sub-heading of linguistics, the notion of the sign being the essence of language. As a consequence of which it became more or less impossible to refer to semiology – even outside the realm of linguistics – without involving the structures of language.

Having followed the work undertaken by Christian Metz after his basic study, I wrote in 1965 in the second volume of my *Aesthetics*:

> It is impossible for there to be a film grammar, for the very good reason that all grammars are based on fixed values, on the unity and conventionality of signs. They can only govern modalities relating to these basic fixed values. Any attempt in this direction has ended in failure and indeed anyone who claims he can submit the cinema to the laws of grammar has a poor understanding of the expressive and semiotic conditions of motion pictures. Since it does not operate with previously established signs, the cinema does not presuppose any *a priori* grammatical rules. Even syntactical rules are unreliable. They may be applied to a particular aesthetic or stylistic principle, but never to the language of film as a whole.
>
> [...] This is why I have grave reservations about the possible syntax for the cinema to which Christian Metz apparently aspires, which, he says, "has yet to be drafted, entirely on syntactical rather than morphological foundations". Since the absence of genuine signs cancels out the need for morphology and, if all syntax is syntagmatic (to use Saussure's terminology), it does not seem possible to govern, with any degree of accuracy, structures which are self-governing through their content and motivated solely by the (infinitely variable) meaning they give to the objects they express[12].

Which was a response in some way to what I had already indicated two years previously, specifically that:

> These same ideas can [thus] be signified in many different ways; but none of them can be signified each time by the same images. *There is no link, no causal quality between signifier and signified –* otherwise the former very quickly becomes an abstract sign devoid of the living qualities indispensable to it.

It is a fact that from 1966 onwards – particularly after the events of 1968 – the theories of Christian Metz and his increasingly numerous disciples (Umberto Eco, Emilio Garroni, Pier Paolo Pasolini, Gianfranco Bettetini, in Italy; Roger Odin, Jacques Aumont, Michel Marie, Dominique Chateau, Michel Colin, in France; and others in the U.S.A. and Latin America) enjoyed an unexpected success.

All this happened at about the time cinema studies and mass communication courses started to be taught in universities. In 1968, those historians and theoreticians capable of running cinema courses at university level could be counted on the fingers of one hand (at the outside). For strictly administrative reasons, in the absence of "doctors of cinema", the majority of the teaching staff came from the literary disciplines where they had written their doctoral theses. And since those who were genuinely interested in the cinema confined their attention to pure stylistic or socio-cultural analyses, the arrival of semiology seemed like manna from heaven. As Roman Jakobson put it: "The cinema seems to me an especially important system of signs. I cannot imagine any semiotic study not involved with the cinema..."

The reaction was that any theory or consideration outside the remit of this discipline found itself rejected as being worthless and unproductive, and anything before it as old hat or uninteresting. Even now, in cinema studies based entirely on semiotics, eighty per cent of books quoted have a purely linguistic origin...

Moreover, the theoreticians of audiovisual communication thought it possible, using moving images – film or television – through an objectivity and precision beyond language – to convey messages and relationships of fact and yet avoid personal interpretation, or artistic judgment. With the proviso that precise meanings could be given to the ordering and relationship of images, in accordance with certain rules. Which is self-evidently wrong but provided them with the ephemeral vision of a possible solution through Metz' syntagmatic structures.

Clearly Christian Metz never had the intention of transforming the cinema into linguistics. Without ignoring the gulf between cinema and language, the purpose of his study was to see how and to what extent it was – or should be – possible to apply to the cinema a codifying system which would be, for film, the equivalent of grammar for language.

Even though he said from the outset: "Semiology can and must rely on linguistics, but it must not be confused with it"[13], his mistake – in my view – and that of all those semiologists who studied the question (Garroni, Eco, Pasolini and others) was to depart from linguistic models and look for analogies in different functions rather than start from scratch with an analysis of the smallest units of the film message and examine how they worked, ignoring any notion of code, grammar or syntax.

Christian Metz' work has enabled empirical methods to be replaced by a rational analysis, and has brought out the processes by which (or with which) a film creates meaning, has revealed how it functions. Yet though semiology is capable of saying *how something signifies*, it has no way of saying *why* it does so. In linguistics the question never arises, but in contrast with words, images are never created to signify. They contain a curious function which turns film into a sort of discourse whose structures, superficially similar to linguistic structures, are totally resistant to any rules of language.

Effective when it comes to analysing or "deconstructing" a film, semiology is of no use when it comes to drawing up laws, codifications and rules applicable to all films. Its systematisations are all *after the fact*. Metz must have accepted this when he declared at the colloquy on cinematic research in February 1977: "I believe that, as a school of thought, semiology has had its day. It may, and even should, retire [...]."

My work was deprecated by dogmatists who must have found it difficult to accept, but a certain panic set in amongst the ranks of the high-priests blinkered by their "established" convictions. After the doubts, the first attacks were mounted. Twenty years after the event came the revelation that the visual and verbal had no point of comparison and that it had been a fundamental error to turn linguistics into the model for all semiology. As G. Deledalle wrote:

> It is understood that the notion of sign limited to linguistic sign may be appropriate for textual semiology but is unsuitable, or at least is not the most suitable for a description of non-linguistic signs, such as a film or any other system based on iconography[14].

Following an article by the critic Raymond Durgnat published in May 1980 in the review *Cinéaste* and entitled "The death of

Semiology", the English film-maker Lindsay Anderson wrote in
The Guardian in March 1981:

> The comparison of film with language and the attempt to
> examine and interpret a work of art using methods borrowed
> from linguistic analysis, are associated with a tendency originat-
> ing as so often in France, which tries to examine the work of art
> from a scientific and logical point of view [...], by trying to
> replace a simple affinity with a Rule, intuition with a Law. [...]
> The structuralist movement in film criticism is harmful [...]
> because it tries to replace interpretation, research into meaning
> and human behaviour, with stylistic analysis.

Then the philosopher Gilles Deleuze, before publishing his
remarkable work *L'Image-Mouvement*, said this in an interview:

> The attempts to apply linguistics to the cinema are disastrous
> [...]. Any reference to a linguistic model always ends up
> proving that the cinema is something else and that, if it is a lan-
> guage, it is analogical or one of modulation. Which leads to the
> conclusion that any reference to the linguistic model is a detour
> to be avoided[15].

However, whereas Christian Metz abandoned structural semiology to pursue a more productive study into psychoanalysis, several
of his acolytes believed that if the taxinomic models proved ineffective it was because they had been applied too "rigorously". The
models deriving from transformational grammar seemed to them
more suitable or more promising. In this regard the work of
people such as Dominique Chateau is not without interest. And
Chomsky's operational transformations are centered on a syntactical system involving their genesis, whereas film significations are
not subject to any limiting function other than the concrete facts
which they reveal.

The product of various different associations, symbolic or other
deal evolved from logic, psychology or psychoanalysis, film signification lies beyond the scope of linguistics or at least its rules – and
the laws of Hjelmslev's structuralism, Chomsky's generative
grammar and Greimas' semantics cannot be applied to it either.

I felt it appropriate to provide a few reasons for this. Which is why, in spite of the editing of the *Histoire du cinéma* (which I thought I might complete much sooner) – and though the semiological frenzy has somewhat abated – I thought I might point out the essential argument in the present modest book. The reader should not expect an exhaustive study here, instead more general considerations concerning a semiology beyond linguistics, for which language, though not a model, remains a basic term of comparison – an "open" semiology, i.e. one without a code, or at least without *a priori* codifications, based on the constantly casual and contingent relationship between form and content.

In fact, we are less concerned to criticise the futile intrusion – now superseded – of linguistics into the formal structures of film than to examine why all the attempts to create a syntax have, inevitably, ended in failure.

As we know, science cannot explain itself using science. In the same way, cinema cannot explain itself using the cinema. Yet, if it is language, it is only insofar as it is representation, i.e. the image of the world and its objects. Now, this concrete representation implies certain values involving perception, the psychology of form (*Gestalt*), and other conditions at least as influential as those of linguistics whose structures, in the final analysis, are only concerned with film semantics and narrativity.

II

Signs and Signification

Defending the proposition that film is a language, I wrote twenty years ago:

Victor Perrot, in an article published in 1919, was the first to speak of the cinema as an *écriture*, a form of writing, or language.

It became usual to regard this means of expression as inconsistent and changeable in suggesting ideas, signifying rather like discourse. However, in a purely metaphorical sense.

The question – from the linguistic point of view – was only considered really seriously by G. Cohen-Séat in 1945[1]. And even he rashly associated the film and verbal languages, declaring that the verbal language was *a priori* the exclusive form of all language and, since the two languages had *nothing in common*, the cinema could not possibly be a language. As he wrote: "If these problems are ever to be resolved, it will not be through the use of vague grammatical analogies."

We could not agree more. For there is no association between the film and verbal codes other than that they are both languages. *Any likeness exists in the structures not in the forms.*

Every thought is formed insofar as it is formulated. Since language is the most direct expression of thought, we may say that the latter is, for the most part, formed in words. But language is an objective reaction whose nature is not essentially different from the majority of reactions which make up human behaviour and for which it can stand as a substitute. Non-formulated thought, reduced to states of awareness, pre-exists and stands outside language and may be translated – or, at least, become manifest – in other ways. Primitive language, as we have seen, was a way of translating states of awareness or mental attitudes by means of purely physical reactions.

Since it is a means of translating the tiny impulses of thought, *all language is necessarily associated* with the mental structures which organise them, i.e. with the operations of the mind which consist in conceiving, judging, reasoning, ordering, according to associations of analogy, consequence or causation.

In this way, we can say that a language is a means of expression whose dynamic nature implies the development, in time, of some sort of system of signs, images or sounds. And the purpose of the dialectical organisation of this system lies in the expression and signification of the ideas, emotions and feelings included within one stirring thought of which these form the actual tiny impulses.

Thus language implies different systems each of which has its own appropriate set of symbols but which *combine in the formulation of ideas* of which they are merely the formal or formalised expression. Thus verbal language and film language express themselves by using different elements in different organic systems.

A film is clearly something other than a system of signs and symbols. Or rather it does not present itself as that *exclusively*.

A film *first and foremost* comprises images, images *of something*. A system of images whose purpose is to describe, develop and narrate an event or series of events. However, during the course of the narration, these images may, *in addition*, become symbols. They are not *signs*, like words, but objects and concrete reality; objects which take on (or are given) a predetermined meaning (however ephemeral and contingent). It is in this sense that the cinema is a language; it *becomes* language to the extent that it is *first of all* representation and by virtue of that representation. It is, so to speak, a language in the second degree. It does not appear as an abstract form to be supplemented by certain aesthetic qualities but the aesthetic quality itself supplemented by the properties of language [. . .]

This distinction between *art* and *language* does not apply to the language of film for the simple reason that this is *always* to be found at the level of the work of art. Whether the work is good or bad changes nothing; it is not a matter of *quality* but of *fact*. The language of film, by principle and definition, derives from artistic creation; unlike words, images are not to be found in the pages of a dictionary. It is not a discursive but a developed language. It is lyrical rather than rational. The language of film is not the language used in conversation but that used in a poem or a novel; and images – though organised according to a predetermined meaning – inevitably leave an area of vagueness around the thing expressed which makes us rather think that it does not encompass or designate a rationally defined thought[2].

Language or discourse?

I believe I was the first to argue, against Cohen-Séat, Dina Dreyfus and others, that the cinema is a language in the linguistic sense of the word, with the following caveat:

It is a poetic language, a language once removed. Film [...] becomes language to the extent that it is developed in time, in the same way as discourse[3].

I began to wonder, however – since language is also speech, since film only appears at the level of écriture and since I do not believe in the existence of grammar, syntax or general codification – whether this notion of "film language" should be reassessed, as masking as many unfounded problems as it resolves genuine ones.

It should be clear that by "grammar" I mean a series of rules applicable to all (with rare exceptions) constructions of whatever kind specific to language. In the sense that Christian Metz means it, for whom "free creative originality is *necessarily* grammatical through its very organisation", it is obvious that any film develops along the "grammatical lines" appropriate to it, but not according to an *a priori* established grammar. As we shall see further on, the appropriate codifications for a film, almost always determined by the content (the form/content relationship), can in no circumstances ever be generalised.

The whole field of intelligibility is formed of significations, but all forms of articulation do not necessarily correspond with linguistic articulation. Thus, if film is language only to the extent that it creates a linkage of signifying relationships, there may have been more point in referring to it (along with Cohen-Séat) as discourse, at a time when I had no way of knowing that the term language, used to describe expression rather than structure, could lead to such unfounded comparisons. Linguistic concepts may be applied to other sign systems but, to reiterate, the cinema is not a system of signs. Metz himself wrote:

> Genuinely linguistic laws cease to apply when nothing is obligatory, when the ordering mechanism becomes free. This is where film begins and is the direct source of rhetorical and poetical codes.

This observation might have made him suspicious of an over-systematic mind-set, for the film semiologists eagerly overlooked the fact that images have no particular function specifically assigned to them, whereas units of speech do have a *precise function* enabling them to organise their combinations according to strict rules.

In the simple sentence *Susan is blond*, the meaning is provided by the functional relationship between subject, verb and predicate. The paradigmatic elements are infinitely variable: *Peter is crossing the road, Louise is coming tomorrow*, etc., the signified is different in each case but the signifying function is the same, formalised by a structure "with intrinsic signification".

In the cinema, where there is no such thing as image-verb, image-subject, image-adjective, where the briefest shot incorporates all these designations, it is not possible for a signification to be distributed by the structure. Which is another way of saying that the shot has nothing in common with the word. It is a unit of construction, but one which includes a whole series of relationships; a *signifying* unit, not a unit *of* signification:

> Thus, the shot is not the equivalent of either a word or a phrase; rather it is the equivalent of a whole series of phrases. Several phrases are needed to describe even the simplest close-up; and a great number are needed for a description of a more complicated wide-angle[4].

Thus if a single shot may be regarded as a statement, the linking of shots may be compared with the linking of phrases. Now, no grammar exists to govern the order of this linking – apart from Chomsky's generative grammar. Yet even this is burdened with paradoxes. To be able to establish any rules in ordering units, the meaning of the units must first be known. The semantic system which, according to Chomsky, must be based on syntactical rules, ends up determining the syntactical rules on which it is predicated...

In fact the linking of phrases is entirely determined by the logic of the narrative. Which means that it would be more natural to compare film structures with narrative structures rather than those of language. No film unit stands on its own and any change is absorbed into a separate signifying unit, as though passing from one sentence to another instead of any grammatical transformation.

Signifying values

Yet, in many instances (notably direct antitheses), shots can act like words because of their impact. Now, the meaning of words is invariable whatever their semantic depth whereas what is denoted by film is always *something else*. Words are *neutral* as lexical signs in being identical to each other, whereas images, in being different from one another, each have a specific value, a personal quality. Words have a distinctive quality only at the phonological – or phonetic – level. Pronunciation, intonation, emphasis all confer value and meaning on the "verbal material", but at the level of speech rather than the written sign which alone may be contrasted with images in that its point of reference is without oral or equivalent intermediary.

The concrete value of the images gives them a different meaning each time. They never repeat themselves. If we were to include only the 500,000 feature films produced in the world since 1912, there would be over 60 million million images. And none of them bears the remotest resemblance to any other. Each has its own specific content, meaning and signification. Which brings us obliquely to the *Fido Fido Theory* proposed by G. Ryle to poke fun at linguistics: the word Fido corresponds to the dog Fido. Adam Schaff writes:

> If we require the word to describe the individual object thereby forfeiting its potential to generalise, we must disregard the whole system of abstract thinking established during the course of history, and then remember an infinite number of words corresponding with an unlimited number of objects and phenomena[5].

There is no grammatical rule which could possibly govern or dominate such a wide range of possibilities. Yet this is almost what the cinema does, without inhibiting the potential for making generalisations from the individual or for "creating abstractions" from the concrete. Having both the content of a single phrase (or several phrases) and the impact and essence of a word, acting either as a complete statement or as a sign, the film image avoids – as I shall try to prove – any causative codification.

Every image is endowed with a semantic content whose significations depend on a whole network of circumstances which are analysable only by giving each of them a temporary value, by dividing arbitrarily the signifying functions into several different levels, in the same way as the tripartition of linguistic signs[6].

A. In essence, the image maintains a reciprocal relationship with what it shows. It is not a *signal*, which would imply a whole series of conventions, but a *duplicate*, a consistent reproduction called *gestalt-sign* by psychologists, *natural sign* by linguists and *direct sign* by semiologists. With no other signification than what it presents, it is the *degree zero* of film expression.

B. The first level depends on the way things are shown, the angle, framing, spatial organisation of the field of view, in short the internal structures of the image. This signification is termed *iconic* or *imaging*.

C. The second level belongs to the formal association of shots in the continuity, indications provided by the denoted objects relative to the film – without these being symbolic or metaphorical, merely *refractive*.

D. Most importantly or most characteristically, the third level is none other than *effect-montage* whose connotative meaning effectively depends on the association of two or more shots. Yet it can also depend on events interrelated within the depth of field. Symbolic, metaphorical or allusive, this signification is essentially *rational*.

As we examine each of these forms, we shall try to see to what extent they approach or diverge from the structures of language, what ensures their intrinsic originality and distinctness, with the understanding that mise-en-scène – the directing of actors – is the art of utilising, harmonising, fusing together all these significations into one single signification – the *meaning of the film*.

III

The Direct Sign or the "Neutral Image"

According to the linguistic definition, the direct sign (natural sign, or gestalt-sign) is a homologous figure, a kind of duplicate where the signifier is coextensive with the signified.

There is no such thing as a neutral image. The neutrality we are considering here is only a hypothesis to allow us to study how the image – photographic or film – is produced, outside the context of the intention which provides its basis. And this image, limited and delimited by the camera lens, is of necessity held within a frame, the result, by reason of the techniques employed, being an interpretation of what is photographed.

There is no lens with an angle of view comparable with the human field of view. The widest angle lenses may contain a similar area but their short focal length and heavy optical distortion have the effect of increasing the impression of depth and giving a slight curve to the vertical lines at the edges of the field of view. At the other extreme, long focal length lenses "flatten" any distances. Only "normal" lenses (from 25mm to 75mm) provide a spatial effect similar to human vision.

We know that our representation of the world depends on our sensory capacities. Totally different representations are therefore perfectly conceivable and may be presumed to be as "true" as the reality captured by our eyes. However, to avoid for the time being any epistemological consideration, we shall refer to the reality of our collective perception as being "true reality", i.e. what is real for us. In which context the effect of long or short lenses may be described as a distortion of reality or an interpretation of the field of view.

In another area, qualities of light are given more or less contrast according to whether the image is formed on orthochromatic or panchromatic film. The same is true of colours. Recorded using optical (additive) processes, colours are matched to produce a perfect photographic reproduction. But only in close shots. In long shots – especially because they are further away – the difference in axis of the lenses involves effects of parallax and produces unacceptable fringing. Which is the reason why the subtractive process is preferred, where the colours are produced by a chemical reaction on three superimposed light sensitive layers. However, this colour reproduction is no more than a technical artifice presenting the *equivalent* of natural colour instead of a direct recording.

All these permutations provide the film-maker with the basis for his interpretation, emphasising or altering them as he wishes. However, to describe these as "transformations" when they are generated entirely by the recording processes seems to me particularly misguided. In fact, the colours of a landscape change according to the hour of the day, the angle of the sun, the density of the atmosphere and other physical conditions, which leads us to wonder what is the "real" – or natural – colour of things. The extension of which is that the impersonal, purely technical reproduction of a photographic recording may seem as true as the appearances of perceived reality.

Having said that, it seems to me that insufficient attention has been paid to the huge difference between the photograph and the film image, a difference not confined to the reproduction of movement.

Photograph and still frame

The photograph is clearly the "direct" sign of what it represents. In the photograph the sign is not only coextensive with the signified, it coexists as a separate entity both different and similar. The photograph of a person retains the impression of his presence. It constantly refers back to him. His going away merely reinforces the impression that this image is the only testimony of what his physical appearance was at a particular moment in his existence.

This is also true of each individual frame of a film. Every single frame may potentially be compared with whatever it represents; the film image, however, which is no more than the action of light and shade projected onto a screen, acts rather differently. It cannot be recorded without a support. It can only exist as the effect of the continual and regular substitution of one frame with another: and *for the image to exist the individual frames must disappear.* When the projector stops, the impression is lost.

Although the frames are the elements composing the moving image, they cannot be considered as a collection of "bits" (or else the word is meaningless), for at the moment the bits become separated from each other, the moving image stops moving. Being deprived of movement they stop being units of movement; yet they are units of dynamic articulation – to be considered as *cinematic* units though certainly not *film* units.

Which is why it is mistaken to regard the individual frame as the equivalent of the second articulation of language, as have certain semiologists too quick to compare film language with actual language and arbitrarily attributing to it similar structures. The simple fact that the second articulation may be seen as opposing the first is for us a sufficient distinction for the moment: it is always possible to place the word and its constituent syllables (or phonemes) side by side, whereas one would be hard put to consider the moving image and its constituent frames together.

By its very stillness the photograph marks itself as a *sign*, whereas the moving image, by reason of its movement, its continual transformation, cannot be considered as the sign of the objects it represents. Unless it is every moment of the object represented at every moment of its representation – which is precisely what the individual frame is, without the movement which makes it a moving image.

The film image is no more the sign of a filmed reality than my reflection in the mirror is the sign of my person (though it is the fleeting sign of my presence). In this image it is I signifying me, seeing me see myself. Exactly as objects *signify themselves* by projecting *themselves* onto a screen; they present themselves as a duplicate which formalises their meaning but avoids being a fixed sign by being their living expression.

Where reality expresses itself in its image

To the extent that the film image is "neutral", i.e. not manipulated; to the extent that it signifies nothing except what is signified by what it represents; to the extent that it *reproduces* (and does not produce) the meaning appropriate to it, we may accept Bazin's idea of transparency and concur with Roger Munier that:

In the cinema [...] the leaf really quivers; it expresses itself as a leaf quivering in the breeze. It is a leaf as may be seen in nature and yet becomes even more than this from the moment that, as well as being a real leaf, it is also, first and foremost, a represented reality. Were it merely a real leaf, it would have to wait to be signified by my looking at it. Because it is represented, duplicated by the image, it has already signified itself, preferred itself as a leaf quivering in the breeze. What fascinated audiences at the Lumière projections, far more than the precise repetition of natural rhythm, was this self-expression of movement in the image. The leaf projected like this was, through the power of this auto-language, more "real" and meaningful in its quivering in the breeze than the actual tree-leaf. What was fascinating was not so much seeing the duplicate as being aware of the photographic power of the expression through the duplicate. Something was being said which had no conceivable equivalent in nature. [...]

He goes on:

Photography is reality-turned-into-expression. Rather like a word of the world. In the photograph the world states itself as world, in its undifferentiated self, before any abstraction or choice. It is pure revelation[1].

Bazin, for his part, reminds us that, in photography,

for the first time, between the originating object and its reproduction there intervenes only the instrumentality of a nonliving agent. For the first time an image of the world is formed automatically, without the creative intervention of man, according to a strict determinism [...]. Photography enjoys a certain advantage in virtue of this transference of reality from the thing to its reproduction[2].

Expression achieved by artifice

However, to say that things signify *themselves* by projecting *themselves* onto a screen is merely a figure of speech. A way of considering a meaning which the things *acquire* as though accidentally through being represented on film for, though it may be true that light automatically records the image of things on the film stock, this same image projected onto a screen is not just the "image of reality", like a photograph, but *reality itself presented as moving images*, a duplicate, as it were, with the specific additional qualities of whatever makes it a genuine *re-production*.

In fact, the camera has an undoubted effect on what it shows. As well as the framing, angle of shot and lighting, its simple photographic quality is already an interpretation. Beside which, since the camera's point of view is necessarily *positioned*, the image only ever presents one aspect of the world, an aspect imposed on our vision. What we are seeing on the screen is what an eye has already seen, which has an automatic effect on the data of the directly perceived reality. The world is no longer *available* to us: *that particular* chair, seen from *that particular* angle, replaces *henceforward* all conceivable chairs – and all conceivable "aspect-chairs". The image is thereby referred back to the concept. It suggests the idea through a form at the same time as it makes the object "unreal" by rejecting the reality of which it is the image in order to present itself as an image. In other words, it is positioned less between reality and fiction than between essence and existence. It evokes an essence through an existence as though evoking an absence through a presence: it reinforces the presence of the chair shown but, *as an image*, it affirms the absence of the chair which nevertheless I can see in it. It affirms a real datum in its very unreality retaining only the forms and appearance of a universe "without substance".

"Virginal" reality or "secondary" reality?

Consequently, to refer to the image as "revelation" is to consider it as a more intensely perceived reality, experienced in its deepest meaning, and not as a "transcendental" reality in the sense Bazin means it (though we need to know exactly what this does mean). The reality of the physical world, to all intents and appearances, transcends perceived reality since the latter is only one aspect of it. Idealism exists to the extent that an *in-itself* is presumed, evoking Plato's Ideas; an In-itself whose "reality-for-us" is the concrete expression and whose existential purity is revealed by the camera merely through its objectivity.

Clearly the camera, which is nothing more than a machine

without memory or consciousness, is capable of recording what Bazin calls "virginal reality". He writes:

> Only the impassive lens, stripping its object of all those ways of seeing it, those piled-up preconceptions, that spiritual dust and grime with which my eyes have covered it, is able to present it in all its virginal purity to my attention and consequently to my love[3].

But this is no more than a notional truth. What I attach to things in the way of accepted, codified meaning, utilitarian, cultural or social signification, I discover in their image (or attach to it) so that, though it may be devoid of any subjectivity, the reality recorded by the camera loses its supposed virginity at the very moment it presents itself to my eyes.

Anything expressed *de facto* by the moving image is not necessarily connected with film signification, i.e. with the arbitrary meaning ascribed to things through the composition of the images, the organisation of the narrative structures, etc. As we have said, this is the *degree zero* of film expression. However, we must clarify certain definitions, in order to avoid any confusion or contradiction.

Though there may be no such thing as an *intentional* expression or signification, what does exist at least is an objective quality deriving not only from the objects filmed, their meaning "as objects", but also from their reproduction. A secondary signification dependent on the way the objects are recorded and formalised. A signification which is not *appended* to the primary signification, as is sometimes claimed, but envelops it and alters it, for it is obvious that the representation alters what it *represents*. Necessarily and fundamentally subjective, the message – even a simple report – conveys only a *mediated* reality.

The impersonal, the abstract generalisation are the property of words. I defy anyone to translate into audio-visual terms: "Every day at the same time the marquise went for a spin in the woods", for an image can never translate the indefinite article. All I will ever see is *that particular* marquise, never *the* marquise or *a* marquise. And always from a particular angle, in a particular context. She must be given a body, the time of day must be specified. She will come out of a particular mansion or apartment

The image reorganises appearances: John Ford's *The Grapes of Wrath*, 1940.

block, she will drive a particular car, a Citroën or a Rolls. She will be seen from close to or far away, in tracking or static shots, etc. So many different methods of saying the same thing, of course, but formalising the same action *in different ways* confers on it a *specific meaning*, an allusive or analytical, informative or dramatic interpretation, according to a slow or fast rhythm. Which is a roundabout way of saying that information, even the most trivial, *inevitably* becomes a kind of personal discourse. The shortest documentary, the smallest news item, whether good or bad, are already *works of art*, or are on the margins of a work of art.

The moving image will never be, could never be, a utilitarian language potentially capable of organising itself towards an aesthetic purpose. On the contrary, it is an artistic expression developed in ways similar to those of language. We might almost say that, whereas verbal language expresses only to the extent that it signifies, film language signifies only to the extent that it expresses.

IV

The Image and Perceived Reality

Up to now semiology has been confined to more or less linguistic preoccupations and very little attention has been paid to imagery as such, i.e. as perceptual information. To my way of thinking, this provides a convenient starting place, specifically to establish what relationships there are between the image and the reality of which it is the image; also what we mean by reality.

Before we consider whether there is such a thing as an "impression of reality", we should define our terms and agree as to what reality is. What better definition could there be than that which obstructs our senses?

Can a concrete reality exist independent of the consciousness we have of it[1]? Obviously there can, but can this be seen as an absolute? In other words, does this reality exist "in that form" previous to our consciousness of it or is it a subjective construction, an "effect of consciousness"? The response is different according to whether one is an idealist, materialist, spiritualist or positivist.

For the Kantian idealist, though phenomena are no more than simple representations, it is clear that they are representations of a reality which transcends them, a reality given to each individual mind, impossible to isolate in fact but which remains in principle the genuine "thing-in-itself". Such that Kant draws a comparison between perceptible reality – or *phenomenon* – and an intelligible reality, the object of reason and, by extension, the absolute reality, which he calls *noumenon*.

Thus, Noumenon merely takes the place of Plato's Ideas, with slightly less mysticism. Though the concepts are different, the kinds of relationship also, the "object-in-itself" is turned into the "in-itself" of the object. What cannot be perceived by the senses is rejected only to affirm it in an "essential" ideal postulated *a priori*.

Even so, idealism finds its psychological expression (not just at the metaphysical level) in the thinking of George Berkeley who postulated the impossibility for the individual to forsake his individual consciousness. Pierre Janet writes:

> Idealism, taken as a whole, requires definition: any system which reduces the object of knowledge to the subject of knowledge. This is how it has been formulated: Esse est percipi; the being of things consists in being perceived by the thinking subject[2].

From this to argue that objects are merely constructions of the mind was but a short step, dangerous to take, but happily taken nonetheless. Berkeley's position, however, was a long way from solipsism and his philosophy, which seems nowadays to be the most up-to-date of all the classical philosophers, does not deserve the ridiculous position into which his disciples unfortunately led it. In point of fact, Berkeley never denied the reality of the external world; he confined himself to proving that it was unknowable except through the representations we make of it: "*Ideas* (or passive objects) do not really exist in the mind except those received via the senses"[3]. In other words, *Esse est percipi* should not be translated as "the being of things consists in being perceived by a thinking subject" but "*for the thinking subject, the being of things consists in being perceived*", which has a quite different meaning, we would all agree. Husserl writes:

> As an absolutely universal rule, in no possible perception, that is, no possible consciousness, can an object be presented as an immanent reality[4].

He goes on:

> All consciousness is consciousness of...

In other words, consciousness does not exist "in itself"; it is not a material form of reality. The object of which I am conscious does not exist within my consciousness; it is a datum of my consciousness – none other than perception itself, fully realised and consummated: a perception which "knows" itself through what is perceived. Consciousness of the object coalesces with the object of which one is conscious. The object is correlative with the perceived reality and perception.

Modern science and philosophy invite us to consider that what we declare as *real* is merely a structuring, an organising of our sensory faculties formalised by what we are conscious of, also by what we are conscious of our own consciousness without ever being able to appreciate the organising functions by which our consciousness constructs itself as it makes us perceive what we call *reality*. A reality which is not an illusion, but is *real* and true *only for us*. In other words, if our sensory capacities, our perceptual frontiers were different, it is very probable that our world would also be different. Reality is not an "in-itself" but one of the many aspects which phenomena may adopt through a particular consciousness of which we can only ever know the surface; it is a "material" world constructed by our senses.

A physical reality which transcends the percept is perhaps an illusion. For the physicist, it is the manifestation of *Energy*. For the metaphysician, it is a manifestation of *Spirit*. Now they each may be merely two complementary aspects of the same *Absolute*, the distinction being merely one of category of understanding.

Having established this, let us examine things from the angle of perception. We know that visible light is only a tiny part of the electromagnetic waves whose frequency varies from one or two cycles right up to millions and millions of kilocycles, from Herzian waves to the frequency of the proton. On a scale somewhere between 380 and 770 million million kilocycles, visible light extends from the extreme red (the limit of infrared) and extreme violet (the limit of ultraviolet) ends of the spectrum. At either end there is a *threshold* beyond and below which the human eye is incapable of perceiving light vibrations.

If, for simple convenience, we term *sensory level* the area between the minimum and maximum thresholds, we realise very soon that all our perceptions, whether in space or time, of any relationships of intensity or movement, and visual, auditory, tactile impressions involve a similar sensory level, limited as they are by the two extreme thresholds. Now this sensory level serves as a *framework*. Acting as a *grid*, it enables us to record certain events, which we call phenomena or objects, but remains unaffected by many others which "slip the net".

At the same time, it would be wrong to think that these "objects" might exist "in themselves" as we perceive them, that they are simply drawn out of a context which remains alien to us, for it is we who structure the forms through which they appear to us, who "make them into objects".

Form and substance

Let us imagine someone lowering a pipette into the sea in order to draw up a sample of water. He then lets out the contents *drop by drop*: the drops thus created originate in the ocean but they do not exist as drops within the ocean for the reason that the ocean is not a collection of drops of water. They are correlative both to the ocean which provides them with their substance and to the pipette which structures their *form*.

Let us recall Bergson's dictum about the runner:

A thousand successive positions are contracted into a single symbolic attitude, which our eyes perceive, which art reproduces and which becomes the universal image of a running man[5].

We know that a flash of red light of a second's duration contains so many synthetically captured basic pulses that it would take 25000 years of human life to be able to perceive each one separately; and that certain vibrations, at the ultraviolet end of the spectrum, involve a greater number of frequencies from the transmitting particle over one second than there have been seconds since man first appeared on earth.

Now, we have only to imagine a ball bouncing discontinuously and randomly at a rate of two hundred bounces a second to realise that, however sharp our vision, we could never isolate each one of the ball's separate positions. We could never expect to remember more than one or two "as freeze frames" (supposing a quasi-cinematic analysis of movement). Yet our minds immediately link together the different positions in a more or less broken line which, *for us*, represent the movement of the ball during the course of that second. This representation is neither true nor false; the ball will, over a period of time, have been in each of the remembered positions but, in the interim, it will have been in many others. In other words, a diagram of the movement will be merely an *abstract* figure, a shape structured by our consciousness to link arbitrarily the perceived positions while "skipping over" the others.

We can therefore say that perception depends on sensory levels, *which mark out objects only to the extent that they limit the data of our senses.*

The piece of metal presented as an "object" before me obviously corresponds to a certain "state" of matter whose organic stability is independent of my percept and the consciousness I have of it. But this state does not exclude other states whose combination is precisely what constitutes the physical reality of the object. Thus, within its apparently static state, the continual movement of electrons, the constant exchange of energies, responding, corresponding and balancing each other out, remain beyond my perception. Which does not mean it exists any the less "at the same time and in the same space": it is the piece of metal, which I perceive as a body from the surface of which visible light bounces back, which resists my touch as well as my vision, and presents itself as an object, a thing, by virtue of the resistance it offers all my capacities for understanding and the fact that my consciousness links, in the form of a smooth and homogeneous shape, the finer points of its impenetrability. And so this "state" really does exist, but not as an "in-itself", not as independent of a number of the other interdependent states without which it would not exist. Now, it is uniquely this state which I perceive, to the exclusion of all others and which, alone, isolated, "abstracted", forms the "piece-of-metal-for-me". The piece of metal is therefore not a part with a separate existence within the whole, but a reality structured by the assembly of the several phenomena – or physical realities – which make it up.

Consciousness neatly avoids what it cannot perceive and constructs an image by creating tighter and tighter links between the elements which impinge on it through the senses. Yet the non-perceived elements are as much an integral part of reality as the perceived elements; the "object" is therefore merely a slice of the totality of the physical world, but reorganised and structured by consciousness into a coherent entity. Correlative with this world and the act of consciousness, it does not involve an "in-itself". There is no possible transcendent "essence" since the phenomena from which it derives are different from what it is and since it exists as an object only by virtue of the act of consciousness which "produces it as an object", as the logical construction of perceptible data.

The real and reality

Perceived reality is real in the most concrete and tangible sense of the word, but it is a reality for us, relating to the conditions of our existence, our physical make-up.

Of course, objects are the expression of a phenomenon which precedes them and extends beyond them; but this phenomenon, alien to their existence "as objects", is not an "essence" of which they are merely the outward appearance. There is no "ideal" form preceding their representation and no more relationship between the stimuli and the perceived object than between a building and the materials with which it is constructed. However, there needs the involvement of a builder. The builder in this case is perception, which is able to build only *within the limits* set by our senses.

Thrust in the midst of a reality extending beyond the limits of human understanding, our consciousness organises, with the means at its disposal, a reality which it is able to dominate because it is the consequence of its efforts. In other words, the direct data of consciousness are the effect of a constant and ceaseless *mediation*. This arbitrary reality is for us the only true reality; it seems direct to us only because this mediation, dependent on our sensory level, it is what forms the actual act of perceiving. Instantaneously structured by this process, our reality is true *for us*, direct *for us*.

For beings endowed with a sensory level different from our own, the reality of the physical world would appear totally alien, such that their "universe" would have nothing in common with our own. The "object" structured by their consciousness using physical events of the same order but whose perceptible data might be different would bear very little relation to the one we might remember. What right would we have in judging it less real "in itself"? An unreality "for us" might very well be a reality *for them*. The object of their consciousness is not more true nor less true than our own. It is merely one aspect of the "physical world" – which presupposes as many different aspects as there are possible sensory levels.

Sensory data (sensations, stimuli) are the "raw material" on which a particular form bestows a particular meaning. Yet this meaning is meaningful only to the extent that consciousness is conscious of it. And consciousness can only be conscious to the extent that it becomes conscious of this form: Form and meaning are the "way" what is perceived *appears to consciousness*. Meaning is therefore inseparable from form, but form is not an *a priori* to which the sensory data must submit: on the contrary, the data are what *determine* it.

To say that these data are "directly informed" (that is, given meaning) is the same as saying (as we have just done) that the structure and meaning proceeding from it are previous to consciousness – which is confined to "recording" the product of the perceptual act. However, though pre-conscious, this act is *already a creative act* for, although the "spontaneous structure" is "what appears to our consciousness", this structure is not *presented* to our perception; on the contrary it is *constructed by* it, though it has the ground laid for it by the sensations in that these sensations are *limited*. Forming a clearly defined "field" by virtue of this limitation, the stimuli offer a network which perception formalises into an organic "whole". Perception creates associations, connections, *structures*.

Perceived reality is the form of our perception, which is *predetermined*, i.e. "framed and limited" by our sensory level. To perceive is to construct a world; to be conscious of it is to present the world *as an object*.

Visual perception

Vision is of particular interest to us. Firstly at the level of direct images called "real" (or, incorrectly, retinal) in order to distinguish them from mental images – photography, painting, etc. As Bertrand Russell notes:

> From the physical point of view, whatever I see is inside my head. I do not see physical objects. I see effects which they produce in the region where my brain is[6].

Clearly, the image forming on the optic nerve exists within the organism. From the physiological point of view, the neural process corresponding to the perceived subject occupies part of this organism; to begin with, the back of the retina where the image is formed. But this image is not what I see; it is what *is seen*. I do not see the effects produced in my brain by the act of seeing, I *surrender* to them. I do not see my vision, it is *given* to me. What I see is the result of that vision, which *appears* in my consciousness and becomes immediately externalised because the retina, displaying all the properties of brain tissue – among which the capacity to externalise perceptions – does not present the forms as being inside or even alongside my eyes but *outside* them. Now, at the same time, because I am incapable of relating to "me" the information I am experiencing and which comes to me "from the outside", I relate it "in intention" to the cause of my "seeing". What is *seen*, and is an image, then becomes *what I see* which I turn into the object I am looking at. The subject of my vision becomes the "object" of my looking. It becomes objectified into that "object" existing outside me, according to a process which is still quite vague but which my tactile perceptions help to bring into focus.

It could never be said that consciousness "becomes transcended *in the direction of* the object", for this would be to see the object as *already* existing in forms attributed to it by perception. Consciousness, simply, "knows itself" *within* the object – and *through* the object.

When I see the red colour of the blotting-paper in front of me, the red is not objective in the physical sense of the word. It is a subjective construction *presented* to my consciousness (since the mediation of the percept is *previous* to it). Consequently, the red is objective "for me". Unable to relate it as a creation of my will, I can only receive it as an external cause. It is thus spontaneously and definitively perceived as a quality of the object. And what is true for this quality is equally true for the object.

The colour does not in fact exist as such in the physical world. It is a vibration of a certain frequency transmitted (reflected) over a surface. The subsequent stimuli are interpreted as the "colour red", but it is a "representation" of reality and not reality itself. This colour red is only true (real) for us because it is directly presented to us. The physicist is right to say that there is no more relationship between these vibrations of light and the colour than between the colour and the word "red" used to describe it – which itself is merely a "sign" of its perceptible qualities.

However, if consciousness is merely the product of a structuring process, rather than the process itself, we may well wonder how the effects produced in our brain by the act of seeing appear to our consciousness.

In attempting to provide an answer, we should examine the act itself. Let us not forget that the retina is made up of one hundred million cells whose messages end up in the brain in a visual zone which is explored, ten times a second, by an associative zone, duplicated by a psychic zone, the whole system enjoying the benefit of an extraordinary network involving approximately thirteen million neurons. It is by means of this "seeing machine" that the stimuli become translated into images.

As we have just described, there is no such thing as a retinal image, if this is interpreted – as it was thirty years ago – as an image produced on the back of the retina as though on a mirror.

The work of Henschen and Wildbrand have proved that the retina does "project" onto the brain. To describe the process more accurately, there are two retinas, one on the periphery which receives the impression of light rays; the other situated in the calcarine sulcus of the occipital lobe, which is symmetrical to it forming the cerebral retina. And each of the two cerebral retinas is related to the two eyes: *it is there that the impressions become conscious*. Establishing the formal links between the imaged data and forming the image into an organic whole, into a *form*, the cortex fulfils perception.

Thus consciousness defines itself in what appears to it. And if it is to be compared with the *surface on which* the image appears, it is tantamount to saying that it is the brain itself, i.e. the whole upper level of the sensori-motor mechanism which acts as a control while observing it.

To put it another way, using as reference the recent work of David H. Hubel and Torsten N. Wiesel[7], the retina, containing over ten million rods and twenty million cones, transmits to the brain via the optic nerve signals which are more or less intense according to the number of photons received. The optic nerve carries out an initial process by the fact that its fibres (estimated at over a million) assemble the impulse into several hundred receptors. A second process is involved at the level of the chiasma, i.e. the point where the optic nerves associated with each eye meet and cross so that each cerebral hemisphere receives the nerve-impulses from both eyes. Which explains why binocular vision is simultaneous and why it is possible to see in three dimensions.

In short, it is the cerebral image formed in the cortex (striated cortex or zone 17) which acts as support for the visual image.

Which is constructed from received impulses and is where memory and any correction relating to the information provided by the other senses play their part.

Real images and film images: movement and illusion

Though the perceptual image ("objectified" visual perception) is inseparable from the perceived objects, the direct image (which we shall continue, through habit and convenience, to refer to as the retinal image – and which is "flat") can be seen as different from the objects shown as images. In other words, the landscape in my view presents itself as a two-dimensional image – though it is a three-dimensional reality. Or, to put it another way, I could place a window between the landscape and me; it would then appear to me through the window as though projected onto it like a film image projected onto a screen.

On the other hand, from the moment we exclude everything but visual perception, we perceive the film image in the same way as we perceive objects. The image of a landscape presents itself to my vision in the same way as a real landscape stretching out before my eyes. Naturally I am not able to sit on the image of a chair; but at the same time nor am I able to sit on a real chair if it is placed on the other side of a window. It is therefore *as though* the world projected onto the screen is a real world as seen through a window. With this important difference: that the image establishes between the elements included in it a series of relationships which do not exist in reality where there is no frame by which a fragment of segregated space can be removed from the world, to be considered in isolation.

Yet in the context of film images, we always refer to the "illusion of movement". Doubtless because this perception is due to the discontinuous linking of a series of images which we *know* to be fixed and whose replacement time is less than that of retinal persistence = a sixteenth of a second in silent films, and a twenty-fourth of a second since the advent of sound.

If movement were to be broken down into a greater number of frames – 50 or 100 per second – the rendering of rapid actions and jerky pans would be smoothed out but by the same token it would have to be described as a "reconstituted" movement, that is, a manufactured illusion. Movement does not present itself as an image: it either is or is not. In the image of objects in motion there is perception of real movement. As René Zazzo describes it:

> Movement is not in addition to the image. It suppresses it as an image, instantly altering it into reality. At this level the feeling of reality is not a construction of the mind or a product of the imagination, it is an immediate reaction[8].

We might add that the perception of movement over a quick discontinuous sequence is less the effect of retinal persistence than a relative inertia of the cortex, called the "phi effect" by Wertheimer in 1912[9].

The perception of real movement is similar. Without delving into irrelevant scientific considerations, we may say very generally that continuity does not exist in the reality of the physical world – the continuity of wave movement is only ever the continuity of alternation. In other words, what we term continuous – what is continuous *for us* – is always a non-perceived discontinuity.

The formation of the television picture provides an example: we know that this image is not the effect of a whole series of frames being projected but the transmission of a series of successive dots. The television tube comprising 816 lines (or 625 according to the system) and each of these lines constituting a thousand contiguous dots, it is the succession of 816,000 dots in one twenty-fifth of a second which reforms the image across the whole of its surface. Remaining visible from the appearance of the last dot by virtue of the calculated inertia of the receiver, the first dot of the first image is replaced by the first dot of the succeeding image, and so on. Now, unable as we are to perceive any discontinuity less than a twenty millionth of a second, all these dots are perceived as a global unit replaced by another at the ratio of twenty five every second[10].

As well as this impression of movement, the "impression of reality" has provoked the most varied and contradictory comments.

Perspective and the "impression of reality"

We know that it is from the data of the *camera obscura* that the theoreticians of painting, like Piero della Francesca and Alberti, defined the laws of perspective, starting from the position of the painter in front of the world, his observation-point, i.e. the point of view providing the geometrical interpretation of the spectacle. The *camera obscura*, equipped with a lens by Jérôme Cardan, then an optical system from 1550 onwards, becoming widely used by engravers during the 18th. Century, encouraged the notion that it would be possible to fix its image using the silver salts which, through Fabricius (1565), Glaubero (1658) and Homberg (1694), were known to darken on exposure to light. But, before the laws of perspective could be applied to an eventual photographic reproduction, they were used by painters of the Quattrocento to represent objects and people according to a vision which, it must be said, does not *translate* the phenomenon but *directly records* it, the light reflected from the objects focussed by the pupil onto the retina.

As we have seen, we perceive the layering of objects in space because perception involves cerebral reactions relating to the coordination of a whole series of memorised sensory data. As Merleau-Ponty points out: "perspective, experienced through our perception, is not geometrical perspective". It is not reducible to this datum alone, but involves mental and sensory adjustments (outside the scope of the present study) relating to our earliest experiences in childhood: movement in space, evaluation of distance relative to the subject, tactile sensations, etc. All of which enables the *stimuli* which organise the retinal image to be "situated", put in place through a conditioning process.

We might recall in this context the sensations felt by certain people blind from birth who have their sight surgically restored. With the image of space being presented to them "flat", they continually bump against obstacles in the external world and only become conscious of spatial reality through a great deal of tentative tactile and psychomotory trial-and-error, allowing the eyes to learn balance: one of them reported that he had to close his eyes (to begin with at least) to be able to find his way about.

Contrary to what some critics think, there is no direct relationship between a pictorial transcription of the laws of perspective and the direct recording of the phenomenon. Alberti's formula was only ever the *reduction* of visual perception to geometrical data enabling depth of space to be rendered on a flat surface as objectively and concretely as possible. It is a *representation* which has never been claimed to replace the real data of perspective.

The pathways of light and its visual reception are not to be confused with the laws of optics. These are laws conforming with the conditions of the phenomenon. The point of departure for "perspective triangulation" is not arbitrary. It is the same as the point of view of anyone looking at the world before him. What we see is determined by the position from which we see it and is limited by our visual field. But, wherever we are is always the apex of what, relative to us, is the "perspective triangle". Transferred to someone not sitting where "the audience sits" (at the apex of the triangle), the point of view would not relate to anything seen since there would be no-one to see it. Also, it is hard to understand the claims made by some critics that "perspective should create the effect of recentering, moving the centre to be fixed on the eye, i.e. assuming the position of the subject", for there is only one centre, that of the person looking or whatever takes his place (the camera). It is the observer who chooses where to place the perspective effect and, therefore, the point of view, for there is no such being as a spectator who is not the subject of what he sees.

In photography, perspective is recorded onto film in the same way as onto the retina. With this important difference: that the pencil of light rays crosses an optical system constructed on the model of the human eye and that the image does not extend beyond its registration on the light sensitive emulsion. The camera perceives nothing, it records mechanically but, when seen by our eyes, the photograph forms a retinal image to which the brain reacts exactly as in normal perception. However, because the photograph is inert, the vanishing-point and dimensional relationships of the objects mean that, though we *recognise* the perspective effect, we do not *experience* it. Space is "flattened" in an image where the data, instead of being represented as in painting, are registered by the light, yet stratified and set.

However, once they are projected as moving images, the movement creates the effect that *depth is experienced, felt as it is in direct perception.*

And the image appears instantly to become separated from its support, indeed does become detached: it is no longer a photograph projected onto a flat surface; it is a "space" I am perceiving. The film image presents itself to my eyes as a "spatial image", similar to the real space stretching out in front of me.

M. Michotte's observations, the consequence of a great deal of study in experimental psychology, confirm this idea. As he says:

> As soon as a technique can be successfully applied to separate the constituent features of an object from the surface which acts as its support, the notion of dimensionality immediately assumes the obvious and sometimes even unexpected features of reality. This result may be achieved by several different methods, among which there is one (particularly interesting from our point of view) which consists in setting up an interaction between the constituent features of the object. The antithesis between the movement of the shape and the immobility of the screen acts as an agent of separation freeing the object from the surface in which it was included. It is, to some extent, 'materialised' and assumes an independent existence; it becomes a 'corporeal object'.
>
> One very simple test, used for many years now (reference to it can be found in the work of Von Recklinghausen dated 1859), proves our point. The shadow of a solid object made of wire – parallelepiped or cube, for example – is projected onto a screen. Observed from close to, the shadow gives a similar impression to that of a simple perspective drawing traced onto the screen; but, for the object to become real, all that is required is to spin it and, in certain viewing conditions, it actually becomes impossible to distinguish the moving shadow from the metal object itself.
>
> This experiment is important in that it reproduces precisely what happens in the cinema where the behaviour of the characters, their gestures and changes of facial expression, even the simple transfer of inanimate objects, must obviously eventuate in a similar effect.

M. Michotte adds that:

> it is easy to ascertain this if the film is suddenly stopped during projection. The impression of relief suddenly disappears, it loses its reality and gives way to the unreal volumes of a simple image with flat perspective[11].

In a sense, the film image is comparable with the reflection in a mirror. Though the latter is a flat surface, the image is of a directly perceived perspective inverted in the virtuality of its reflection but perceived as though in direct reality. On the screen the image appears as though perspective were *being reproduced* in and by the recorded movement. The impression given is of the filmed world being imitated on the screen while at the same time happening in a real space on the other side of the screen.

We should add that, since the movement is always "actual" (we only ever perceive the present), the world presented as an image is not only spatialised by the effect of the reproduced third dimension but *presentified* by virtue of the perceived movement. As Christian Metz observes, "in the cinema the impression of reality is also the reality of the impression, the real presence of movement".

Under this definition, the notion of monocular recording which has dinned our ears (with reference to geometrical laws and their application in painting) is of secondary importance. Binocular vision only comes into play as far as relief is concerned and is only perceptible in close shots. In distances beyond twenty metres, it becomes confused with perspective as perceived by a one-eyed observer as well as observers with normal vision. To prove this, all one has to do is look at the world with one eye closed. Though the axis of vision is different according to each eye and though the visual field is apparently more limited, the vanishing-point remains exactly the same.

Perspective and ... ideology

Having said this, not intending to add fuel to the controversy raging between *Cinéthique* and *Les Cahiers du cinéma* over the interpretation of the "impression of reality", it is surprising to see to what extent critics as informed as Marcelin Pleynet, Jean-Paul Fargier, Jean-Louis Baudry, Pascal Bonitzer, Jean-Louis Comolli and others have been able (for entirely ideological purposes let it be said) to relate the photographic recording of perspective to the Quattrocento code, associate them to the point of confusing them by reversing the problem as though the camera, built according to laws of optics to capture light and receive the image of objects, was established following pictorial conventions drawn from these laws in order to represent artificially their effects.

Arguing that film reproduces or reflects existing ideologies, the writers of *Cinéthique* hypothesised and then declared that the impression of reality was the inevitable expression of the dominant ideology, which would have constructed the camera according to the principles of the *camera obscura* in order to "dress up reality for the masses" and use a fiction to indoctrinate them in prevailing ideas and feelings. In short, to make them believe the moon is made of green cheese. Marcelin Pleynet writes:

> The cinematic tool is purely ideological. It produces a perspective code directly descended from and built on the model of the Quattrocento's scientific perspective[12].

This idea, related to the work of Francastel and Panovsky, is based on a mistaken interpretation, for neither Panovsky nor Francastel ever spoke – at least in this sense – of real space, but represented space created by the painter's brushes and colours. For them, it was a *representation*, not an objective recording.

Now, as Jean-Louis Comolli and Jean Narboni add:

> It is not the world in its concrete reality which is captured by a non-interventionist tool, but the vague, unstructured, untheorised, unthought-out world of the dominant ideology [...] The camera is therefore encumbered from the outset, from the first foot of film exposed, with the inevitability of reproducing, not things in their concrete reality, but refracted by an ideology[13].

In other words, through its very nature, the camera is "likely to produce a specific ideology" directly connected with the dominant ideology which, it is no surprise to learn, is the old chestnut bourgeois ideology. We give our theoreticians the benefit of the doubt that they mean "camera", not only in the sense of a recording apparatus, but also all the technical processes whose purpose is to record and reproduce reality mechanically by implementing the laws of light production. But, leaving aside the "vague, unstructured world" about which we know very little except that it displays a rather surprising idealism in its so-called marxist thinking, we are entitled to ask how it is that the cameras and technical processes used by Soviet film-makers (which are exactly the same as ours) are capable of producing as impersonally, as passively and with no organic changes, ideologies so totally at variance.

Jean-Patrick Lebel puts it accurately:

Confusing the use of the cinema made by the dominant ideology and a "natural" contamination following on from this, the effect and the cause become reversed and the cinema becomes "in essence" an ideological tool. If care is not taken, ideology finally becomes, through this process, the metaphysical essence of the cinema.

He adds:

This belief in the "ideological nature" of the cinema as a tool is itself revealed as idealistic when Marcelin Pleynet, pushing the theory to its limit as he tries to "rewrite history", suggests that the cinema was literally invented by the dominant ideology, that it was in some way "propelled" towards its own discovery[14].

An idea which I rather ridiculed when I wrote:

Those various articles which, invariably, put the cart before the horse, would have us believe that discoveries and inventions only appear because of the ideologies which inspire them, because of an interest which at a given moment would have created them anyway. As though, for instance, capitalist society in the nineteenth century, seeing that gas lighting had had its day, waved a magic wand and "invented" electricity[15].

When Pleynet argues that "the camera has the impossible role of maintaining an objective association with reality, he is partly right in the sense that he ascribes to the camera a non-contingent role. Taking into account the minor differences indicated above, the camera objectively records the reality in the view-finder. If the image were not similar to whatever it is the image of, i.e. our vision of things, we would reject it as false.

The confusion apparently stems from the fact that Pleynet describes both image and film under same heading. More accurately, he confuses (or regards as the same) the *effect of reality* and the *impression of reality* which, though complementary, are two entirely distinct phenomena. One is the relationship of the image with what it shows us, the other the relationship of the film with what it tells us.

The *effect of reality* is a purely cinematic effect dependent on the simple duplication of objects in motion. Free of any intentionality and therefore any ideology, it is the characteristic feature of the moving image, which signifies nothing more than what the filmed objects themselves signify. To which we should loudly proclaim that, though the camera may objectively record a real piece of information, it only ever records what we choose for it to record. From which it is clear that the camera cannot maintain a direct association with reality, but no less clear that any subjectivity belongs to the film-maker and not the camera (which lies outside its capabilities).

Now, according to Pleynet, from the very fact that light only registers on the film emulsion having passed through an optical system constructed on the model of the human eye (or the data of the Quattrocento...), it is impossible for the *actual production* of the image to be objective. How far must he go in order to discredit the word!

Having said that, the film image is not produced *upon* a flat surface as is the case in painting – or photography – but *against* a flat surface which reflects it back into an imaginary space where its moving shapes take on a three-dimensional form. Which is what produces the "effect of reality".

As for the *impression of reality*, this is an aesthetic effect which validates a fiction by giving the audience the impression that the data of the fiction have not been invented but are natural, arising from elements whose "effect of reality" indicates that they are reproducing a "true" reality. Yet, between the substance of the film and the film itself, there is a similar association to the one between individual bricks and the building created by their arrangement.

Even so, it is undeniable that any film which is the expression of an auteur contains an ideology within it. However, this is a rather different problem from those concerning us in this chapter. It remains the case that, by virtue of the projection which "objectifies" everything projected, connotations frequently appear as the direct forms or specific qualities of the denoted objects. Which is the origin of the ideology which emerges "insidiously" from this obvious but imperceptible manipulation, which fools no one but those who are blinkered and one or two rather misguided critics...

From criticism to Critias

Moreover, if certain truths are pushed beyond their boundaries, the consequence is sophistry worthy of Critias. For instance, basing his remarks on Godard's rather silly aphorism: "the cinema is not a just image, it is just an image[16]". Clément Rosset has this to say:

> The area (of just images) relates to a cinema where the cinematic expression of reality is not expected to be found except where it already exists, in the subject of reality, in preformed ideas, a pre-representation ready to be filmed. The justness of the image is proportionate to the nature of its own illusions of reality[17].

I am not sure that my "representation of reality" is an illusion arising from a preformed idea. I rather think that it is the formation of a concept. If the image of a tree is formally identical to the tree it represents (whose reality is obviously at the limits of my perception, controlled by it), if I recognise the one through the other, then I would say that the image is just. And, indeed, it would have to be, otherwise I would not recognise the tree. Rosset goes on:

> The image is the expression, not of reality, but of the significa-tion presumed to be contained within it [...].

I cannot see how such a signification could be presumed. It might be an "addition" or "modification", the image being a duplication before it is – and in order for it to be – a signification: either I know the reality in question, in which case I have no need to presume or presuppose its meaning; or else I do not know it, in which case I have to create an idea of it – an illusion – which my perception will eventually correct. Rosset concludes by saying:

> As always, reality appears alongside the specific (just an image), the illusion alongside its duplicate (the "just" image providing merely an illusion of the reality which it "justly" claims to evoke).

If this reality did not exist, the camera would be obliged – justly or unjustly – to give me an image of it. Which image would obviously be no more than an aspect of reality, and not a purely conceptual "in-itself". But, wherever I am, I personally can only ever see one aspect of the world.

Clearly, this kind of sophistry is no more than word-play. With the proviso that the cinema "is capable only of turning reality into unoriginal duplications and unsurprising representations" (which is to recognise implicitly that they are accurate relative to the reality), it would be "totally wrong to evoke this reality as it is". Now, the word "evoke" is ambiguous. The image has no purpose to "evoke", since it represents (re-presents). Evocation suggests distantiation, difference. Only words, which describe the object, and painting, which interprets it, are capable of evoking it.

The "ontological deficiency" of the cinema thus resides in the fact that it is not reality in its duplication, only the duplication itself ... which brings us back to the self-evident truth (already quoted): "The cinema is not the reality of which it is the image, otherwise it would not be its image [...]"

Another piece of sophistry: to prove the unreality, or non-reality, of the "film within a film", Jacques Petat writes, of Fritz Lang's *Fury*:

> The cinema is not introduced into the film [..] in order to prove the reality of the facts. On the contrary, the compositions and angles of the shots prove that Joe has produced a proof out of nothing[18].

Now, how is it that Joe has been able to produce these images of the rioting crowd when they have been recorded while he was in prison? Undoubtedly, he might have been able to choose them, assemble them, edit them together in order to create a more convincing proof, but he has not created them... Jacques Petat continues:

> The images do not relate to reality but to the characters them-selves, to the images Fritz Lang gives us of these characters.

Indeed! They relate to the reality of the fiction, the only reality in question. It happens that the events filmed during the action provides the events with a quality of true reality: the film pushes the filmed reality back to reality but the image can only relate to the image because the filmed reality – true or false, authentic or imaginary – is presented as an image.

The association between "fiction-images" and the "images of the image" does not exclude reality any more than the images of any film – or, for instance, the association between filmed news events and the film reality in *Citizen Kane*. Whether the images represent a true or fictional reality or, as in this fiction, an aspect of the latter, the represented/representation duality remains the same. Except that in the last instance the representation is at one remove. It is the representation of a representation taken as the representation of true reality.

That the proof has been "produced out of nothing" by Fritz Lang to lend credibility to his story and to Joe's accusations is not in doubt. But Jacques Petat's argument is pure sophistry, claiming, for instance, that conversations between characters in a novel come from the novelist rather than the characters and extrapolating from this a philosophy of reality by contrasting the unreality of the fictional reality with the reality of the fiction.

Yet another piece of sophistry: having given credit to the film-director for everything, here is a context in which he is denied everything. It is not the film-maker who makes the film, it is the studio – far from my notion, the idea of minimising the influence of the producer and the technical crew. But this influence has a bearing on films, types of film and, more particularly, on men and the role they have to fulfil. There are films where the work of the cameraman is of prime importance, much more so than the set-designer or screenwriter. There are others where the reverse is true. Sometimes the director is all-powerful, sometimes he is merely the executor of a script controlled in the finest detail by the producer and the scriptwriter. All generalisations are equally absurd. Nevertheless it still holds true that, even when a film is no more than a well-oiled, well run product, whenever there is a recognisable style, (whoever the producer and his collaborators) that style, that form, that signature comes from the director. This fact is irrefutable.

A film is never the work of a single person, that much is true. But it is also true of cathedrals. Without ever placing one stone on top of another, Hardouin-Mansard is still the creator of Versailles, just as Lescot is of the courtyard of the Louvre.

Yet this whole new reassessment itself comes directly from literature (or rather the literary criticism currently in vogue).

Following various very useful studies by Michel Foucault and Lacan, it was thought good form on the margins of the "new criticism" to deny the individual creative role of the writer. Elevating a few aphorisms into rules of conduct, making a habit of generalisation, it became convenient to refer to "it writes" instead of "he writes". And since many of those writing about the cinema would have considered themselves behind the times had they not quickly adopted the most extreme positions of linguistics and psychoanalysis, for them to be or appear to be "up to the minute" they had to sing the same tune, albeit with different words.

Now, saying *it* writes is absurd to the extent that a system is created in order to define or contain the ambiguities of the *Self*. It is clear that the individuality of any thinking, acting being is not an entity and is the consequence of a whole series of different influences. Whether it be the innate personality, inherited character traits, or the personality acquired through education, culture, the whole social environment, it is true that these infinitely variable and changing influences are assimilated by someone, who is me. And in a very specific way, which makes me what I am, different from all others.

The *It* is none other than what is *within me* and which I describe as *me*. Not an idealistic "in-itself" for which I am merely the unconscious puppet. Whether I am a writer, filmmaker, painter or composer, I am not a sleepwalker under the influence of an impersonal *It* buried in the mists of my unconscious. On the contrary I am conscious of the unconscious within me, which guides me and makes me what *I am*. But if we were to flush out all the sophistry which abounds in cinematic literature we would be here for ever...

V

The Shot

As we said before, a shot is made up of a series of frames contained in a short scene filmed in one block, thereby forming an indivisible segment between two joins. It is a *construction* unit involving a larger or smaller assembly of people, actions, events, a complex unit with a global meaning rather than a unit of meaning. A whole sentence is necessary to describe even the simplest close up, and a whole paragraph for a detailed wide-angle.

Now, of the expressions in current usage, the term shot is one of those most easily misinterpreted through its many meanings – and has been since at least the 1950s when considerations of form were so radically overhauled. As Pascal Bonitzer writes:

The idea seems strangely unstable, inconsistent, ambivalent, continually veering between various different meanings not necessarily connected or complementary. The expression 'shot' varies according to its description: close-shot, shot-sequence, static shot, for instance, do not necessarily mean the same object – "shot"[1].

Semantic arguments about the meaning of this word in fact arise from the different ways the character of the shot has developed. Its significations have been made conspicuously different, whereas the technical process on which they are based has maintained the same position.

Twenty years ago, giving as precise a definition of the shot as I was able, I wrote:

When, after D.W. Griffith's first explorations, the cinema began to become aware of its resources, i.e. when the technique of recording scenes from many different points of view became commonplace, the technicians were compelled to give names to the different 'shots' in order to distinguish between them. To do

Medium long shot: John Ford's *Stagecoach*, 1939.

this, they used the position of the main characters as reference, dividing the space up into planes perpendicular to the axis of the camera [translator's note: French uses the same word *plan* for 'plane' and 'shot'], describing, if you like, the distance from the camera guaranteed to be in focus[2].

Wide medium shot, *The Last Laugh*, F.W. Murnau, 1924.

Close shot: Lilian Gish in *The Birth of a Nation*, D.W. Griffith, 1914.

In fact, since the only lenses used before 1915 (25mm, 35mm and 50mm) were in focus across a very deep field, the problems of focus only appeared with wide aperture lenses whose short depth-of-field enabled the field of view to be fragmented. However, every time the scene was shot from a different angle or with a different framing, the camera had to be moved. Since most shots were static, each one involved a different set-up; consequently, shots and set-ups could be regarded one and the same thing. Only *tracking-shots*, which, since they moved, were able to record a whole series of different fields of view, angles and shots, broke the mould. Yet they represented perhaps a tenth of scenes shot. Thus, it was possible to define individual shots in terms of a short scene filmed from a particular angle and at a particular distance from the camera; or of an autonomous fragment inserted between two joins, i.e. like a unit of editing. Since the division of shots in terms of size – from close-up to long-shot – was only ever a convenient

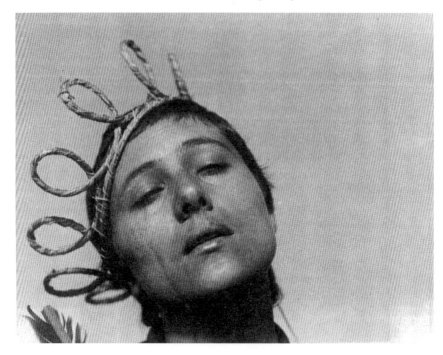

Facial close-up: Falconetti in *The Passion of Joan of Arc*, by Carl Dreyer, 1928.

short-hand, it is possible to imagine as many different shots as there points on the optical axis of the camera.

After 1940, the huge increase in the number of moving shots, and particularly the appearance of shot-sequences, broke down the similarity between shot and set-up by suggesting contradictory definitions, such as the description of *Rope*, shot in 12 continuous takes (each one involving at least twenty shots), as a "film composed of only 12 shots"...

At the height of Bazin's influence, I criticised the use of the designation "shot-sequence" as being employed too freely, because it contradicted the definitions both of the *shot*, based on incontrovertible notions of optics and geometry, and the *sequence* made up principally of a series of successive shots relating to various different significations.

Referring to one shot-sequence in *Citizen Kane*, I wrote:

In effect, when an image shows us a face in *close-up* on the extreme right of the frame and, in the rest, in mid-shot, two or three people behaving in a particular way, others in long-shot and, in the background, someone coming into the room, we are hard put to define the shot according to established terminology. How might we describe it? – establishing-shot, long-shot, what?

It would seem correct to call it an *establishing-shot* [...] but then the relative positions of the characters must be precisely defined (in the *script*), since they are all (except Orson Welles) of equal importance and the man entering from the background causing such different reactions might very well be the *main character*[3].

According to the normally accepted scale, the shot description defines the area in the view-finder, but, whenever the mise-en-scène exploits depth-of-field, it is the content of the whole field which defines the shot and not the area of the field itself. Which is what Bonitzer himself indicates:

the idea of shot-sequence is paradoxical in the sense that it describes a shot which may contain *several shots*. The relationship between container and content obviously presupposes a different notion of shot [...][4].

Now, this is where the problem starts – also the ambiguity. For the same word is being used to describe both the geometrical *place* or *places* where the action occurs within the field of view in the view-finder and the unity of the shot enclosing that field of view. Similar meanings are now diametrically opposite. But the same word cannot describe two completely different things. A choice must be made.

As long as the shots in question are static, as is the case with the majority of shot-sequences in *Citizen Kane* or *The Magnificent Ambersons*, the problem is avoided. Indeed, all shots stacked up in the depth of the field of view are on the same plane of focus, since the wide-angled lenses used were in focus from 0.75m right up to infinity. In this sense, the shot-sequence may be understood as a single shot since there is no optical differentiation to interfere with its universalising geometry.

This is the case with the shot in *Ivan the Terrible* quoted by Bonitzer where two contrasting themes are shown in the same shot:

Depth-of-field and shot-sequence: *Citizen Kane*, by Orson Welles, 1941.

The snaking line of people moving towards Ivan in his castle and, right in foreground, the angular profile of the Tzar with his pointed beard.

According to Bonitzer, the depth is "flattened" in the sense that Eisenstein emphasises the formal relationship between the linear designs more than the spatialisation of the field of view. Yet the spatialisation exists nonetheless. Mitry wonders:

> Are we dealing with a close-up of Ivan or a long shot of the people? Both, without a doubt. But are we to see in them two shots, as Mitry would have it? No, the image is made up of one shot, created for the purpose, in rhythmic opposition to and harmony with the shots immediately before and after it[5].

I agree entirely – except that Bonitzer makes an insulting gener-alisation of my argument. As with the previous example, what we are dealing with here is a *single general shot*. It is like saying when

The snaking line of people and Ivan in the foreground in *Ivan the Terrible*, by S.M. Eisenstein, 1944.

looking at a landscape: this tree is in the foreground, this in the background, without the need to dilate or contract the pupil in order to see each one separately. So we can say that the shot refers to a simple or complicated action within a space undifferentiated, undivided by any sort of optical system. Dividing shots up in terms of scale achieves nothing, but the term shot nonetheless retains its dual descriptive function, defining both the fragment, the unity of the set-up, and its content.

Now, it is a different matter when the shot-sequence contains a moving shot involving, within the same space-time unity, in a single flowing movement through a single camera take, a whole series of different places, angles and shots, instead of small fragments of space and time associated arbitrarily by being edited together. In that case, as Bonitzer describes it:

The unity of the film splits in two, the shot and the take, and it is no longer possible to glue the pieces back together[6].

In point of fact, it is the word which splits in two and describes two things which are no longer interchangeable. Except in terms of static shots, with or without depth-of-field, the film unit stops being the *shot*, but the *take* since, however long and convoluted this may be, the take forms an indivisible fragment, exactly like a *single* shot. But continuing to refer to these constantly varying fragments as *shots*, using a previously equivalent description is meaningless. As is the case with the zoom, which is neither shot nor sequence since it contains a continual transition from close-up to wide-angle (or the reverse) and, as a lens, is only ever used to cover a detail or quick effect.

It is not just a matter of using the correct terminology, but what lies behind the words themselves. It does not really matter what the word is and if we must find one to describe the static or moving units previously referred to as shot, why not *segment*, the word shot reverting to its original purely technical function and referring exclusively to an internal designation or the analytical description of relevant places included within the different spaces recorded by the camera.

Close up

All the slightly wider shots (mid-shot to establishing-shot) include a number of details whose meaning carried through into the subsequent shots ensures the development of the action, its dynamism, while keeping the audience's attention through all the missing, dissociated links of the chain of meaning, through everything inviting a complementary meaning. Each shot is in effect a more or less complex series of signifiers and signifieds whose associations with previous significations give rise to ideas or feelings which explain the events being described.

There is too much that is suggested or implied within a shot to be able to associate (as is so often the case) the meaning of shot-relationships with that of word-relationships.

Since meaning is conferred because the fragment of time and space represented is formalised, it is easy to see that the isolated shot is already, through the relationship of its form and content, a *statement* equivalent to one or more phrases. It is futile to look for a "smaller unit of signification", as various semiologists have attempted to do.

It would take at least a sentence to describe the smallest close-up of an object because the object, having a necessary *position*, cannot be totally isolated like a word in a dictionary. Nevertheless, since it is the only signifier concerned, it may be associated with the word which describes it and therefore act – contrary to all other shots – like a *linguistic unit*.

With this important difference: though the word "gun" for instance may describe a concrete object and signify the concept with which it is associated, the close-up does not possess the denominative or demonstrative function ascribed to it by Christian Metz. The close-up of a gun does not say "here is a gun" or "this is a gun". It merely *shows that the gun is there*: *that particular* gun and none other. As with every other kind of shot, although in a much more meaningful way, the close-up assumes a specific character only in the context which determines it. Yet if it becomes eclipsed by what it reveals, it proves nothing. If it signifies anything, it is immediately the idea suggested by the associations which the gun has with the events described in the sequence of which it is part.

From which we can see that though the close-up acts like a sign, it leaps over genuinely linguistic significations in order to reach directly the narrative or discursive significations where the association of sign and signified is always accidental. This is doubtless true of most shots, but the significations of the close-up have a symbolic quality which distinguishes them from all other shots whose quality is mostly allusive, suggestive or simply descriptive.

Meanwhile, it was this facility for possessing a constant "potential as a sign" which surprised and excited the first theorists.

Moreover, as well as the ideas and feelings of which it is the ephemeral sign, the object presented in close-up inevitably draws attention to its perceptible qualities, to everything which *makes it different*. It appeals to the emotions but these can only be felt, experienced by seeing it. In isolation it becomes a "whole" relative to the frame which sets it apart, within its own constituent parts, the internal components which subdivide it, whereas, in wider shots, it is submerged under the vast number of relationships between the objects and the whole of which they form part.

The close-up thereby presents a tactile, sensual impression of objects. It concentrates on the object, on its forms, all the recognitive and dynamogenic operations relating to the knowledge we have of it; and this before it makes any appeal to the intellect. Of all shots, it is the most concrete, most objective through what it shows, the most abstract, most subjective through what it signifies. Any emotion is contained in the represented object, but also in the forms of the representation and the ideas suggested – as it is in all other shots, obviously, but in a much more relevant and, especially, more meaningful manner. Thus, in *The Battleship Potemkin*, the pince-nez hanging off the steel hawser gives, at the emotional level, the impression of a disaster – but of a ridiculous disaster. Not only does it "represent" the doctor who has been thrown overboard (or rather his absence) by showing the part for the whole, but it also symbolises, not without irony, the collapse of the old order represented by this officer.

Since there is nothing intelligible in the cinema which has not been given through the senses (visual perception evoking all sensations, tactile and others, relating to a given object), the main criticism to be levelled at structural semiology, beyond the blind alleys it has frequently taken, is that it considers significations only at the level of what is intelligible, totally ignoring what is felt, as for instance rhythm which offers many possibilities for analysis totally disregarded by structural analysis. As though temporal relationships do not represent one of the most basic elements of film structure. So much so that, as the raw material of art transcending mere communication, emotional qualities play a considerable part in significations, the signified being almost always filtered, expanded by the emotion, as much by what cannot be expressed as by what is expressed.

Shots do not just present a difference of scale or a more or less extended spatial field. Using the represented objects to compose a suitable *form*, a "specific quality", each of them acts differently on the percept and, therefore, the consciousness, the emotions, the intellect. The same script, shot first in wide shots and then in tight close-ups, would provide two entirely different films, even though they would be following the same dramatic development, the same narrative sequence. The story might be the same, but the impressions, the ideas and feelings expressed would be quite different, would have a different value, a different meaning – particularly if the rhythms were also changed.

We have only to imagine Dreyer's *The Passion of Joan of Arc* shot in wide-shots rather than close-ups and mid-shots: nothing would have the same meaning.

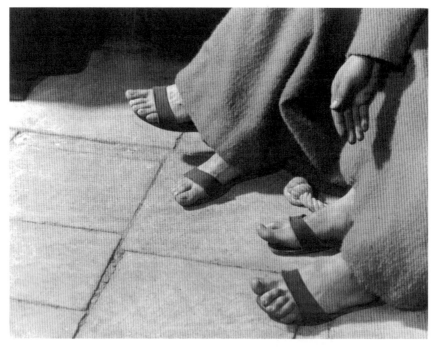

Details in a downward tilting close-up: Carl Dreyer's *The Passion of Joan of Arc,*
1928.

This example enables us to cover a sub-section devoted to facial
close-ups used – mainly – to give emphasis to a reaction which
might be imperceptible but reveals the psychic state of the character, such as trembling lips or fluttering eyelids, a sudden
movement of the eyes, etc. These close-ups always follow in a
sequence of wider shots and are, as often as not, the *enlargement* of
an expression begun in the preceding shot.

Facial close-ups

Towards 1915, when the use of close-shots (of actors, not
objects) had become widespread, their integration within the
sequence was very different from what it is today. In the most
important films (those of Griffith, Ince and twenty or so of the top
level of directors), transitions to close-shots were made in straight
cuts. An action begun in one shot was followed through into the
next. Matching movement had not yet been discovered, therefore
changes in the camera axis had to be used to disguise the jump-

cuts and overlaps but the dynamic continuity remained intact. In poor films the solution was simple: a subtitle inserted between shots softened the transition from one to another, such that it was difficult to exploit any sort of associative effect or "signifying montage". It was another process altogether in standard cinema. In these films, made for a mass audience, instead of a continuity of movement from establishing-shot to close-shot, the *same gestures were repeated in the same axis and within the same time.*

If, for instance, there was a courtroom scene in which a woman had to give evidence, the scene would be recorded by two cameras set side by side. While one was filming the whole scene, the other would be *simultaneously* shooting the woman in close-up.

Which would give:

A. The woman stepping into the witness-box, raising her right hand to give the oath, glancing furtively at the accused (off-screen), looking anxious then settling herself. Fade down and iris-in/iris out to:

B. Close-shot. The woman makes the *same movements.*
Fade down and iris-in/iris-out to:

C. (same as A). Continuation of the movement: the woman settling herself. The judge asks her a question.

D. Subtitle explaining the question; etc.

The close-shot (or close-up according to the context) was therefore merely a way of showing a closer view of what had already been seen, drawing attention to something the audience might have missed. It was merely an addition included, *as a shot*, in the body of the film, not included, *as a movement*, within the dynamic continuity of the action. Which explains the constant marking and unacceptable repetition of time which we find so irritating nowadays when we watch reruns of old films.

The face as the "mirror of the soul" was a pet-theme for a time of various theoreticians towards the end of the silent era: "The face is psycho-analytical", Jean Epstein wrote. And Béla Balázs: "It is a mirror in which the source, the essence of the soul is reflected." Now, the face is able to reflect this "state of mind" only when its expressions are related by the audience to an event, to passions whose effects we imagine they translate. As with everything else, it is purely a question of relationships.

In some silent films the *close-up* (the reason it was called close-up in the first place) was surrounded by a circular mask: an iris

An "expressionistic" close-up in John Ford's *The Long Voyage Home*, 1940.

outside the camera. Its use was abandoned around 1920, however. From then on, faces were recorded "full-screen" and, even later on, framed alongside a significant detail. In Dreyer's film, shot almost entirely in close-ups, we can see that Joan's face is placed almost invariably between parts of other faces (chopped off by the frame) or in front of characters (monks or soldiers) shown in mid-shot. Except for the sequence where she is alone in her cell, there are very few shots in which her face is totally isolated. It contrasts therefore with other similar close-ups (Cauchon, Massieu and others), for the film is a confrontation of faces. Here they are never enlargements introduced into the narrative sequence for the sole purpose of emphasising the actors' talent whose close-ups are unwatchable because they interrupt the narrative flow contributing nothing but a worthless additional expression. On the contrary, the disruption caused by the close-ups of objects are *dynamic* disruptions. They are not perceived as disruptions because they *generate meaning*. In effect, a facial close-up *does not signify*; it *expresses* and almost never acquires the quality as a sign which the isolated object assumes. Except, that is, in *The Passion of Joan of Arc*:

contrasted and juxtaposed in a kind of abstract representation, the facial close-ups become, as it were, *the sign of what they express.* This is what makes Dreyer's film so characteristic and, sometimes, certain of Bresson's or Bergman's films.

Pans and tracking-shots

Amongst camera movements, the simplest and oldest (1896) is obviously the pan, which is the same as the vision of someone standing still and turning his head to the left or right, or the tilt, which is the same as someone lifting his head up or down. The camera remains fixed and pivots on its axis.

The term *tracking-shot* has various different meanings: either it is a shot "in motion", i.e. filming the countryside from a moving train, car, cable-car, etc. The camera remans fixed and moves with the moving support on which it is set. This type of tracking-shot is as old as the cinema itself (*The Grand Canal in Venice*, shot by Promio in 1897).

More generally, we mean it in the sense of "trucking" the camera on a platform mounted on rails or rubber wheels. The camera moves in relation to one or more characters, ahead of them or behind them, getting closer or further away, etc. This type of camera movement, used in conjunction with the actors' movements or any moving object independent of the camera, was used for the first time – apparently – by Griffith in 1909.

The shot which tracks in between static characters (restaurant, theatre), the camera picking up the behaviour of some of the characters in the drama or representing one of them moving relative to the others, is rather more recent. It was used for the first time by Murnau in *The Last Laugh*, in 1925.

Since the advent of talkies, cranes (1929) and "jib-arms" (1935) have enabled all movements in space to be combined, but the widespread use of portable cameras during the 1960s (and the advent of "steadicam") has made a marked difference to the style of films providing a freedom of movement previously unimaginable. A freedom which has also produced effects as intolerable as they are unsuitable.

Made to translate the speed with which we turn our heads, "zip-pans" work against their own intentions. In fact, when we quickly turn our heads and our eyes take 1/6th of a second to move from a field of view 2 or 3 metres away to one 7 metres away, any objects caught in our vision are not seen as though "zipping" from one to the other. Moreover, if the field of view is very close – 50cm to 1 metre – the objects are reduced, leaving as it were a trace behind them. Even so they are not blurred.

Firstly because, in not being limited by a frame, the visual field is unaffected by its isolating effect, and by its associated structure. Secondly, and more importantly, because we are unable to move our bodies (or eyes) faster than the minimum time for visual perception, that is, the perceptual threshold which varies (according to the lighting of the field of view) from between 1/50th and 1/100th of a second (nothing to do with retinal persistence which is associated with it in a different way and is related to a short-circuit in the cortex called the "phi effect"). In other words, to perceive images as if in a zip pan, we would need to spin on the spot at a rate of something like 20 or 40 turns per second.

The camera, on the other hand, recording at a rate of 24 frames a second, will record only 4 frames in the same time (7 metres in 1/6th of a second). And because the shutter speed of the camera is not fast enough relative to the speed at which the camera is moving, each of the four frames will be blurred, which is what gives the zip-pan effect.

I am teaching grandmother to suck eggs. Every member of the camera department knows this. And yet there are still cameramen who persist in panning the camera at speeds based on the human body. Trying to be true to life, they are consistently wrong – moreover, they startle and upset the stomachs of even the sturdiest of audiences. A similar speed would be conceivable if it were possible to record an even greater number of frames in the same time. Eight frames in 1/16th of a second for the same distance would make quick pans at least watchable. Filming – and projecting – should therefore be at 50 f.p.s., which has many advantages, since the reproduction of movement is smoother the more the movement is broken down into a greater number of frames. This camera speed, technical considerations apart, was proposed by many cameramen at the beginning of the talkies. It was only rejected for reasons of economy, since it would have meant using twice as much film-stock. However, it would have allowed silent films to be projected "normally" by tripling each frame in new prints...

Editing against the movement of the camera

Moreover, the development of film style during the course of the first twenty years of the century, using editing rather than camera movement, has surprised many critics and theorists with scant knowledge of the history, not only of the cinema, but the conditions of work – producing, directing, photographing – over this period. We should let Christian Metz take up the story:

The history of the cinema between 1900 and 1915 invites a striking observation: the indirect technique – more questionable in some senses, less immediate – has played a more vital role than the other; montage, and its corollary, the shooting-script [translator's note: literally, 'technical breakdown'], have helped to liberate the camera in a more decisive way than camera-movements themselves. Of course, panning and tracking movements were not dismissed, but the most important consideration lay elsewhere. Camera movements do not really exist as such in Griffith's films, although he exploits certain of them in a quite wonderful way. The great events of these fifteen years are not represented by the first appearance of the panning shot used for dramatic effect (E.S. Porter's *The Great Train Robbery*, 1903), nor the famous camera 'displacement' in *The Birth of a Nation*, but the first use of cross-cutting (F. Williamson's *Attack on a China Mission*, 1901), parallel editing (E.S. Porter's *The Ex-Convict*, 1905), changes of angle (in Porter's films), and also the notion of inserting a close-up into a sequence of long shots (A.G. Smith's *The Little Doctor*, 1900), then of exploiting the close-up for expressive purposes, rather than as a simple 'study in detail' (Griffith's *Judith of Bethulia*, 1913; Thomas Ince's *The Fugitive*, 1914): in short, the effects of montage[7].

It is no accident therefore that André Malraux and Albert Laffay cite the shooting-script as a corollary of the camera being liberated[8], whereas Béla Balázs[9] and Jean Mitry[10] consider it to be montage. These writers choose not to reveal that this contains a paradox: it is not camera movements which have made the camera more mobile. They write as though the transformation of the cinematograph into the cinema centered on the problems of the succession of various images, much more than on an additional modality of the image itself – such as 'camera movement'[11].

This may well have "gone more quickly to the core of the problem", as Christian Metz suggested but, at that particular moment, no one could have known this... The truth is much simpler. As paradoxical as it may seem today, montage was used in preference to camera movement precisely *because it was much easier*. For reasons which ought to be explained, before the 1920s, tracking-shots represented on average only 10% of shots. All (or almost all) shots were static. Since each one involved a separate take, a separate fragment, it was normal for them to be spliced together according to the order required by the dramatic action – without taking account – before 1906 – of any signification produced by the specifics of the ordering. It was only as it was put it into practice that it was realised that this "association of shots in a particular order" produced a meaning, an unexpected signification. Which was immediately exploited, developed, refined by Griffith as well as a dozen or so others during the period 1910–1914, and enabled critics to discover rhythm and montage.

Why were there so few tracking-shots? It was not very difficult to mount a camera on a dolly. However, any movement involved altering the focus, and cameramen turning the crank-handle (with their right hand) would have found it virtually impossible to operate the focus ring at the same time with their left. Moreover, controlling the focus would have required using a through-the-lens view-finder. Now, at the time, the view-finder was used only for "framing" purposes. It was closed during the take, so as not to fog the film. A "sighting mechanism", parallel to the filming axis, enabled the actors' movements to be controlled, but not the framing or the follow focus. Which was of no significance since the shots were static. In addition, with the exception of the very rare and very brief movements "in depth", if the camera moved (mid-shots or long-shots) it always maintained the same distance between it and its object.

From 1915 onwards (1912 in the case of Ince, Griffith and one or two others), the camera-operator had an assistant beside him to alter focus according to reference-points chalked on the ground during rehearsals. Towards 1923–4, the new cameras were equipped with light-tight (with rubber eye-pieces) view-finders adjustable to the eye of the operator, allowing him to frame up through the lens during shooting and, from 1926–7, the widespread development of automatic cameras, whose internal electric motors eliminated the need to turn the crank, freed the operator's hands. From then on, tracking-shots became more numerous. Cranes, dollies and, of course, the hand-held camera took over. Which is how, like it or not, film aesthetics comes to rely on technicalities – themselves dependent on research prompted by intentions which may be described as ideological. The same is true of *depth of field*.

Depth of field and the deep field

We must be careful not to confuse what is termed *depth of field* (or use of depth in the spatial field) with an interpretation of space, with the field which is only *deep* relative to the given area.

Depth of field is a means of expression which appeared in 1942 with new lenses of short focal length, so-called "wide-angles" (16mm and 18mm), used for the first time and developed by the cameraman Greg Toland in Orson Welles' *Citizen Kane*.

A *deep field* is produced by 50mm lenses used in the cinema, as in photography, from the very beginning. Fixed to the most basic of box-brownies, they allowed focus to be maintained over a "total field", i.e. from 3 metres (subjects framed from head to foot) through to infinity.

If a technique is to be judged by its complexity or its effects, then the most extraordinary movement within a "deep field" was produced by Griffith in 1916 in *Intolerance* when Cyrus's armies enter Babylon driving the crowds before them. Yet it is obvious that what is shown is a *descriptive* simultaneity. The characters have no other connection than of being there and being involved, despite themselves, in a global event. Now, in *Citizen Kane*, what we are being shown is not just two or more characters acting simultaneously, but *reacting differently to the same cause*.

However, though the space contained in this way corresponds more or less to the visual field, its image in no way conforms to normal vision. In fact, the wide-angle distorts perspective (in itself the source of some significant effects) and focus over the whole field is artificial. If we focus on an object in front of us, it appears sharp but everything beyond it soft; if we shift our focus to the background, then this becomes sharp whereas the object becomes "duplicated" through the effect of our binocular vision.

Certain cameramen tried to translate this peculiarity of vision

A "deep field": the grand entrance into Babylon in David W. Griffith's
Intolerance, 1916.

into film. By altering focus gradually, distant objects at first soft became progressively sharper as the foreground objects became blurred – and vice versa (with no duplication, the camera being monocular). This technique also became fashionable (between 1935 and 1940), but eventually excruciating. In point of fact, in reality, this perfectly natural process becomes more or less imperceptible because of the chosen focus-point, whereas the image, imposing on us both points *at the same time*, one of them blurred, the other sharp, gives it an annoying emphasis.

On the other hand, a photograph composed with "depth of field" comprises a totality which the eye sees according to separate perceptual fields and presents an image *uniformly in focus*. In other words, we see a *representation* relating with the same sharpness objects which appear as near or far only by the effect of perspective. Which is the same as saying that the inaccurate and interpretative reproduction which maintains focus over the total field presents a "corrected" equivalent of normal perception whereas a consistent translation ends up being a false representation.

Inflicted like a torture on the audience's eyes, this interplay of blurriness and sharpness thankfully disappeared in its turn – except in television where electronic cameras are almost able to achieve the instantaneity of visual accommodation.

In an image registering depth of field, the effect is as though the space is related according to two separate shots imposed on top of each other within the same frame – creating a kind of *caesura* establishing a associative effect similar to that of montage; a kind of montage *within the shot*, for though keeping focus over the whole field underlines the homogeneity of the space, the 18.5 draws attention to the separation of the areas which make it up (closer foreground/more distant background) and enables what normally would have been shown in two successive shots to be combined.

The field and what lies outside it

Remarks about what lies outside the field and the endless discussions about the notions of continuity and discontinuity derive mostly from epistemological platitudes. If the following from Pascal Bonitzer is not a platitude, then I do not know what is:

> The cinema utilises as much what it does not show as what it does show [and] cinematic space is made up of a space-inside-the-field and a space-outside-the-field, of what is seen and what is not seen[12].

Through its limits, the field clearly implies and defines what lies outside it; but what lies outside it is not excluded. It is not terra incognita, another world; simply "what is not seen", which may be seen in the succeeding shot, which is always there potentially, outside but to one side. And not neutral as a non-presence but acting more or less directly on the events in the frame; either through information suggested by looks "off-screen" whose character may have a decisive effect on the behaviour of the characters "within" the frame; or through noises which inform us about the immediate surroundings and create a meaningful atmosphere. In 1927 Béla Balázs was already referring to "indirect vision" with respect to information outside the field perceptible through their effects and more meaningful than merely suggested. We should

Effects of depth-of-field in Eric Von Stroheim's *Greed*, 1923; diagonal
composition in *La Nuit de San Lorenzo*.

remember among the best-known examples: Edna's massage in *Public Opinion*, the completely naked young woman out-of-vision at the bottom of the screen, with the movements of the masseuse's hands moulding the shape of her body. And, in the same film, the train the only part of which we see as night falls being the platform lights reflected in the carriage windows as it draws into the station, then again as it pulls away with Edna leaving frame, effectively "climbing onto the train". The murder of the trapeze artist in *Variety*, which happens off-screen where what we see (for symbolic reasons) is the marriage-bed. The aeroplane shot down by Charlie Chaplin in *Soldier Charlie*, where we see Charlie take aim at a Fokker bi-plane, then follow the expression on his face, the direction of his eyes, as the aircraft falls from the sky[13]. But there are many more examples. As many in Chaplin's films (one of the first from 1914 to exploit the suggestive power of off-screen events) as in many others, for instance Renoir's *Nana* quoted at length by Noël Burch, whose effects were already commonplace by 1926. Nowadays they pass unnoticed.

Burch points out that there are not only the four off-screen possibilities on either side of the frame, but also the "fourth wall" – face on to the camera, or the painter in the case of a painting. However, this other wall acts as such only in a limited space enabling what is "off-screen" to be related to the field of view. The best known example in this respect is Velásquez's *Las Meninas* where, within the painting, the mirror reveals the King looking at his children framed in the doorway.

Mirrors enable action placed in the axis of the camera to be included in this way, the action becoming the image of an image, reflected in the mirror set in the field of view. A striking example of "off/on screen" is in John Ford's *The Prisoner of Shark Island*. A military guard is shown in close shot by the prison gate pinning into a glass case the names of prisoners condemned to death, including that of Doctor Mudd. Having disposed of the piece of paper, the soldier closes the glass case, in which the anguished face of Mrs Mudd is suddenly reflected, introduced thereby into the field as though "captured" by it, while remaining physically outside the field of view.

Yet beyond a certain distance, the space where the spectator (or the camera) would stand cannot be considered as "outside the field of view". It is the place to which someone looks, implying a

The "fourth wall" included in the frame by a "mirror effect" in John Ford's *The Whole Town's Talking*, 1935, and in Joseph Losey's *The Servant*, 1963.

certain distance without which that someone looking becomes looked at himself. Which is effectively a definition of the frame without which the image would be incapable of being outlined. Though its limits are not to be compared with the visual field, the frame behaves in the same way as our body, creating in reality a material distinction between the Self and the non-Self.

We might imagine a landscape painter wanting, through some crazy impulse to push realism to its limit, to reproduce everything included within his visual field. He would realise that, in front of him in the foreground, would be his painting on its easel. He would then have to include them in his painting. But, on the painting represented within his canvas, he would have to represent the canvas which he is representing himself as painting. And on the painting represented in his painting, another painting representing that painting. And so on, in a regression to infinity, like the advertising posters on which a black worker is shown holding a tin of cocoa on which a black worker is shown. . ., etc.

In conclusion we would agree with Noël Burch that "it is obvious that any camera movement involves the space outside the field changing into the space of the frame, and vice versa"[14].

What is also obvious but has been rather neglected by critics is what corresponds at the temporal level to events happening outside the field. Ellipses, for instance, are the equivalent of the "indirect vision" described by Béla Balázs.

As Pascal Bonitzer observed, it is clear that the space outside the field is in no way *imaginary* in the sense that it cannot be seen; rather it is *imagined*; the characters in the film do not stop existing when they leave the field of view, their existence being capable of consideration only at the level of fiction. It is also true that the "cinematic image is haunted by what is not found within it" and that what happens outside the field of view has a "quality of uncertainty, even angst, which confer on it with an enormous dramatic power". However, when critics refer to the "incompleteness of the film image" we have to ask them to define their terms. Whether on film or not, all images are incomplete since they are only ever the *particular* representation of a *particular* fragment of the world, inasmuch as, if something is incomplete in the film, the following shot completes it with an incompleteness completed in its turn, and so on in a continuity which can only ever be a particular look at a particular aspect of the world. It is also true that at the level of this continuity, the image, no longer considered as a fragment in the context of the represented space but as an element in a signifying sequence, ensures its semantic autonomy vis-à-vis the meaning which it helps to produce.

Moreover, some clever minds would have it that the cinema – whether inside the field or outside it – is a "mystifying" force. Doubtless the illusion here has a more formal, more insidiously "realist" basis from the fact that it is a duplication of reality, yet because film shows us what seems to be there but is there no longer, it confirms the absence of things behind their formal presence – and this is, must be, a *snare and delusion*. Yet are those who would have it thus so naïve as to believe that only film images are illusory? I will not go so far as to cast doubt on the reality of the world but, as I have already suggested, this reality is only ever a datum of our senses picking up fragments of phenomena which our consciousness turns into a reality which is "effectively real" for us.

When we look up at the sky, we know (but overlook the fact) that no star actually exists where we see it, with the exception of a few thousand whose light takes between ten years (Sirius) and four hundred (the Polar Star) to reach us. The others – hundreds of millions – are much further away. At the speed of 300,000 kilometres a second, it takes a hundred thousand years for light to reach us from the Milky Way and more than two million years to cross the distance separating us from the Andromeda galaxy near our own. Further out, the galaxies stack up at between 50 million and 15 trillion light years distance. When we observe the Andromeda nebula, therefore, we are not seeing it "as it is" but as it was two million, two hundred thousand years ago. Where is it, how is it today? We have no idea; indeed we do not even know whether it still exists. We will know it – so to speak – only in two million years' time.

Thus when we look at the sky, what we are seeing is the past, a distant past. The vault of heaven is peopled with ghosts: a rather more consistent delusion than that of film!... But is it not also a delusion to extend the idea of the present to the whole universe? The illusion is concealed in the hidden depths of reality...

Looks to camera

As I mentioned above, "the space where the camera would stand [...] implies a certain distance without which someone looking (the spectator) himself becomes looked at". This "fourth wall" of the scene marks an unbridgeable separation between two universes. Communication cannot and "must not" exist, without exposing the fiction by revealing it as such. Acceptable, at a pinch, in the theatre – in comic rather than straight plays – the "aside to the audience" is intolerable in the cinema where nothing must appear to have been contrived "for" an audience witnessing a supposedly true event rather than knowing that the story is purely imaginary.

Even as early as 1909, Frank Woods (one of the first serious critics) was writing in essence:

> A good director constantly asks his actors not to look at the camera, and good actors try not to. Many of them succeed; yet is the simple fact of not looking at the camera enough? Should there be a complete indifference to the presence of the camera?
>
> By turning his face to the camera, the actor betrays the fact that he is acting, shows there is someone in front of him, hidden from the audience, whom the actor is addressing. The impression of reality disappears instantly and the hypnotic illusion capturing the audience's spirit vanishes[15].

This was the case with the Rigadin series (1909–1914), where the actor, not bothering to preserve the impression of reality, instead emphasised the artificiality of the story by making the audience a kind of accomplice "let into the secret".

This kind of aside to the audience, still common in comic films made before 1915, disappeared a long time ago. It has been replaced, however, by what nowadays is called – rather clumsily – the look to camera, a look which demands various conditions. As Marc Vernet asks:

> In what context is it possible to refer to looks to camera? The question begs a whole grey area in evaluation of the direction of looks and the way they are filmed. The expression "look to camera" is a poor one since it attempts to explain in terms of *filming* an effect produced when the film is *projected*, viz. the *spectator* has the impression that the character in the narrative is looking straight at him in his seat in the cinema. So, three different spaces are being lined up: the filming process, the narrative universe, and the cinema auditorium. Nothing surprising in

that, one might say, since the "look to camera" has precisely the effect of producing this alignment. Yet, cause can become confused with effect. Also: does this alignment actually occur except for the spectator?

For the moment, let us confine ourselves to the filming process. To achieve a "look to camera" the actor must look into the lens without any other actor or object coming between him and the camera. He must stand quite close to the camera so that it is possible to see the direction of his look in the image: he must therefore be shot in close-up (or mid-shot) as front on as is possible. His look must also be focussed on the focal plane of the lens or camera (he must bring the "focus" of his eyes forward) in order to give the impression that he is concentrating on something or someone – otherwise his look appears empty, with no counterpart or purpose, stuck in no-man's land. [...] Moreover, it is worthy of note that what is called "look to camera" is the union of visual data (the look "into the lens") and sound data (a speech or comment). It is obviously very tempting to explain in terms of a look information deriving from the voice and sentence structure, even gestures (an arm raised to the camera). It is easy to see how a parallel may be drawn between a look and a "voice-over", which is a purely vocal speech to the audience[16].

But looks such as this occur rarely in the cinema. They are much more frequent in television where, without any contrivance, a narrator, in referring to events illustrated on the screen, speaks to listeners rather than to spectators. Such is the case with Alain Decaux whose look is *not* focussed on the focal plane of the camera, precisely in order to avoid giving the impression that he is looking at someone *in particular*, instead anyone looking at him.

In fact the only justifiable look to camera is when the actor (not necessarily in close-up) talks to the audience during the film in order to poke fun at the film in which he is acting. Or when the subject is the film in the process of being made (as in François Truffaut's *La Nuit américaine* [*Day for Night*]), where the director and his crew wish to give the impression that they belong to the same world as the audience, thereby dismissing the drama they are in the process of filming as an obvious fiction.

There is another look which directors are almost always at pains to avoid, for the reason that they confuse it with the look *to camera*, and that is the look *towards the camera*, i.e. towards the space "alongside the audience", to which it is equally possible to look as to the space outside the field of view to the right or left. In this instance, either the character is talking to someone not seen and needs must give the impression of looking at him without focussing on the plane of the camera; or else he is simply looking at what is before his eyes, people, houses, landscapes, while he soliloquises like Belmondo in *A Bout de souffle* [*Breathless*] – a film which, in a revolutionary way, proved merely that looks directed towards the camera were in no way, or were not necessarily, looks directed *at the camera*.

In the case of singers singing directly into the camera (in the example quoted by Jim Collins, referred to by Marc Vernet), as in American musicals, when "various shots are seen where the audience plays a narrative role" it is no more than the equivalent of shot/reverse-shot. The camera takes the place of the audience instead of that of the other character in a two-handed scene.

Technique and ideology

It is not the purpose of this study to be polemical and I have absolutely no intention of downplaying the influence of ideology – ideologies – on the development of the cinema. But, as I said with reference to perspective, this does not mean that we should constantly be putting the horse before the cart, at which Jean-Louis Comolli was a past-master when he was writing his theories in *Les Cahiers du cinéma*[17].

According to him, the reason the use "depth of field" was more or less rejected between 1928 and 1942 was not technical or aesthetic, but economic and ideological "dictated by the interests and power of the ruling classes".

It is obvious that technical considerations were not entirely responsible, technicalities being subject, as anything else, to the circumstances of any given society. However, it becomes necessary to speak plainly, to sort the chaff from the wheat with respect to close-ups, perspective and depth-of-field.

For a start, we should point out there has never been an "eclipse of depth-of-field", if this is meant in the sense of huge wide-angles including the whole depth of space. There were hundreds of examples during the thirties. If, on the other hand, it is meant in the sense of the aesthetic conditions developed in Orson Welles's films then, effectively, there was an "eclipse" since the majority of these conditions were unrealisable before the development of short focal-length lenses, i.e. before 1942[18]...

The truth is that there was a particular fashion during the years 1928–40 to film the majority of scenes shot in the studio with lenses with wide apertures and, therefore, limited depth of field. This had to do firstly with the widespread use of panchromatic stock from 1927–8. Insensitive to the blue end of the spectrum, this stock made it imperative to replace arc-lamps with incandescents whose spectrum tended towards the yellow end and burned with intense heat. Since their power was less than that of arc-lamps, cameramen were forced: either to use more of them, which meant that filming had to be interrupted constantly and the lamps switched off in order to reduce the unbearable heat in the studio (make-up would start to melt...); or else to "open the lens up" to its maximum in order to expose the film correctly with less available light. Which was the choice most often made. As a consequence of which, mid-shots were sharp against an out-of-focus background.

Talkies also put an end to arc-lamps, because they had a tendency to "spark", making sound-recording impossible. However, from 1932, silent arcs burning yellow light (using tungsten arcs) enabled normal conditions to be resumed. But cameramen – and directors – having become used to creating "hazy" images and to use many more close-shots relying on editing, continued along this track "because it was the right way", and also because it allowed them to play with rhythm and shot-contrasts.

Thus there was no compulsion, except for a very short period, at the level purely of technicality. And even less so, at the level of ideology... The same is also true of close-ups. Why is it that (with very rare exceptions) there are no close-ups in any film before 1912? There was no problem in bringing the camera in closer nor of using "portrait" lenses similar to those used by still photographers. What happened was that, as in the theatre, characters *had* to be shown from head to foot. Henri Fescourt, who directed for Gaumont from before 1914, relates in his book *La Foi et les montagnes* that Léon Gaumont made him redo shots which accidentally framed only half an actor's body. Gaumont used to shout at him: "You should know that heads can't walk by themselves. . .!"[19]

It was much the same for every country in the world. Ideology? Just as it was in the first years of the century for shots following each other according to different points of view, it was a matter of cultural tradition, ideology suggesting economic-political agenda irrelevant to the question.

As with tracking-shots, the reasons and conditions governing the cinema's development are often unexpectedly much simpler – and more complicated.

Note relating to the close up

It is odd to realise how far certain critics, even the most experienced, will sometimes go in following dubious misinterpretations. For instance, in an article in the Belgian review *Gros Plan*, Philippe Dubois quoting from some rather confused remarks of Sadoul on *L'Arrivée d'un train en gare de La Ciotat*, observes that:

> This train, which approaches from deep in the field of view and moves without stopping through the whole space, quite literally makes us feel the *strange forces* associated, not with different sizes marking its journey like the compartments of an empty structure which it fills bit by bit, but with the constant *transition* from one to the other, with a release from the system, a crossing over. Through its continuous movement, *The Arrival of a Train* bypasses all articulatory structures, avoids the imposition of a "scale of shot sizes" seen as an a priori optical-technical system, with its various degrees, its distinctive criteria, its preestablished patterns.

But this is precisely what depth-of-field is. Which then leads him to inveigh against:

> A shot presented as such, clearly identifiable, isolated, separate, discrete in the linguistic sense of the word, that is cut off from the others by a barrier marking a distinctive frontier – and which by that fact sets up a preestablished, strict, structural system: the *system* of a "scale of shot sizes".

But this "scale" has never existed anywhere except in "film grammars" established during the thirties by theoreticians for want of classifications. As I have said a hundred times before, these arbitrary distinctions, these divisions into segments are only a shorthand used for convenience sake. There are as many shots possible as there are points between the lens and infinity, the real distinction being marked by the spatial margin "in focus" by virtue of the focal length, the lighting of the subject and the size of the aperture. Philippe Dubois goes on:

> If there was a genuinely distinctive *effect* created by Lumière's film apparatus (and all historians seem to think there was) it was the *effect of the close-up*: *impressing* the audience with surprise, or shock, or even terror, to the extent of making them jump out of their seats and run away from this increasing, overwhelming, all-consuming image. To quote Sadoul again: "In *The Arrival of a Train*, the locomotive rushing from deep in the frame towards the audience made them jump back for fear of being crushed".

Now, there are no *close-ups* in the film in question. The closest the locomotive comes is into medium-close-shot leaving frame on the left. The closest any of the passengers come is into mid-shot. What frightened audiences was not the shots getting progressively bigger but the movement of the locomotive getting progressively closer. And it was only the initial audiences which were alarmed. We must not forget that before the existence of the cinema, it was not possible to record movement – the genuine movement of real objects. There was indeed something novel and therefore surprising in their reproduction, particularly the setting of a train. However, audiences soon became used to the idea and the notion that there was a "collective fear" is a myth.

What may be surprising in this context is to read, under Bonitzer's byeline, that:

> The close-up, by absorbing within it the scale of shot sizes, actually cancels them out; by violating the distances imposed on our eyes, it breaks up the hierarchy.

Also that:

Close-ups tend to destroy depth-of-field (that is, the alignment of shots according to perspective) and, with it, perspective "realism". Because of a natural partiality of our vision this realism is carried through to a point of consistency: of pleasure, horror or terror embodied in the close-up.

Now, whether it be of a face or an object, the close-up by definition fills up the majority of the screen. Thus it could never cancel out what is outside the frame or hidden by it. And if it is a close shot, leaving the rest of the field of view open, Lumière's film is proof positive that standard lenses, not only do not destroy depth, but actually help to align the shot right into the distance.

Thus, it is difficult to see why, or how, the close-up could only be "purely superficial", to use Bonitzer's words.

To conclude with these "film grammars" quoted yet again, whose intentions should not be underrated, we can say that the rules they lay down for editing, framing, angles, reverse-angles, etc. are all *true*. However, we can turn these definitions on their head and say that the *reverse is also true* (depending on the context, of course). This is not to say there are no rules in the cinema, merely that no single one is relevant, no single one has the force of law.

VI

Iconic Significations

If the film image, at the level of the shot, may be considered as a kind of *gestalt-sign* in which the signifier and signified form a single entity, it is also true that genuine film significations begin only with a way of showing things, organising them relative to each other, where, like the linguistic sign, the signifier has no common measure with the nature of the signified. But, before we consider the organisation of shots within a film narrative, i.e. editing, we must first consider the organisation – or reorganisation – of the space within the field of view, i.e. the significations of the image itself.

Though I have written elsewhere that reality is in its own image "like a duplicate supplemented with the specific qualities of its reproduction", this should be seen only as a metaphor, for the image is in no way the "duplicate" of reality as some critics would have us believe. The duplicate of an object is of necessity a *different object*, similar but separate, whereas the image of a chair is not a different chair but the *same* chair presented as an image. The image has different properties from the real object, but in *terms of its shape and form*, it is that object and none other.

Thus to refer to the signified or referent is, at this level, one and the same thing. In verbal language, the referent is alien to the word which designates it. On the other hand, in the cinema, it is *contained within* the image; it is the *image itself* which would not exist without it. The represented has no other referent than its own representation: the image of the chair does not refer to any *other chair* but to the chair of which it is the image. It is futile to search for a different reality from that provided by the film unless it is to use it to compare and contrast with a concrete reality potentially serving as a reference but not a referent.

In my *Aesthetics*, I suggested the term *analogon* to indicate the similarity and difference of reality and its representation. Now, the film image is not an analogon. In fact the term can only be used in reference to painting. In Van Gogh's painting representing his bedroom, the chair with the straw seat is the analogon of what we might suppose served as his model or which we might imagine through it. But the painted chair only exists by virtue of the painting. However similar it may be, it is separate and autonomous. In the cinema, it is not possible to imagine an object both separate and similar: *we see the real chair at the same time as the image, as an image, confirms the absence of the object which nevertheless is perceived as present.*

The purpose of the signifying process is not necessarily to load an object with a meaning it does not possess. This may be limited to deleting redundant significations in order to emphasise others which have a temporary relevance. It then becomes a *subtraction* rather than an *addition*. Be this as it may, through the effect of the *frame* (which is not limited to giving prominence or attention to particular characters, objects or shapes, any more than to enclosing the image, but defines its internal structures and causes a genuine *recentering of the field of view*) the image assumes a meaning which is not additional to the initial meaning, but merely a modification, thereby creating a new signification *through which genuinely filmic significations can begin,* for – and it is as well to make this clear – there is no film signification which is not based on the signification of the objects filmed: *in the cinema we refer to objects with the objects to which we refer.*

The cinema is in effect an art of the concrete, turning concrete objects into signs – or significations. An art of structure and structuring, which is in no way comparable with structuralism, since there is no such thing as film structure containing meaning in itself, the signifying form being entirely based on – or with – the form of the content.

In other words, by exploiting the relationships between objects, forms, and position, it is possible to compose an expressive image and give a particular meaning to the represented world. The reality presented as images, which seems to us immediate, is always of necessity – and with good reason – a mediated reality.

The elements captured by the lens are re-organised, structured in terms (and by virtue) of the frame with which they are associated. The image becomes a *form*. And since what the representation denotes is always from a particular angle, it is already in itself a sort of *connotation* – one which might be described as *iconic* so as to distinguish it from the "discursive" connotations arising from the ordering of shots. Thus the image is not, like the word, a simple denotation. First and foremost, it bears witness to the significations relevant to the represented object, but *by it* and through it the object assumes a new meaning. The image therefore has more weight, more meaning than the sum of its parts. Which leads to the deduction that *any object presented in moving images gains a meaning – a series of meanings – which it does not possess in reality, in other words, in its real presence.* As we have said, *the representation alters what is represented.* The image causes objects to be compared. It is a summation of reality which constantly makes us think *about* the objects at the same time as it makes us think with them.

Certainly, the film image seldom draws attention exclusively to its structures. Except in Expressionism where plastic values relate all significations to a formal symbolism.

In which sense, we should make a distinction between *framing*, which separates out a fragment of space so that the elements included within the frame balance each other and the composition of a world made *from a frame* acting, exactly as in classical painting, as a compositional parameter.

Any stylisation in this instance relates to the sets and is made *before* shooting. The signifying modalities exist in the interplay of light and shade, in the relationships of volumes, lines, surfaces, which the camera records according to a symmetrical or asymmetrical arrangement of a limited and constricted space.

The information provided by the frame in general takes on meaning entirely from the context, which means that iconic significations work at their best when the image behaves as a separate autonomous unity, for instance in Expressionism where formal relationships are emphasised by the permanence of the frame. In fact, these become rather less evident in moving shots, but since any alteration of the image always relates back to the same frame, what the audience feels is a transformation of the plastic values; maybe in a less obvious sense, but no less definite.

Represented and representation

The image is therefore fundamentally attached to its frame. Any plastic signification depends on it. And yet the screen gives the impression of being a window on the world. The boundary limiting the represented reality is part of this window. The world continues somewhere beyond it. But, whereas the image presented in a still photograph gives the impression of depth while being confined to the flat surface, the film image, through the movement which it reproduces, emphasises this impression, which becomes a real *sensation*. And thereby allows it to *become detached from the flat surface on which it is produced*. Relief and depth, perceived as in reality, make the screen appear as though it were an opening into a space *on the other side of the screen*, and not like a flat surface at all.

At the level of representation, however, objects *presented as images* are no less *associated phenomenally* with the frame containing them: whereas in reality I can move closer to the window to see a wider field of view or move to one side to see the space hidden from me standing centrally, in the cinema there is no point in moving to the left or right, because I would see the same image. All I would achieve is to see a distorted image...

In other words: *as represented*, the film image is similar to the "direct image" of consciousness, but *as representation*, it is an aesthetically structured form. Which creates a perception on two levels which, together with various other phenomena to be examined further on, form the basis of film fascination, its magic.

We do indeed experience (whether consciously or not) the "frame-effect", which makes the plastic components more or less contrived. Yet we do not see the film data as an image: I do not see the image of a cowboy riding the image of a horse, but a cowboy on horseback. *I observe the real object through the image presented to me of it*. Which involves:

A. a direct perceptual level which presents a form outlined by a frame whose pictorial or plastic effects have an effect on our feelings.

B. a perceptual level relating to experience, to *judgment*. The represented objects are understood as real data through an instantaneously accepted formalisation. We know that the space shown within and *limited* by the frame is in no way *delimited* by it.

The mistake made by many theoreticians is to consider only one of these two aspects. One or the other, but one to the exclusion of the other, because of their apparent contradiction. And yet the *represented* is only ever perceived through its *representation*. From which it follows that, because they are similar in form, film perception also works at two levels. The directly perceived image imposes its structures on the filmed reality in which it shares. The *window-on-the-world-effect* becomes superimposed over the *frame-effect*, but in various different degrees allowing for any number of stylistic forms according to whether it is the image which takes priority (at the extreme, Expressionism) or the recorded reality (Neorealism, or "direct cinema").

Whatever the case, though reality becomes "divested of its reality", though it occupies a "different space", we *become involved* in that reality, we enter that space, whereas it is only ever through convention or a voluntary act of consent that we become involved in the "represented" reality of the stage even though the action might be happening in the same physical world as our own.

This involvement may be caused by several factors but more particularly camera movements or shot changes. Because the effect is that we appear to be moving within the represented space, we endow it with an apparent "reality" and "involve" ourselves within it.

The frame presents reality objectively and makes each of us audience members into observers, responsive but "outside" the drama. It introduces a kind of distantiation between the characters and us, a distantiation made more obvious by the impossibility of any contact: a man walks forward into the foreground from deep inside the set. He moves towards me – it seems – but no sooner is he close to me than he disappears from my field of view. He will never reach me. He cannot cross over from his space; a space to which he is attached, on which he depends, and outside which he is nothing. We are a world apart...

At the same time, through the mobility of the camera, the possibility of a number of different shots, I can be everywhere at once. It only requires me to be involved, to play the game, to let myself go. I am "gripped". Not just captivated but quite literally "captured", absorbed by the alien and fascinating space onto which a screen has opened. The heroes of the film are suddenly closer to me than the person in the next seat, so close that they appear to be able to touch me. I follow the movements of first one, then the other; I move with them, see with them, act with them, at the same time as them; I become involved in their drama which, for the moment, becomes "my own". I am no longer a spectator; I am well and truly an "actor". I know that I am sitting in a cinema but I feel that I am inside the world before my eyes; a world which I can experience "physically" by identifying with one or other of the characters in the drama – or, alternatively, all of them.

Which is tantamount to saying that in the cinema I am both *inside and outside* the action, *inside and outside the space*. Having the gift of ubiquity, I am everywhere and nowhere.

Absurd effects

Since the "frame-effect" was virtually unknown during the 1920s, there were some fairly far-fetched theories and practices as a consequence. So, for instance, we had cameras being tilted horizontally in order to represent what someone lying down might (or ought to) see. Consequently, walls were shown to be horizontal whereas the floor and ceiling axis was vertical – which in no way corresponded to any real vision of things, since someone lying on their side sees his bedroom walls as though he were standing up.

This is produced by a regulatory function whose purpose is to maintain balanced perception and guarantees that observed objects keep a constant position and orientation whatever the movement of positions of the observer. This function is related to the Brunswick constant according to which the apparent dimensions of objects do not diminish in inverse proportion to their distance from the observer as the laws of perspective (quite arbitrary as it happens) require.

These effects were well-known before the existence of the cinema, discovered through the experiments of Helmholtz and his disciples, before being taken up, developed and refined in the decade after 1910 by the Gestalt psychologists. Not only does the frame limit and delimit the image, but it uses a kind of isolation to separate the fragment of space from the space from which the fragment has been taken, apparently occupied by the observer.

It is this isolation which, by creating an opposition (or distinction) between object-subject, observer-observed, appears to transfer onto "the other side of the screen" the space contained in the frame whose variations, if incorrectly managed, create disastrous effects. A perfect example of this is contained in Andrzej Wajda's *The Wedding*. After the wedding sequence, the guests throw themselves into a kind of "skipping" dance. With the obvious intention of providing an "impression of truth", the hand-held camera also starts to skip, following the movement of the dancers. Like them, it jumps up and down, maintaining them at a "fixed point" in the framing. But when it is projected, because the screen is static, it is not the dancers jumping up and down but the whole space – the framed universe – which seems to have been subjected to a sort of preposterous St. Vitus dance: the walls jump about, the ceiling spins around and the spectator feels as though he is on the deck of a ship in a storm, seasick for good measure. In trying to be "true", everything is false – or falsified. We might assume that this has to do, not with realism or lack of realism, verisimilitude or lack of verisimilitude, but, more simply, with accuracy in the simple "perceptual interpretation". No dancer sees the walls spinning; no one jumping on the spot sees the walls jigging about...

The same is true of "dutch tilts" [translator's note: where the camera is tilted off its axis either to the left or right] fashionable for a decade or so. Someone leaning sideways does not see streets tilted sideways. Objects may be viewed from top to bottom but, whatever the angle of view, the incidence of the angle is only ever one aspect of a global perception. It is precisely the limitations and delimitations of the frame which draw attention to this incidence and define is as an upward or downward tilt. Obviously, it is acceptable to show a tilted view of a part of a whole whose horizon is hidden beyond the framing; but not the "whole" itself. It may be tilted up or down, but the horizon is never "sideways", even when we tilt our head to one side. Thus if the intention is to give the equivalent of real perception, the camera must never show the horizon sideways on, whatever the position of the observer it replaces. In the interests of being "true", that particular shot set the horizon on the diagonal...

The so-called "subjective" camera

It is also the frame-effect which allows what has come to be known as the *subjective camera* to be used. Various film-makers, wanting to destroy the apparent objectivity of reality – manipulated or otherwise but always "distantiated", seen from the outside – had the idea of letting the camera temporarily take the place of the hero so as to share in his point of view and, by extension,

enable the audience to adopt or better understand his feelings, his
state of mind. The technique was sketched in by Abel Gance in *La
Roue*, in 1921, but used more generally by Ewald André Dupont in
Variety, in 1925.

The point of view of the narrator relating facts in a purely
descriptive way was alternated with what one or other of the characters in the drama could see: images whose subjectivity was
restricted to a *view* of the outside world (not associated with a
mental or imaginary image) which, in order to be recognised as
subjective and capable of being associated with an individual,
required that that individual be placed, beforehand, in a position
to be an observer relative to the objects or persons observed, i.e.
that he be framed therefore in the preceding shot. If, following a
general shot showing a young girl walking from the distance
towards a young man, the camera shows her placed in the axis of
the young man's vision, then of course I will be able to identify
with him. But if the young man has not been conveniently set in
the general shot, the image of the young girl walking towards the
camera will be absorbed into the anonymity of a perfectly objective
view.

In 1926 following Dupont's film, it occurred to several young
critics, myself included – as well as Pierre Porte, Paul Ramain,
Henri Hughes – that an entirely subjective cinema was possible,
i.e., one in which films would be told in the first person. Only
what the hero would see would be shown; the camera would
constantly take his place. Gréville went so far as to imagine a
drama in which the hero would be none other than the audience
led to recognise itself guilty of a murder committed in tragic
circumstances. The idea which provoked many discussions in the
Dôme and the Deux Magots was given expression in the various
articles advocating or denigrating the virtues of the technique.

Talkies reactivated interest in it again by providing, through
speech, an apparent body for the invisible hero, allowing him to
tell his story or comment on events. It was several years before
Robert Montgomery's film *The Lady of the Lake*, based on this
principle, added a full-stop by demonstrating the futility of the
technique. It is not our intention to pick over any further explanations made over many years, the subjective camera being recorded
as "subjective" only insofar as it is related to the vision of a character objectively present[1] which, let us remind ourselves, was the

case with *Variety*. It has become common currency and films with a hero identified throughout as the camera are no longer made. A totally subjective cinema (at the level of vision) is one which "objectively" relates the vision of someone hiding behind what he presents for us to see. Which proves fairly convincingly that any theory which extrapolates valid data from concrete experience and elevates it into a system often ends up contradicting itself.

An art of association and suggestion

By reason of framing (over which we should linger for a moment), also by reason of optical and photographic transformations, we could never overstate the fact that the most realistic image is not a reproduction, or imitation but an *interpretation*. Though similar, it only ever represents one aspect among a whole series of arbitrary relationships which provide the filmed objects with a temporary signification set within the body of the film. Thus, a chair seen from three-quarters back suggests the uncomfortable stiffness of its back, whereas, seen from the front, it reveals the softness and comfort of its cushions. This being so, either one or the other of these representations may eventually involve a more general symbolic signification (in the right context. . .).

Which is the same as saying once again that, in the cinema, there is no such thing as pure denotation. As I suggested above, denotation – at the level of the shot – is always a means of connotation. One might also say that iconic connotation is the actual form of denotation. Yet this connotation, belonging to the "imagistic data" must be regarded as entirely separate from the narrative connotations produced by editing. One might say – crudely, using a linguistic comparison – that iconic connotations are similar to lexical polysemy whereas, at the level of the narrative, any connotations produced by the arrangement of shots are of the same order as semantic functions.

Thus, if it is exactly the same thing at the level of the shot (or isolated image) to refer to the signified or the referent (since the signified is none other than the represented object in the form of its representation), it is clear that, at the level of the syntagma (association of shots), the *signified is quite different from the represented reality*. Involved through various semantic functions and

A downward tilt expressing the desire for power much more effectively than the usual upward tilt: *Citizen Kane*, 1941.

not through the formalisation of the "imagistic data", the connotations remain purely conceptual.

Though at the level of the image they act as a group of *stimuli* to create various emotional reactions, at the semantic level they depend on intellection. It is in this sense that I have said, and continue to say, that connotations must remain implicit.

It is clear that the connoted signified is "unhooked" or "uncoupled" from the denoted[2]. Long before the semiologists came along, it is what I and several colleagues were saying – using different language – around 1927–8 (in *Cinéa-Ciné pour tous*) when we spoke of the cinema as an "art of association and suggestion", with the suggested idea apparently emanating from the represented facts.

It was also by reason of the expressive conditions of the moving image that I was able to say that the "literal message was a necessary support for all film signification", accepting the "literal message" to mean the narrative and not at all (or not only) the denotative, as some critics would have it. Indeed film is just as inextricably bound up with narration as the image is with representation.

Semantic connotations almost always end up as symbolic or metaphorical signifieds but iconic signifiers most frequently (except for analogical connotations) open onto indical signifieds.

VII

Indical Significations

Referring to Charles Sanders Peirce's definition, it is obvious that indical connotations are different from analogical connotations in that they imply a causal link, a factual motivation. Indical significations are only one of the forms of iconic signification but they extend beyond them in the sense that they are dependent on context. The meaning does not come from the isolated shot, from its internal structures, but from the image understood as an element in the narrative sequence, even though in this context the relational associations of montage have less of a part to play than that of simple connected relationships within the shot sequence.

Curious index: a bed-cage on the plains of the Far West. John Ford's *The Wagonmaster*, 1950.

The juxtaposition of two shots may apparently suggest an idea or a feeling but it could never be said that any relationship of shots has (even potentially) a similar effect. As Roland Barthes observed: "It is possible to imagine purely epic, a-significant sequences; but it is not possible to imagine purely signifying sequences." And relational significations are allusive or indical as frequently as symbolic or metaphorical, contrary to what many theoreticians believe, for whom signifying is creating metaphors...

The following represent a few examples relating to an object whose connoted meaning is either indical, allusive, or symbolic.

In a shot showing the corner of a garden, a doll can be seen lying on some stone steps. Inevitably, the toy suggests the presence of a little girl. It is an *index*. But it is only an index if we have not yet seen the little girl. In fact, her presence is not guaranteed, at least in the immediate context. On other hand, if we observed the doll during the preceding shots, it would be *allusive*. But, if we learned that little girl has disappeared and if we were shown, after a wide-angle showing the parents looking for her, a close-up of the doll, then this object becomes a *symbol*.

We can immediately see that allusive or indical images connote through the bias of an unexpected or unusual detail, a detail picked out of all the elements making up a medium or general shot, with no interruption unlike the symbolic image (or image-sign) whose ephemeral, but relevant, meaning is emphasised by the way the close-up behaves as a synecdoche.

Shot polysemy

We intend to return to these questions later on. What matters for the moment is to see how the same things may have, in turn, an indical, or allusive or symbolic meaning; not only in each separate instance, as in the example above, but within the separate phases of the same action, the same global event, as may be seen in a short sequence from *The End of St. Petersburg*.

An old Bolshevik worker under surveillance from the White Army lives with his wife in a basement flat where the only source of daylight is a window at street level. A medium shot shows them sitting at a kitchen-table. The woman has just poured tea into each of their glass cups, but the old man realises he has run out of tobacco. Swallowing a mouthful, he leaves to go to the nearest

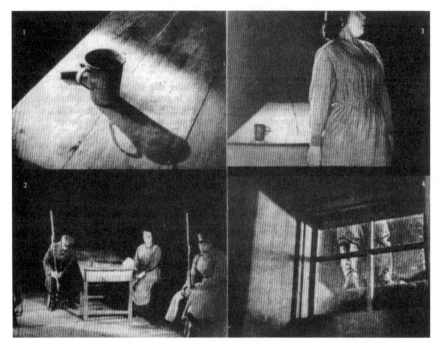

The cup sequence in *The End of St. Petersburg*, by Vsevolod Pudovkin, 1927.

shop. A close shot then shows, slightly tilted downwards, the cup full of tea on the table. This shot showing the temporary absence of the old revolutionary alludes to the danger he is in. The door suddenly opens; a junior officer marches into the lodging, looks around, interrogates the woman who swears before God that her husband has left town. Then the soldier notices the cup full of steaming tea. The index is obvious: the old man is not far away. Swaggering with self-importance, the officer waits while the woman, shaking with fear, looks out for her husband returning. He stops to roll a cigarette and she notices him through the grill. She immediately picks up the cup and throws it at the window. His attention alerted, the old boy leans down, sees the policeman and takes to his heels. A close shot then shows the cup broken into shards of glass on the floor.

These images, in turn allusive, indical and symbolic, assume in a constant transformation of meaning, significations involved through facts, with such an unrestrained and instantaneous mobility, impossible for words to achieve imprisoned in their own meaning.

In fact, every word has a defined, codified meaning, whatever the modalities it may suggest. Linguistic polysemy is only very relative. If verbs possess a relatively wide semantic spread (for instance, the frequent confusions deriving from the use of the verb to be), the semantic density of a word always relates back to its primary meaning; the verbal image always refers to a property of the denoted.

Though it is not possible to compare a shot (even a close-up) with a single word, only with one or several phrases, any individual object contained in the shot may be related to the word which designates it. Now, though it may connote in many different ways, the word cup will never be able to signify (especially in one or two short phrases) first that the old man is not there, then that he is close by, then that he has been alerted, then that he runs away. Whereas the word – as a written or spoken sign – always remains identical whatever the context in which it appears, the constantly differentiated image always signifies *in a different way* something different.

In most shots – general shots or medium shots – it is not, as we have seen, the whole of the shot (except in the case of the close-up) which is allusive, indical or symbolic, but certain objects within the shot emphasised by the framing. The objects are thus repeatedly involved in a narrative reality with a beginning and an end – a purpose. Or rather a *praxis*. The requirement that they be accessible is mandatory. They cannot help but belong to an action which is alien to them but involves them in it by the very fact that they are *evidence* of it.

To all intents and appearances, the clock above the fireplace in the room where a drama is happening has no part to play. It can do nothing. And yet, it marks the time and thereby provides us with *information*. In any case, it is there, forming part of the drama. The same is true of all the objects, furniture, nicknacks which make up the setting; the setting which contains the drama and in some way reflects it by imposing on it a certain structure. Setting, characters and objects are involved in the same action. It is the same space subject to the same time sequence.

Which means that it is vital that the "time of things", always placed in a predetermined and determinant space-time context, be preserved. The image is the *image of space and time*, of a fragment of the space and time within which and during which the events take place.

Duplicated shots

As I have already indicated, it is not possible to duplicate the same shot showing the same action or movement.

A sequence from *Monsieur Verdoux* exactly demonstrates what must be avoided. Chaplin tries to signify in shorthand M. Verdoux's repeated journeys in search of rich fiancées, and repeatedly shows locomotive wheels turning at high speed. Which would be perfectly fine if it were the *same shot* showing from the *same angle* the *same wheels* of the *same locomotive* turning at the *same speed*. Edited first of all into M. Verdoux' first journey, this shot represents a precise moment within the time sequence of the drama. A moment which no other moment in the diegesis can represent, except by repeating something that cannot be repeated a second time. An action may be repeated but not the time within which it happens.

The same device is used in *The End of St. Petersburg*, where Pudovkin tries to signify the sudden explosive effect of the 1914 war and opens the sequence with a shell-burst, throwing up a huge shower of soil. It is an excellent symbol. But, much further on, he signifies the October Revolution in the *same way*. It would have been acceptable had he not connoted the same idea with the *same image* of the *same shell-burst*. Just as in *Monsieur Verdoux*, Pudovkin falsifies reality by duplicating a "fragment of time" and turning a concrete fact into a clichéd sign which does not merely refer back to a concept as a word might but *represents* it. Taking the contrary position to my thesis, Michel Colin would have us believe that:

> Though it is obvious that only the rhetorical function of the close-up remains when it is integrated into the narrative and becomes a genuinely signifying unit, the repetition of a detail corresponds to a well-known linguistic phenomenon – focus.
> John is coming.
> He is coming, John.
> Moreover, as in speech, focus implies in this context repetition (*anaphora*) [translator's note: a rhetorical device describing the repetition of the same word or phrase in several successive clauses]. Thus it is possible to consider the inclusion of close-ups (repetitively) to correspond to a much greater exigency than

the development of the narrative: the linguistic structuring of the iconic message[1].

Which is certainly true at the level of language. But Michel Colin does not take account of the fact that, in verbal expressions, repetition of the same word is less frequent than repetition of the subject: *John – he...* Also (more especially), because it has no "intrinsic materiality", words have no genuine time value. The time it takes to read or speak is implicit only in the reader. On the other hand, if I show: *John crossing the street* (descriptive shot), this action involves a certain time value, that of the shot. If then I repeat the shot – the same set-up – it will not be the action, the movement I repeat but the time it takes for them to take place. But time never repeats itself: "No man can bathe in the same river twice", as Heraclitus put it 2500 years ago...

This is not to say that anaphora cannot be used in the cinema; it must be used differently. An action may be repeated for semantic emphasis provided that it is a *different* action, in a *different* shot. For instance:

1. The politician waves to the crowd (descriptive shot).
2. The politician waves to the crowd (similar gesture but *different*, shown in a closer shot).

In language the same word may be repeated, particularly since it acts as a substitution. "Similar to nature/similar to a coverlet/ similar to thought..." (Michaux) "People who walk upright/ people who think laterally/people who..." (J. Prévert), etc. In the cinema, if we see in the same shot the politician waving several times in sequence, it is merely a repeated gesture that we are observing. On the other hand, if there is a change of shot (size, angle, framing), as in the example above, then the emphasis becomes clear. It is not substitution any longer, but confirmation – it being that anaphora is one of the specific functions of editing. It is no longer a case of *He is waving, but he is waving, he is waving.../Once again, he is waving, the politician.*

Michel Colin's example once again proves that it is impossible to think, act, speak, structure using images as one would using words. Which even the most blinkered semiologists would acknowledge, though they might continue to act and think – from force of habit – as though it were irrelevant.

Excluded from these remarks are comic films, dream or fantasy sequences, nightmares and the strictly formal games which we see on video where this kind of repetition may have an appeal, but has nothing to do with the expression of a supposedly true event occurring in the objective reality of the world.

As soon as it is fantasy, the question becomes irrelevant. A proof is the wonderful sequence in Fernand Léger's *Ballet mécanique* where we are shown, in a gentle downward tilt, a woman bent double under a heavy burden struggling up a flight of steps. No sooner does she reach the top than she has to start all over again from the bottom, making exactly the *same movements*. Five or six times in succession, the *same shot* is repeated. And it is marvellous. But it has nothing to do with realism!...

Certain of my detractors, irritated by my unreasonable rationalism and logical positivism, would have it that I would be appalled by the absurdities of Mack Sennett or Buster Keaton. On the contrary, I think they are wonderful. Work it out for yourselves...

To sum up, whether the film image is analogical, indical, or allusive, whether it is an isolated shot or (as we shall see later on) a relationship of shots to each other, it is always laden with meaning. As we have said, representation alters the represented objects, but nothing – be it structure or form – has an *a priori* signification, except for these objects and their direct meaning. Representation is not a "model" which, by definition, may be applied to the represented: on the contrary it depends on it.

Contrary to the way language behaves, where the signified exists by virtue of its signifying qualities, *film signifiers do not exist except inasmuch as there is a signified*. Verbal signifiers, conventionalised and unmotivated, become signs only by a grammatical decision, in the context that objects, facts and actions create, in their ordering and formalisation (within the limits of a given logic and in specific circumstances), the meaning chosen by the narrator. Film signifiers are not abstract forms around which or from which specific generative laws can be erected. They are concrete facts which may be used, within a given context and in the right circumstances, to create the forms of the expression, that is, the expression of an idea or a feeling. Forms which are valid only for *a particular film* – exist only in terms of these structures – and which disappear as soon as they appear to give way to other ideas and feelings as the narrative unfolds...

VIII

The Inferences of Montage

If by montage we mean the splicing together end to end of segments – shots or tableaux – then montage is as old as cinema itself, especially since, from the very beginnings, various directors – Méliès most notably – used cuts and connections like tricks in a similar way to superimpositions, lap dissolves and other photographic processes. But, before 1910, no film (apart from very rare exceptions) contained montage as it is understood today, that is, as a *signifying structure*.

With Méliès, in films like *Le Déshabillage impossible*, *Les Luttes extravagantes*, or *La Dislocation mystérieuse* (1900–1901), all he did was edit out frames here and there and join them together in order to displace the action or break up the movement. These cuts signify but in no way do they "create meaning". To put it more clearly, because linguistic comparisons are always being made, if I take a word such as *superimposition* and remove one syllable or another, I can obtain *supposition, posit, position*, and even anagrams such as *trippers* or *merit* but no new meanings (at the semantic level of course). On the other hand, when Apollinaire joins together terms like *Soleil cou coupé* [*sun neck cut*], he creates a metaphor. This is montage. ... Or at least this is what has been understood as montage ever since critics started theorising about the cinema and since this sort of structure became normal practice; or, to put it crudely, since Eisenstein (except that it is not just a question of metaphor, but more to do with very different connotations).

Before 1910, there were in fact very few exceptions since, apart from reverse-angles, cross-cutting and change of point of view (1903–1904), it was through films like *A Corner in Wheat* and *The Drunkard's Reformation* (D.W. Griffith, 1909) that the associative significations deriving from montage became apparent.

It was between 1910 and 1914, with Griffith, Thomas Ince, Larry Trimble, Reginald Barker, Colin Campbell, Loane Tucker

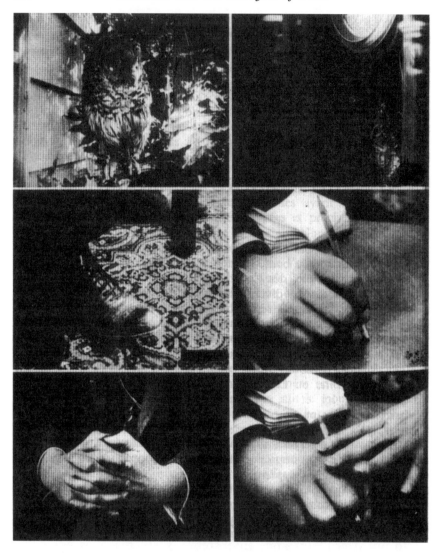

Relationship of details in D.W. Griffith's *Avenging Conscience*, 1913.

and one or two others, that these ideas became developed, to become with *The Birth of a Nation* (1914) one of the basic principles of film expression. Yet the first theories did not appear until a few years later, as a consequence of the celebrated Kuleshov experiment.

As we all know, it is these famous experiments which are the origin of the linguistic theories relating to film and which enable the functional capacities of montage to be demonstrated, considered not merely as a means of constructing the narrative or as an element of rhythm, but as a creator of meaning[1].

And yet, when we take a closer look at the "Kuleshov effect", we see that the process involving the audience's understanding is much less cinematic than it appears. For instance, in the "Mozhukhin/naked woman" example, because neither one nor the other is expressing anything (anything which might related to the relationship *arbitrarily constructed* by the simple juxtaposition of two completely alien images), nothing allows us to suppose that the man loves the woman or, simply, desires her; or, by the same token, that the woman is flattered, or indeed feels anything. It is solely the *man looking/woman looked at* association which evokes and *signifies* the notion of desire. From this juxtaposition an emotional reaction arises in which we all recognise – or rediscover – the meaning of our own experience. Whereas a child who knows nothing of sexual desire cannot understand the meaning of these images, the adult *projects* his own reactions onto the man who it would be normal to suppose desires the woman he is looking at. In other words, the relationship described above is no more than an *idea* already existing in the mind of anyone conscious of the nature of love. We are moved by an idea, not by a concrete fact. Because the image represents a concept, we pass from the abstract to the concrete without the freedom, as with words, to conjure up a personal fiction resolving into these precise images. Though visual, the process is anti-cinematic in that it moves from the idea to the emotion instead of the other way round.

The Kuleshov effect only becomes really filmic from the moment the *looker/looked at* (and, more generally, *object/subject*) relationship is based on concrete facts.

Then it is the emotion which suggests the idea and not the idea which creates the emotion. It means more especially, since idea and emotion are connected, that the image must not be the result of an idea *already formed* but the creation of a meaning, the inspiration for an *available* idea.

Though they mark an important date in the history of the cinema, these experiments (not limited to the images of Mozhukhin supposedly looking at a plate of soup, a naked woman, a corpse, etc.) have sent many researchers down blind-alleys. By drawing attention to the signifying capacities of film, they have led theoreticians to explore verbal statements in order to find types of structures capable of being applied to visual expression. Indeed it was by basing his work partially on Kuleshov's data that Eisenstein developed his theories of montage. As he wrote:

> Pudovkin defends an understanding of montage as a *linkage* of pieces. Into a chain. Again, "bricks". Bricks arranged in series to expound an idea. I confronted him with my view of montage as a collision. A view that from the collision of two given factors arises a concept [...]. The point is that the copulation (perhaps we had better say, the combination) of two hieroglyphs of the simples series is to be regarded not as their sum, but as their product, i.e. as the value of another dimension, another degree, each, separately, corresponds to an object, to a fact, but their combination corresponds to a concept[3]. [translator's note: In the last sentence Mitry paraphrases Eisenstein. A literal translation of the French is as follows: The juxtaposition of two fragments of film resembles their product more than their sum in that the result of this juxtaposition presents a quality (or meaning) not produced by either of the fragments in isolation.]

Excessive generalisations

These ideas, soon generalised into theories by various critics, took on the appearance of a rule of syntax according to which an association of any two shots A and B, necessarily involved, by definition, a signification C.

Which is false, since the meaning implied by the association of shots A and B essentially depends on the nature of the shots, on what they *represent*, according to a process which cannot be reduced to an A/B = C formula.

The *primary responsibility* of montage is to ensure the film's narrative flow; in which regard Pudovkin is correct as far as general structures are concerned (but not specific instances). If the ordering of shots endows each sequence with a meaning it would not have organised differently, it is a dramatic meaning relating to the events on screen rather than connotations which, however frequently they may occur, are not necessarily symbolic or metaphorical. They may be confused feelings, vague impressions.

In the golden age of Soviet cinema, I compared this effect with simple sentences where subject verb and complement have meaning only relative to each other. Since then, semiologists have made a much more obvious comparison between relationships of shots and those of the different elements in a semantic structure, but once or twice the comparison has assumed the shot to be the equivalent of a word. Now, as we have seen, the shot is not a unit of meaning (apart from the *close-up*). The mistake made by Eisenstein and the theoreticians who followed him, fatally fascinated by the close-up and its effect, was to concentrate exclusively on this unambiguous signification; and to interpret every shot, be it close shot or wide-angle, as nothing more than a global signified related to a single unit of meaning.

At the level of the close-up it is certainly true that the association of a signifier A and a signifier B brings about a signified of connotation C. This is true of the "cream separator sequence" in *The General Line*, where close-ups of the apparatus in action are cut against close-ups of peasants standing and staring in wonderment. It is equally true of the association made by a close shot showing a piece of action and a detailed close-up of the same action, as is the case with the example always quoted from *The Battleship Potemkin*.

In close-up we see a "pince-nez" dangling by its braid from a steel hawser. What could this image mean, isolated from its context? Nothing, apart from being a pince-nez dangling by its braid from a steel hawser. Which is precisely what we see. But, it happens that the pince-nez belongs to a doctor Smirnov, the ship's surgeon. We have seen him toy with it throughout the preceding sequences, to the point where this object has come to characterise him as forming part of his habits, his idiosyncracies, his behaviour. It has become a kind of indicator of his personality.

Moreover, we have just witnessed the mutiny of the sailors of "The Potemkin", during which their officers have been thrown overboard – among them, Dr. Smirnov. Hung up by his feet, stabbed, bundled up like a parcel, he has just been flung overboard, in spite of his shouts of protestation. We have seen him struggling and losing his pince-nez in the rigging.

Immediately, this image assumes a *meaning*. The pince-nez "represents" Dr. Smirnov or, more accurately, signifies his "absence". Nothing remains of this arrogant and rather contemp-

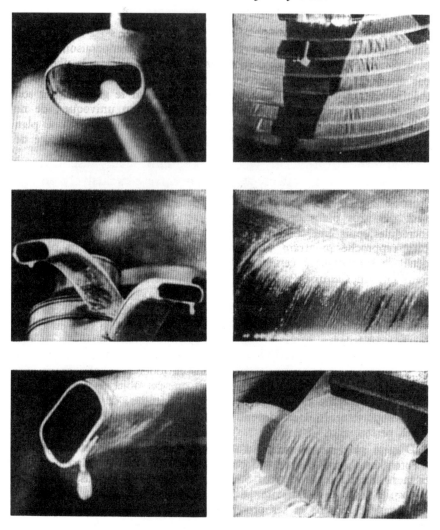

The cream separator sequence in S.M. Eisenstein's *The General Line*, 1929.

tible officer than his ridiculous pince-nez foolishly dangling at the end of a rope. The part replaces the whole; but it is precisely the most insignificant detail which reminds us of the character, inviting our contempt of him. There is more: through his position, his rank, Dr. Smirnov, a sample of the ruling class and pro-Tzarist aristocracy, "represents" that same class. So much so that the pince-nez comes to signify in a single moment the downfall of the bourgeoisie, literally "thrown overboard". There is nothing left of this class, symbolically, than a ridiculous substitute implying the worthlessness and stupidity of what it represents.

As we have said, *the specific language of the cinema consists in referring to objects with the objects to which we refer*. But, whatever the signified idea, the represented object is confirmed in the first instance as an object. Consequently, though the image signifies through what it shows, it can never behave like words transparent with their signifieds: the image is always relative to what it shows. And it is because it acts as a screen for what exists beyond the meaning of the represented objects that it can assume a signification outside its own signification. In the above example, it is not the pince-nez which is the signifier but the relationship of that object with the preceding shot. The image of the pince-nez assumes the quality of a sign only because we intuitively objectify in it the idea suggested by the relationship of which it is one of the elements containing the greatest potential signification. This is how it comes to behave like a sign or a symbol. And yet, this structure, containing the smallest possible syntagma (two shots joined by an associative structure) is a signifier only *within the context* of the film. By itself it is devoid of meaning. Someone with no knowledge of Eisenstein's film would find no meaning in it at all. The sequence: officer thrown overboard/smoking chimney/flag flapping in the wind, etc. would not tell him any more or any less. In order to decipher this association (for there to be an association in the first place), he must see all the previous sequences, for it is these alone which give the object a meaning by showing the pince-nez as specifically belonging to Dr. Smirnov. It is this "current of meaning", carried by the film, which turns these two successive shots into a coherent entity. Without which they are merely two individual shots arbitrarily brought together: there is no discernible connotation (or rather there is every possible connotation depending on the taste of each individual viewer). It is thus the context which determines these structures, which gives them the power to signify by loading them with a meaning for which they act as agents. In isolation, the syntagma loses its identity: its associative meaning disappears.

Whereas in linguistics the syntagma has meaning beyond and independent of the context which may – or may not – alter or complete it, there is no such thing as a film syntagma beyond the causal entity through which the syntagmas are formed as such. In other words, by virtue of its predictive structure, the smallest linguistic syntagma contains an *internal* association which gives it meaning, whereas the signifying association of the film syntagma (making it what it is) almost always comes *from outside*.

... and excessive signifiers

Thus, though the *unambiguous* signified is (or may be) the consequence of the relationship between a medium shot and a close-up (the relationship of wide shots involving a number of *different signifieds*), this meaning could never be contained within a succession of close-ups each possessing a more or less symbolic quality, without the need to use intermediate descriptive shots. The "Gods sequence" in Eisenstein's *October* is significant in this respect.

Showing successively a Baroque Christ, then the ancient Greek Gods, Hindu, Mexican, African, etc., Eisenstein claimed that he was "discrediting the idea of God" and, by extension, the futility of the concept. According to him:

> While idea and image appear to accord completely in the first statue shown, the two elements move further from each other with each successive image. Maintaining the denotation of "God", the images increasingly disagree with our concept of God, inevitably leading to individual conclusions about the true nature of all deities[4].

His analysis has merit, but it is one made *after the fact*, at the editing-bench. Films, however, are made to be *seen*, and must be immediately decipherable – for the most part at least. Now, as they appear in the film, these divinities tell us nothing of the kind. They are perceived as a collection of ornaments or statuettes. As regards any connoted values, these are *associated* in our minds within the same global concept: the idea of religious or pagan beliefs; and ridicule of these beliefs and divinities. Though the spectator may well recognise these as distinctive – effectively denoted – signs, he can never be forced to see them as signifying the "discrediting of the idea of God"...

In other words, the same signification is ascribed to each one of the signifiers. The whole is perceived as repeating the same meaning under various different guises.

Once again, this is using images like words without realising that words are separate signifiers relating to a meaning an appropriate concept, whereas images, relating to a concrete reality, are separate only at the level of the denoted and not at the level of a value judgment bearing on the concept to which the denoted refers. Images connote nothing (or very little) in themselves[5]. It is clear that, in this instance, the denoted is a symbolic representation with a connotative value. But Eisenstein assembles a series of *readymade* symbols which, taken together, suggest no more than each one signifies in isolation. Thus, though the global signified associating these signifiers – the notion of "God" – is perfectly well defined, the separate signified assuming a different *value* in each is not. This means that instead of what Eisenstein intended – separation – we have *comparison*. His "dynamisation of the subject" turns these into a series of abstract signs whose meaning, confined within the representation, becomes stiff and lifeless (if it does not disappear altogether behind it).

When the principles of "montage" were first applied, one or two film-makers went too far, on the basis that, once a rule has been established (this is a well-known fact), it is used to explain and resolve everything by relating everything to it. Thus, a "montage released from arbitrarily selected attractions, independent of the actual action" should have made it possible to signify by means of symbolic or metaphorical effects. Now, Eisenstein's theatrical experience already proved to him the difficulties and limitations of such a method. In the cinema the main objection is that such a technique is valid only inasmuch as it uses living elements (in the dramatic sense of the word) from which it takes its emotional power at the same time as a concrete symbolic signification. It stops being valid when it acts with symbols *arbitrarily selected* and applied to reality instead of being implied by it. Eisenstein frequently fell into this trap by over-systematising his discovery, ending up in a kind of abstract formalism, forcing his chosen elements into an ill-fitting strait-jacket.

In his first film *Strike*, which traces a strike in a metal foundry, put down by the Tzar's soldiers, he contrasts shots showing workers being shot down with shots of a bull being butchered in an abattoir. The effect is impressive, but though the idea is signified, the narrative logic is somewhat distorted. In order to create a symbolic expression, the slaughter-house scenes are arbitrarily included in an event totally alien to it.

One might argue that the scenes in the slaughter-house (which conceivably is in the same area as the factory) are as realistic as those in the factory, that the plight of the workers is to all intents and purposes the same as the bull's and that, however arbitrary the metaphorical association, it is still manifestly justified. Be that as it may, it has no shock value.

On the other hand, in *October*, where he sketches out what later on he would term *cinedialectics*, Eisenstein became preoccupied exclusively with the 'idea', and frequently overlooked, if not the authenticity of the events, at least the logic of their linking or their association.

Such is the case with the attack on the Winter Palace during the second Soviet Congress, where the Mensheviks' speeches of compromise are intercut with shots of women playing harps. The idea (literary in the extreme) is to give the Menshevik speeches the tone and appearance of lyrical whining, mind-numbing blabbering. However, though the idea is valid (if perhaps a trifle forced), we are left wondering what the harps and harpists are doing dropped into the *objective, concrete* reality of the meeting.

In the same film, just as Kornilov prepares to march on Petrograd at the head of the White Army, an image shows the general sitting arrogantly and forcefully (one might say 'Napoleonically') on his horse. The impression is reinforced by the angle of the shot – an upward tilt. Yet Eisenstein does not stop at this; he juxtaposes an image revealing, from the same angle, an equestrian statue which confirms and reinforces the ludicrousness of the posture. All well and good. But what is this statue doing in the *realistic* logic of the action and, more particularly, on the Russian Steppes?

Elsewhere, we see Kerensky in one of the huge rooms in the Winter Palace. He rehearses a speech, walking to and fro, waving his arms about and looking at himself in various mirrors. One of the shots revealing the tiny man lost in the vast proportions of the room adds to the impression of overwhelming solitude and neglect around him. However, on one of the mantle-pieces in the room, there stands a statue, a bust of Napoleon. And predictably, Eisenstein is quick to contrast it with different shots of Kerensky posing arrogantly in front of the mirrors. This association is possible because the statue is *present* – particularly since Kerensky has repeatedly passed backwards and forwards in front of it, looking at it. Suddenly, however, the doors open with a loud crash. The Winter Palace has been taken and the Red Guards are breaking into the rooms. Kerensky has barely enough time to escape. Now, at the very instant the doors burst open and the revolutionaries run in, a single shot shows Napoleon's bust lying shattered into fragments on the floor. Who dropped it? No one – except Eisenstein himself, with the intention of "manufacturing" an idea...

Yet, it would have been easy enough to incorporate the symbol into the concrete reality: Kerensky might have accidentally knocked it off, as he rushed past the mantle-piece, waving his arms. Then the sequence would have been as follows: the bust is knocked off; the doors burst open; Kerensky makes his escape. With the coda: Napoleon lies shattered on the floor. So simple that Eisenstein, mesmerised solely by the idea, never thought of it or chose not to think about it (or had not foreseen the effect in the script and consequently not included it in his shooting and had to create it *after the event...*).

Shortly before this scene, we have seen Kerensky enter the Winter Palace surrounded by his ministers. As he climbs the huge staircase leading to the imperial apartments, we are shown a series of shots intercut with subtitles indicating: Minister of War, Minister of Navy and Airforce, Minister for Foreign Affairs, Minister of the Interior, Generalissimo, Dictator – pointing out, not without irony, that he has appropriated most of the portfolios. But the staircase has only thirty steps to it; he only reaches the first floor. Thus we are seeing – from different angles – Kerensky repeatedly climbing *the same stairs*. The idea is to signify the futility of his action, his vanity and absurdity: he is climbing but getting no further up the stairs. And yet the reality is fabricated. One might say that it does not matter since one stair looks like any other and the constant change of shot cancels out the most obvious reference-points. Further on, when Kerensky reaches the first floor, an upward tilt shows him in such a way that one of the statues above him on the balustrade (Glory holding a crown) appears to be crowning him with laurel – a dictator in the fullness of his power. The reverse-angle shows his minsters, his personal bodyguards, stiff and rooted to the spot, like the columns beside which they have stopped. In this case, the irony is all the more effective that these images do not shock. And they do not shock because Eisenstein was using a statue and columns which were actually part of the setting, objects with a genuine place in the genuine space of the drama. He was *using reality, interpreting it instead of falsifying it.*

One of the lessons to be learnt from these examples is that simile is impossible in the cinema, unless the term of comparison is not part of the space which includes what is being compared, unless it is involved in some other way in the actual drama.

The image of the equestrian statue alongside General Kornilov is rather as though Eisenstein were saying: 'Arrogant, ambitious, self-interested, Kornilov sat his horse like Napoleon himself and already considered himself an Emperor'. But, in the verbal sentence, the comparative image is entirely conceptual; it is not at the same level as what is being compared. The verbal structure and the abstract nature of words eliminate the allusive from the narrative – which is not the case with film images, which are, whatever their content, objective and concrete and place objects – all objects – at the same representational level.

Obviously, this "representation" may signify, express, translate a thought or judgment, but within a subjective process which (in silent films) it is impossible to present at the same time as an objective relationship; and even less so within that relationship itself: because the elements of discourse and those of representation are the same, it inevitably means that they must have a different way of being organised. For it is obvious that these "distortions of reality" exist only to the extent that the film in question is observational, when it is merely recounting true facts. When there is a mental relationship (dream, memory, imagination, judgment, etc.) such contrasts are perfectly acceptable. But emotional logic has nothing in common with the objective nature of social realism. If I have said it once, I have said it a thousand times…

If reality is no more than raw material subjected to the processes of discourse, the dialectic logic which replaces factual logic enables these "fragments of reality" to be organised according to the processes of this discourse. However, the film can no longer hide its true nature and show itself as something it is not. These are the same contradictions with which Dziga Vertov struggled.

"*Cinedialectics*"

If the intention is to express the *meaning of things*, social events, individual or collective actions, the signifying process has to take account of the logic of the term of reference. Which does not mean that "reality must be imitated". It must be turned into semantic elements, but not contravene the primary meaning of the denoted by treating it as a metaphor. Now, it was by speculating about the capacities of montage and the significations of the close-up that Eisenstein came to develop, among his less risky theories, the principles of what he was to call *cinedialectics*. A "cinelanguage" for which he attempted to establish signs based on associations between objects but in which, as with the verbal code taken as a model, the meaning of the signifier/signified relationship remained invariable. He gave as an example various ideograms in Japanese writing where the combination of two images (two objects represented by a graphic sign) gave rise to a concept, as for instance:

A dog + a mouth = to bark
A mouth + a bird = to sing
An ear + a door = to hear, etc.

By forming similar signs belonging to linguistics through their structure and to hieroglyphs through their form, overlooking their content to concentrate on the ideas suggested by their logical linking, it would have been possible, so he believed, to organise a kind of discourse. However, though the link was made at the ideas level, moving from one image-sign to another, the sequence of represented objects lost all its meaning, since the objects became involved merely as semantic elements within the chain of signifiers, with no reference to the factual logic constantly subjected to the internal exigences of the discourse: the film was turned into a huge picture puzzle. Taken to its extreme, it would have rendered superfluous the projection of the images onto a screen. It would have been easier to simplify them, schematise them on paper, in order to rediscover the original ideograms. But this sort of experimentation made it abundantly clear to Eisenstein that the linguistic model could not be applied to the cinema, moving images, since the objects themselves resisted the arbitrary nature of signs.

Returning to his own ideas, he made this, among other statements, in an article published in 1938:

The error lay in placing the main emphasis on the possibilities of juxtaposition and in paying less attention than we should, as experimenters, to the elements of the juxtaposition[6].

It seems that, in this article, Eisenstein is anticipating, and answering, the extreme claims made for his *cinedialectics*, by certain critics entirely obsessed with the *dynamic cutting effect* of montage. Which was to ignore the fact that, in a film, the meaning of the connotations depends on the relationship of the objects denoted and that, for them to have a meaning, the objects must be arranged in a narrative sequence – probable or improbable, continuous or discontinuous, objective or subjective – but logical at the level of the causal linking of the represented facts.

The sign loses its potential signification unless, as a *signifier* (a *temporary* signifier) it is *determined* by a specific context. It becomes unreadable, undecipherable: any meaning can be read into it. Or else, it is a cliché, in which case, it becomes stiff and lifeless and loses the living, ephemeral contingent qualities characteristic of the cinema, turning it into a riddle or a Chinese puzzle.

Coincidence and consecutiveness

The extreme formalisations of montage were replaced twenty years late by the extreme formalisations of shot-sequences and depth-of-field.

In his assessment of the originality of *Citizen Kane*, André Bazin criticised, in the name of the "respect due to the objective reality of the world", all "arbitrary manipulations" and accepted montage as a process of construction, the signifying values in his view depending on relationships within the shot (which is strange in view of the fact that Orson Welles always claimed that he relied more on editing than mise-en-scène...).

As we have said in the preceding chapters, what happens in the "shot-in-depth" is as if the space in the frame were being considered according to two separate dimensions (or different planes) imposed on the frame. Which creates a kind of *caesura* establishing an associative effect similar to that of montage. Contrary to what happens in the previous examples, it is a kind of montage *within the shot*, for when the whole field of view is in focus the space seems to be homogeneous, whereas the 18.5 emphasises the association and difference between the elements which make it up; it enables what otherwise would be shown in two shots to be combined.

Of course, this means of expression in no way diminishes the value of fragmentation whose meaning and purpose are quite different. In fact, instead of being a function of the narrative, the signification in this case *depends on the special position given to the object (or character) in the spatial organisation of the field of view.* Produced in space rather than being established in time, it becomes the effect of *coincidence instead of being the effect of an association* (which presupposes consecutiveness). In this respect, Susan's glass (in the poisoning scene, soon to be as famous as an example of "depth" as the pince-nez in *Potemkin* was of effect montage) provides the perfect example. We are shown: Susan lying down and, on the night table beside her in close-up, the glass, spoon and sleeping tablets. In normal editing, the idea that

As though space were being seen on two separate planes, related within the same frame: David Lean's *Oliver Twist*, 1948.

she has tried to poison herself would have been *generated* by the succession of the two terms. The glass would *imply* the idea of poisoning; it would have become the sign, the symbolic representation.

In the total field, on the other hand, the idea is not generated, it is directly understood. From being associative, the sign becomes syncretic: Susan's glass is in some way the "signifying part" of the field from which it is apparently separated. As a consequence of which it *no longer implies* the idea of poisoning; it *provides evidence* of it. It becomes the sign of a fact, an action rather than an idea. While controlling the symbolic expression, the event is understood in its factual reality instead of being merely suggested. It is in this sense – and this sense only – that "realism" (a more obvious, more concrete, realism) can be referred to relative to depth-of-field.

Then there is the *"transparency of reality"*, definable as an event perceived in its totality, i.e. not fragmented, not reorganised. Related to a sufficiently wide and deep field of view, it is presented such that its ambiguity might be said to be preserved and the audience given the possibility of choosing a relevant meaning from among the myriad meanings "objectively" offered by the facts, the responsibility of the film-maker being to avoid distorting these by providing a preselected or additional meaning implied by the montage, and using the frame only to limit the field of view, like a window opening onto it.

It is obvious that if one shows:

A. a character sitting at a desk, staring at an object placed outside his field of view;

B. the lamp on his desk, shown in close-up; the character is clearly staring at the lamp presented (imposed) for him to look at.

If, on the other hand, we see him in a wider angle staring at the lamp contained in the frame along with a number of other objects – the lamp might even be in foreground – we ascribe to him a much greater freedom of action. He may choose to look at something else. Instead of relying on editing, the purpose of his look relies on staging. Yet, the effect for the audience is "as though" the man has freely chosen to stare at the lamp rather than his tobacco-pouch; *as though*, at the level of the image, the world had been perceived in all its potentiality, uncontaminated by any ideology or intentionality, the formalising intention being apparent only at the level of the story (even though the way that shots and sequences are organised and linked together is subsumed in the primary appearance – or freedom – of the facts).

Naturally the film-maker has the option to let events, when they are relevant, speak for themselves; but also deliberately to direct them – visibly – when it becomes necessary to emphasise a specific meaning. But this is no more than a question of style, of general aesthetics even.

Where Bazin makes his greatest mistake is in claiming that the audience has freedom of choice, that, "called on to construct significations from among those offered to him, the spectator himself produces the meaning". Clearly, he is being invited to decipher a meaning, to be interpreted as he wishes, but in no sense does he create the meaning, since this is determined by the facts which he must register as they are offered to him. Unless, of course, none of it has any meaning or that he is presented with a blank screen... But he does choose an action, a fact which would not be explicit relative to the represented action. Indeed, whatever its potential ambiguity, this action is involved in a dramatic sequence which gives prominence to a meaning or an act. The image in a film is not an isolated element.

In the shop scene in *The Best Years of our Lives* (quoted by Bazin) the audience is not free to concentrate on the characters in the foreground rather than the girl hidden deep at the back of the set, for the very fact that she is the only important character there, the preceding shot having shown her walking in the direction of the shop. Thus it is on her that the audience concentrates as soon as she is seen.

We might say, in contradiction of Bazin, that "our eyes are drawn, in all images, to wherever the maximum interest or signification occurs, indicated by the action itself, i.e. by the implications of the drama and the signifying linkage".

I examined all these questions twenty years ago in my *Aesthetics and Psychology of the Cinema*, and many others beside me have sifted through this idealistic phenomenology which these ideas of a "world presented to our eyes in all its existential independence" have become embodied. It would seem necessary to go over this ground again, because of the continual irritating insistence on these notions of transparency and pure imagery, frequently placed at the door of an illusory dialectic.

Far from "revealing" a "true" reality, as Bazin presumed, the image is only ever one aspect of things; a *chosen, restructured* aspect. Whether the consequence of an apparent linearity (shot-sequences, shots-in-depth) or an apparent discontinuity (short shots, dislocation of time), film continuity is created from a series of fragments whose apparent continuous progression is entirely illusory. It is the continuity of a *story*, and not of reality.

Effect-montage, whether achieved through consecutive images or caesura, successive or simultaneous, is always directed towards producing a deliberately selected meaning. There could never be a *"more than reality"*, as Bazin wished, any more than there could be a *"less than reality"*, as Jean-Louis Comolli proposed; only a *different* reality, an entirely *separate* reality achieved by means of the image of the world and its objects. Consequently, film discourse is necessarily *materialist* and *symbolic*. Only its aims and aspirations can be realist, idealist, or whatever. Abstraction in the cinema does not exist except by virtue of continually mediated concrete facts, a mediation which is itself guided by a formalising intention, an ideology whose signified is then the reflection or expression.

The question of matching

Any shot change, "in depth" or not, necessarily involves the question of matching. Now, just as there is no value in hypothesising about what lies outside the field of view, so there would be no purpose in theorising about matching were it not for the untruths which have clouded the issue. It is surprising to read, under Noël Burch's byeline, that the purpose of accuracy in matching "was to make shot changes imperceptible". But the purpose of accuracy in editing together separate shots has never been to "cover up any discontinuity", but to ensure the space-time unity of a sequence of actions occurring in places relatively close to each other. However perfect the matching, it in no way disguises the discontinuity of shots. What bad cuts make apparent – when they ought to conceal them – are not contrasts from shot to shot which *must be perceived* because they carry meaning, but discontinuity of movement, *dislocated* actions, i.e. jumps and overlaps. Discontinuity of shots or angles is not to be confused with discontinuity of actions contained within these shots.

Before film-makers learned how to match movement correctly

(which happened around 1925–26, notably in Pudovkin's films, but did not become widespread until talkies appeared), it was rare to see matching *along the camera axis*, the change in angle allowed the imperfect matching to be concealed. In the preceding chapter I pointed out that where there was a matched cut along the camera axis, there was always a a lap dissolve between them which "ironed out" any flaws in matching. Most frequently, intertitles avoided the problem.

To ensure a continuity of action or movement across a *discontinuity* of shots is precisely the purpose of movement matching, the rules for which are laid down in editing tables. If the intention is to ensure a perfect space-time unity when cutting from one point of view to another (as for instance from one angle to its reverse) then matched cuts are essential. Yet no one has ever claimed that this unity is mandatory. It is often interesting to ignore it. I shall simply point out that when editing for "shock" effect, the cut producing the meaning loses its effect through the meaning it produces in such a way that, though there is a formal discontinuity between the shots, there is still an impression of continuity. Any "breaks" in editing are perceptible only when they are redundant...

The "fascination of seeing"...

I would add that, in the cinema, there is no such thing as an *empty* sign. When an image signifies nothing, i.e. when it signifies no more than is signified by whatever it is the image of (in which case it does not produce meaning, but *reproduces* it), then it is no longer a sign, empty or full. And when shots are "too long" (such as shots where time seems to be passing), it is not that the meaning, signification, or whatever, is missing. On the contrary, there is a *meaning*, but one which remains as it is (suspended, so to speak) in a signifier which says no more than it has just said; a signifier therefore which is not empty but inoperative, non-productive and, by that very fact, irritating. There is no residual significance (as in *suspended time*, where the purpose is quite different); it is paralysed.

Then there is the *fascination of seeing*, which is entirely different from film fascination. Linked to the movement of the images, to everything by which cinema sets itself apart from the other arts,

Matching along the camera axis and in action continuity: David Lean's *Brief Encounter*, 1945.

film fascination is produced by the superimposed identification (comparison) of two complementary (as much as apparently contradictory) impressions: the impression of reality, due to the represented reality, and the impression of unreality, due to the forms of the representation.

The *fascination of seeing* has associations beyond film images. It is an attentive state close to contemplation. Which presupposes a quality worthy of being contemplated, a quality *full* rather than *empty* of meaning, a period of time during which consciousness dominates the object, envelops it, explores it, but when it dwells on it too long, immediately reverses its effect: then it is the object which absorbs consciousness and paralyses it. Consciousness becomes dissipated into whatever it is that has held its attention and fascination is turned into a numbing of the brain similar to being drugged. There are those who are quite happy to stare blankly into meaningless space, but that has nothing to do with film expression...

What these observations make abundantly clear are the endless discussions about vague terminology leading to pointless abstractions. As though the forms under consideration carried with them a special meaning, and involved a signification applicable in all cases, in short as though there were laws of grammar, structures of syntax or codes of description.

The signification of the close-up, the implications of montage, the realism of the shot-in-depth are argued over endlessly, but the close-up *of what*? The depth of what field, what space? The juxtaposition of what action with what other? Long or short shots relative to what rhythm, to what feeling of time, in what context?...

All these arguments in favour of one or other of these forms are equally valid; all are both true and false, logical and absurd, since everything depends on the events being narrated, the circumstances involved, the meaning ascribed to them or intended for them; in short, on the content, through which, for which and relative to which these structures are effective or ineffective. The cinema is not yet cured of the childish affliction of needing external rules and laws. Now, while comparisons are generally useful, in this context, whether close or distant, they only lead to dangerous conclusions.

Because there is no fixed link between the signifier and signified, the film image – close-up or otherwise – cannot be compared with the linguistic unit, even though in certain circumstances it might behave similarly. And it is precisely because it is not the sign of anything that it is able to connote the most widely diverse ideas or feelings. Centered on the events being described and on the articulations of the signifying linkage, its semantic range is unlimited, like its narrative potential, i.e. like life itself.

From which we may conclude that the film language is a *language without signs*. Not only does the image ensure a function not contained within it but, because of the concrete nature of the objects represented there, ideas become identified with a formal quality. It becomes intelligible only through the perceptible. Which is how visual expression – even in the most mediocre films – comes to be poetic. Which is what I meant when I wrote that the cinema is a language only at the level of a work of art, that it is *expression* before it is *signification*.

IX

Concerning Syntagmatics

We know that a syntagma is a group of words, the smallest group of words containing sufficient grammatical elements to make up an utterance. It is midway between a word and a phrase. However, the word (a lexical unit) *indicates* an object and names a concept. To say that it *signifies* is to underline its quality as a *sign* and to use it to extrapolate the meaning of the indicated object. The syntagma, on the other hand, is a much more flexible, more precise linguistic unit, for, as A. Martinet observes, "it is behind the screen of words that the genuinely fundamental features of human language appear"[1].

Thus the syntagma responds to the definition of semantic unit formed by the "presence of two terms and the relationship which unites them".

A phrase such as the *apple is ripe* is divisible into: a nominative syntagma, the *apple*, and a verbal syntagma, is *ripe* (Chomsky). Yet, from a strictly grammatical point of view, *is ripe* signifies nothing without a point of reference. In this order of ideas, the simplest propositional forms, such as *Peter is big*, *Andrew walks quickly*, and even shorter propositions, such as *the sun shines*, *the clockwork runs down* may be considered as the smallest possible syntagma.

Before semiology appropriated the cinema, the short sequential fragments containing shots relating to a moment in a drama were called *scenes*. This term deriving from the theatre and used to describe the *said* rather than the *saying* was apparently judged inadequate for the purposes of structural analysis in not accounting for the notion of *segment*, such as the shots or groups of shot forming a signifying linkage, like linguistic units. These shot fragments have also been termed *syntagmas* by Christian Metz, by virtue of their similarity with the word groups which form propositions (although this would imply that scene and syntagma are one and the same, the one relating to form and the other to content, with any scene capable of being broken down into one or several syntagmas, just like a phrase).

Main objections

An initial objection, however, comes to mind: however much it may *necessarily* signify, the associative organisation of shots is not subject to any rules similar to those controlling the association of words. It is similar to the linking of phrases whose order derives from the logic of the story. The shot, moreover (which is the smallest segment of film), corresponds not to one but to several phrases. Which means that the film syntagma is in fact a *syntagma* of *syntagmas*. It is no longer a group of units of signification (words) but complex signifiers (shots) considered both as units insofar as they are syntagmatic components and as utterances in reference to the signified.

Obviously, the structure of the syntagma remains the same, but the way it behaves is different, especially since, in the shot, the signified does not depend on the linear succession of elements which are separate and capable of being broken down, but on a dynamic and indivisible whole, a global movement occurring in a limited space according to a predetermined time sequence.

Moreover, if there are no rules governing the linking of shots, there is no such thing as a film syntagma except for the causal entity which gives its meaning and makes it what it is. If we take, for instance, the cell formed by two shots in *The Battleship Potemkin*: a. the sailors throwing an officer overboard; b. a pince-nez dangling at the end of a steel hawser... it is clear that this cell (which is the smallest possible syntagma: two shots joined by an associative relationship) carries meaning only *in the context of the film*.

As we saw in the previous chapter, this relationship, considered outside its associative context, signifies no more than what it shows – no connotation can be read into it.

Whereas the linguistic syntagma possesses an *internal* association through its grammatical organisation, the association which gives meaning to the film syntagma (which is what makes it a syntagma), as we have said, almost always has an *external* origin – but one which is part of the internal structure of the film, its core, rather than belonging to an external body outside the film itself.

The second objection is as follows: Christian Metz distinguishes two basic groups within the different syntagmatic forms, each one of which, more or less codified, involves the same production of meaning: *a-chronological* syntagmas and *chronological* syntagmas.

The first group is divided into *parallel syntagmas* (governing events which are contrasted, juxtaposed or compared) and *embracing* [translated as 'bracket' by Michael Taylor] *syntagmas* (governing events associated within the same global conceptualisation).

The second into *descriptive syntagmas* (governing events considered successively but having the same existence in space and time) and *narrative syntagmas*, themselves subdivided into *linear narrative syntagmas* (governing consecutive events in a series of autonomous shots, episodes or sequences) and *alternating* [translated as 'alternate' by Michael Taylor] *syntagmas* (governing the simultaneity of separate events).

All this is true. But, without wishing to doubt the importance of Christian Metz' work, we might observe that:

1. *Alternating syntagmas* govern non-simultaneity as well as simultaneity. It is possible to use these to link two events separated in space but occurring at the same time or two events occurring in the same space but separated in time. The alternation: *Here | somewhere else | here | somewhere else* also presupposes the alternation: *today | yesterday | today | yesterday...*

2. Parallel, comparative, or associative syntagmas also derive from the same form of montage, variously described by film technicians as alternating montage, parallel montage or cross-cutting. The technique is one of making shots alternate according to a A/B/A/B/A/B..., etc. sequence. When there is a juxtaposition of events similar or with the same meaning (simultaneous or otherwise), interacting at the level of the diegesis, there is an *associative* syntagma. On the other hand, when there is juxtaposition of different events but showing a factual or ideological similarity, then there is a *comparative* syntagma. Thus, in *Storm over Asia*:

Monks clean the statue of Buddha.

The English officer shaves.

The statue is polished.

The officer's wife powders her face.

The statue is decorated with various adornments.

The officer's wife does up the clasp on her pearl necklace.

The officer puts on his uniform decorated with his medals.

The statue is dressed, etc.

3. In the same way, descriptive syntagmas and narrative syntagmas (the difference between them is superficial) derive from the *same type of linear montage* A.B.C.D.E., etc. The hurried, broken nature of so-called non-linear montage derives entirely (in this sort of syntagma) from the *elements being contrasted in this formal juxtaposition*. In other words, what differentiates these syntagmas is their content, the nature and character of what is represented, rather than strictly codified organising principles. It is clearly possible to relate these forms to various large structures, as Christian Metz has proved, but to those described above (which are the most frequent) many others can be added.

Specifically: *false alternation* such as Belmondo's escape in *Pierrot le Fou,* shown in various different aspects, when he has not yet left.

Imaginary alternation, like the sequence in *Midnight Cowboy* where we see: a. the young man in his room writing a letter to his uncle; b. the uncle on his ranch receiving and reading the letter; c. the young man still writing his letter, then tearing it up after thinking about it.

Dual alternation where present and past both become absorbed, combined, confused within each other, confirm or contradict each other, as in *Lenny* or *Star 80,* where the actual facts (eyewitness reports, interviews, investigations) do not serve as a commentary on a completed action constituting what actually happens in the drama, but constantly reactivates it. The list of examples is endless, but this structural schematisation, convenient at the level of analytical study, is valueless from the moment an attempt is made to draw general rules or definite codifications.

Moreover, these classifications, relevant only in signifier/signified relationships, at no point bear on the *rhythm* which, as we have said, controls relationships of time. Now, though rhythm may not provide an intelligible meaning to the syntagma, it does provide it with an emotional value not to be underestimated, film being as much expression as signification. Yet rhythm also exists *by virtue of what is turned into rhythm,* and not, as is the case in music or poetry, by virtue of preestablished structures or rules.

We may say, in a general sense, that *implication* is one of the basic conditions of film expression, if not the most important.

Implication is not a closed system but a generative function constantly open to possibility. Similar to semantic induction, it is different in that, just like semantics itself, it is limited by syntax, conditioned by it, whereas the sole bases of implication are the logical, psychological and other principles which we intend to examine later on.

Be this as it may, it is not important that the resulting significations should be obtained through montage (alternating, parallel, comparative, contrasting, linear, broken, etc.) or by its absence (panning, tracking, camera movements, depth-of-field, etc.), since the different syntagmatic forms exist only by virtue of *what is shown* and not because of some law or other.

"Alternating montage tells us nothing about what should be put into the images," Christian Metz tells us[2]. Now, in my view – which the evidence seems to support – it is precisely what is put into the images which governs their structure. Only objects which are comparable warrant being compared; alternating them will not make it otherwise. In linguistics, grammar is not what creates alternation (a fact of construction and analysis) but it is what governs, controls and orders it. The represented is not made up of abstract signs but concrete objects, therefore having a form – the *form of the content*, a material substance which, when organised, constitutes the *form of the expression*. Without a doubt it is this which gives the content its entire meaning, but it is the content which imposes – by virtue of the meaning ascribed to it – a certain form. In other words, *there are no grammatical rules in the cinema, only rules of rhetoric*.

What aligns cinema and language, at least externally, is the fact that significations in both are essentially relational: relationships of words or images, shots or syntagmas, phrases or sequences, every one concerns "the relationship of two terms". A relationship which, in the cinema, is not always created by actual montage but by the transition from one shot to another in a continuous movement or by the association in depth of two separate pieces of information, these effects being termed "effect-montage" for convenience sake.

Which is the same as saying that the term *montage* is inadequate for the purpose of defining the exact nature and prerequisites of these signifying structures. In fact, structure does not depend solely on the association of one shot with another but more on the place, the precise moment the cut is made (or transition or caesura) to ensure that the link has a meaning. Because of which it would be more appropriate to refer to *signifying cut*, rather than montage.

Logic or grammar?

Yet, according to Christian Metz:

This code of rhetoric, *because of various other aspects, is also a code of grammar*, and it is the responsibility of the semiology of the cinema, as Pier Paolo Pasolini so rightly argues, that the two codes, rhetoric and grammar, should be inseparable.

Why can the codified and signifying arrangements of film be regarded as a grammar? Precisely because these arrangements not only organise film *connotation*; they also, and primarily, organise its denotation. The specific signified of alternating montage involves the literal temporality of the story, the primary message of the film, even though the alternating arrangement inevitably carries with it various connotations[3].

Now, denotation is not arranged according to grammatical rules but according to simple factual logic – also according to narrative logic which organises into discourse the events in question or the elements of the denotation. Moreover, alternating montage – as we have seen – is not concerned with the temporality of the story alone but also with comparative, spatial and other relationships.

Lastly, attempting to take the Metz formula a stage further, Dominique Chateau and Michel Colin struggled hard to create a formula to encapsulate the potential for syntagmatic forms. Dominique Chateau writes:

Metz makes no prediction, even approximate, as to the probability, within the narrative context, of syntagmatic types occurring which might be listed in any way systematically. Now, it is obvious that an almost infinite number of films use the so-called "linked" type (juxtaposition of images illustrating a theme), whereas all use a great variety of "sequences"; the large syntagmatic category [translator's note:. Michael Taylor's translation of 'la grande syntagmatique'] provides no indication as to the structural conditions of the actual variety of the sequential type.

As regards empirical data, the model of cinema which, ignoring other examples, proposes a typology of sequences, would be a great deal more useful than the large syntagmatic category. The neutrality of the latter, which prefers the equality of possibles to the distribution of probables, *sanctifies the originality of the theoretical level*, inasmuch as it produces rational forms, a strict respect for which (the so-called rule of relevance) does not imply, through its power alone, a deep knowledge (as a phenomenon) of the object under consideration[4].

One might argue that the premises enabling such a probability to be established are a good deal less stable (always varied and uncertain) and it seems just as absurd to establish this as to establish, for instance, the probability of the letter A occurring in the latest Robbe-Grillet novel. Dominique Chateau goes on:

It is obvious that the large syntagmatic category relies on another of Christian Metz's propositions: the linguistic and grammatical phenomenon is a good deal wider and involves the *most basic transmission structures of all information*. This postulate suggests that we should be looking for, not just *linguistic structures in the cinema*, using raw material provided by linguists, but the *cinematic structures themselves*, by adapting linguistic models to their theoretic representation[5].

But, whether applying to the cinema "a preestablished armoury of rules carefully respecting their formal characteristics", as Michel Colin describes it, or abandoning established cinematic structures and referring, like Dominique Chateau, to syntactical forms in order to find an approximate model, changes very little and does not prevent them both becoming bogged down in the mire of linguistics (albeit generative rather than structural linguistics...).

Although the model suggested by Dominique Chateau *directly* concerns film structures and uses linguistic models only by *analogy*, he only refers to these as an imposed limitation. Now, at the level of film, a hundred possible models can be found – perhaps even more – and none of them would claim to be elevated to a generalisation.

To repeat, film language cannot be turned into a theory – or model – for the simple reason that syntagmatic ordering is not governed by rules, but by the logic of the story. The intelligibility of syntagmatic types is a function of the plausibility of the facts set before the logic characteristic of the given genre.

Moreover, if relationships of shots in syntagmas are as important as the shots themselves, then it might be possible to consider the relationships between the elements forming each shot – characters, objects, setting – as a series of articulations. Yet there is, in my view, an unbridgeable gulf between this and the assumption, made by Pasolini, that this represents the equivalent of a second articulation. As he says:

> We may refer to all the objects, forms and actions of reality within the cinematic image as cinemes, by analogy with phonemes [...] Just as words or monemes are composed of phonemes and such a composition constitutes the double articulation of language, so the monemes in the cinema – shots – are composed of cinemes[6].

This argument seems to me indefensible. Not because there are very few phonemes in language whereas there is a countless number of "cinemes", but because, by virtue of the constant mobility of images, the endlessly variable cinemes create a motivated and separate meaning whereas phonemes, articulated in words in a way that is unchangeable, create through these an unmotivated ambiguous meaning. What is more, the comparative association between the cineme and phoneme forces Pasolini to regard the shot as a moneme, which is all the more inadmissable for the fact that the shot creates many different significations whereas the word is only one single unit of meaning.

Though we might accept Pasolini's distinction between the cinema of prose and the cinema of poetry (a distinction by no means new), we are completely at odds with him when he argues that there is a genuine language of cinema.

Linguistics has supplied film analysis with a more appropriate terminology; it has provided film theory with a huge system of reference but one which, though it enables various useful comparisons to be made, contributes absolutely nothing at the level of significations. These comparisons are interesting only at the narrative, discursive level. When these structures have to be organised, however, at the level of units of meaning, language and film expression have no common measure.

This frantic research, this need to discover a second articulation within the structures of the moving image – individual frames or cinemes – shows to what extent, in the minds of semiologists and certain critics, film expression cannot exist without having recourse to rules which can be established in no other way than by reference to linguistics – starting with the double articulation without which, according to Hjelmslev, Martinet and others, language could not exist. This may be so in respect of verbal language, since this is its essential characteristic. But would it be wrong to conceive of a language which had no double articulation?

If in fact language means the simple linking together of signifier/ signified relationships based on writing, we can quite imagine (like Christian Metz) a language *without speech* and, by extension (as I see it myself), a *language without signs* and, therefore, without grammar, code or system.

In fact images only become signs through induction. They only ever involve what they show and they only signify relative to a given context. As André Martinet himself confirms:

Whenever motivation exerts such a strong pressure on the signifier that it alters it every time it occurs, it is impossible to attach a constant signification to an expression deprived of stability. Thus, it is impossible to impose rules on it...[7]

X

Codes and Codifications

Having examined why the film image might (or might not) have a status comparable with that of a linguistic sign, Christian Metz eventually came little by little to abandon this idea of sign to replace it with the notion of *code* – much as Emilio Garroni and Umberto Eco had done. He writes, notably:

> Without objecting to the notion of sign as such, we should note that nowadays it represents only one tool of research and that it no longer enjoys the special and central role it has played since Saussure or Peirce. [...] Which is one more reason why the search for distinctive units of film should not be associated with the precise study of the cinematic sign.

He goes on:

> It is not true that the identification of the smallest unit is a precondition for the whole of cinematic semiological research[1].

We heartily agree. However, we must recognise that it is the pursuit of the double articulation and the smallest unit of signification which has tempted most semiologists and Metz himself has tried to draw a parallel between the image and the sign.

Unable to find a distinctive unit within the modalities of the shot, Metz looked for it in potential codifications. He writes:

> We should begin by separating off and distinguishing between – isolating – the main cinematic codes and sub-codes [...]. It is to the extent that each of these is clearly defined that the smallest unit appropriate to each may be determined (through the internal correspondences within each, and not the cinema[2].

Now, in my view, there is no such thing as a cinematic code –

specifically to do with film – any more than there are grammatical or syntactical codes.

Defining terms

Firstly, we must agree about the meaning we are ascribing to the term *code*: we may say that a code is a collection of distinctive features enabling us to recognise a thing, an object, a quality or to establish a necessary relationship between a signifier and a signified, codification being merely a way of making meaning universal, reducing it to its essence at the level of a culture or ideology. As Sartre writes: *"In themselves objects have no meaning; they need only to be there."* It is we who give them a quality, a value by virtue of the relation between us and them and by the use we make of them. Thus, any object, any reality in the external world implies a codification which might be called *natural* in being associated with the nature of things and, most frequently, it is used to mean the direct meaning of these things.

Custom, habit, our way of understanding, classifying and judging by reason of a particular ideology or accepted rules, involve in their turn a whole network of social or socio-cultural codifications deriving less from society itself than from civilisation in general. Rooted in secular culture, in the very conditions of existence, generally compared with perception, they too are understood as the *direct meaning* of experience.

But these are *habits*. They are (or may be) interpreted variously, according to the time, place, culture, even the individuals involved. They are codified only *after the event*. In other words, codification *depends* on these habits; it defines them, contains them but does not establish them. It allows a large element of free will to their interpretation.

The *code*, on the other hand – as I understand it – exists *a priori*. According to the generally accepted definition, it is the arbitrary and restrictive imposition of a precise *function* onto a given system. For example, the highway code, the civil code, the postal code. Or else it is the description of a biological function, such as the genetic code, or biophysiological code (produced in the same conditions the same impulses provoke the same reactions). And yet no one would ever think that, if the stomach has a digestive function, it is by virtue of a code... As Mikel Dufrenne so rightly points out:

> If the code is indeed an established system of restrictions, certain objects may be regarded as encoded (such as traffic signals or road signs) but the world is écriture only metaphorically, and our perception is what deciphers it as such: the habits which our bodies adopt relative to the perceptible are not to be confused with the cultural systems of signs; we may say that the body, when it is communicating with the perceptible, is decoding, but it is not decoding a text preexisting it as a code[3].

Clearly, the codifications of language are generally recognised as code in that they are associated with the distinctiveness of signs. It is quite obvious that, in the cinema, whatever is expressed, shown, told relates to a code, since represented objects are inseparable from their meaning. In this context they are forms of content, not forms of expression. The produced "film" is in fact referred to a number of codes but the majority of them are *extrinsic*. They deal with *filmed objects* and not the *filmic*, and I still believe that a specific code for the cinema is precluded as soon as the image stops being an unmotivated sign and as the signifier/signified relationship ceases to be a stable one involving a fixed meaning within strict rules. Metz writes:

> If a code is a code, it is because it provides a single field of commutation, that is, a (reconstructed) "zone" within which variations of the signifier may correspond with variations of the signified, within which a number of units take their meaning from each other. A code is homogeneous because that was how it was intended, never because that was the way it was observed[4].

Rules that do not exist

Now, though variations of the signifier may involve variations of the signified, these differences are entirely unpredictable. According to the particular film, the same signifier may involve quite different signifieds and the same signified may be created by very different signifiers.

Westerns are not made in the same way as thrillers, comedies in the same way as epics, and the enlightened film fan will be able to recognise a Hitchcock or Von Sternberg film from the first few frames. Thus obvious codifications do exist but they influence the type or style of the film, not its language. Doubtless we might codify certain techniques or their meanings. If we could decide that: *superimposition* = *ghost*, it would be a code. However, it is nothing of the kind.

In his study on experimental cinema, Dominique Noguez wrote:

Characters appearing as superimpositions have an obvious diegetic status: they are ghosts[5].

Now, though this may be true of certain fantasy films or dream-sequences, it is not the case with many others. In the course of a single year (1913), the Danish director Holger Madsen used superimposition to represent ghosts (*Opium Dreams, The Spirits*), whereas Griffith exploited them to indicate, in *The Avenging Conscience*, the worry and anguish of his hero and

Superimposed characters "from beyond the grave" in Victor Sjöström's
The Phantom Carriage, 1920.

Victor Sjöström used the same device to suggest memories in *Ingeborg Holm*. Superimposition enabled the "visions" of a symbolic or metaphorical character to be materialised (*Intolerance, Civilisation, J'Accuse*), as well as representing characters "from the hereafter", an image which became widely used in 1920 with Hayes Hunter's *The Ghoul* and Victor Sjöström's *The Phantom Carriage*. A few years later, hallucination scenes became popular with *Secrets of a Soul* (G.W. Pabst), *Waxworks* (Paul Leni), *The Student of Prague* (Henrik Galeen), etc. Thus we are not able to plot the development or change to a rule which had not yet come into being...

In linguistics, punctuation marks, such as question marks or exclamation marks, are signs. Full-stops, commas indicate both linking and separation. In the cinema, so-called "punctuations" are almost always articulations. The *fade to black* suggests a lapse of time over a long period, but it can also mark the end of a sequence (in which case it is being used as a full-stop). The *lap dissolve* links together events separated in time at the same time as it indicates that separation, but it also can link together events separated in space and, as in *Citizen Kane* (in the singing lesson sequence), it can be used in the frequentative mood. Moreover, these linking mechanisms are by no means compulsory, as is proved by contemporary films where jump-cuts have become acceptable. During the thirties, it became fashionable to use *wipes* to indicate a change of location. These are seldom used nowadays. Doubtless these techniques were codified then employed for specific purposes over a certain period, but a code is not to be confused with a passing fashion. Indeed, a code is *all-powerful* (within the limits set on it) or it is not. If the highway code were to change every six months, it would cease to be a code...

What is true of superimpositions and dissolves is also true of other techniques. They can all be used in ways different from or opposite to what is expected, since none of them has an *a priori* defined function.

There is cliché, on the other hand, when a technique or stylistic feature relies on acquired habit, on a code: fixed in its meaning as in a book of rules, flicking through the pages of a calendar has become unacceptable.

Free expression

As I have always maintained, every film *imposes and creates the rules appropriate to it alone*, the codifications suggested by it existing only by virtue of an all-powerful context. Whereas signifying structures preexist the verbal expression, this is not the case in film: *they depend on it* and, by that fact, they are not "exportable". In his study of *Muriel*, Michel Marie recognised in his turn that "text invents its own codes and these codes are specific to that text and not relevant to any other text"[6].

Whereas Pierre Sorlin pointed out that:

Film, through the systems of relationships which it carries with it, organises its own codes, creates its own signs, transforms into indices or semes data which are, *in essence, indeterminate and indiscernible* beyond the relational level in which they occur[7].

It can never be overstated that two actions edited to intercut with each other, for instance, are not being compared by the simply fact of the intercutting, i.e. by a syntagma whose structure might in itself indicate the comparison, like a phrase whose grammatical organisation provides an *a priori* meaning. The nature of the syntagma, undefinable except *a posteriori*, depends on the nature and meaning of the events which compose it. Events whose intelligibility (the effect of understanding that they are being compared or contrasted) depends on the dramatic circumstances, the actions and situations, whose clarity is supported, where necessary, by dialogue or voice-over. This is endorsed by the fact that so-called film codes almost always refer back to a body of socio-cultural codes, which are understood only because of the fact that they are encoded. So much so that, quite frequently, subtle effects are created by contradicting them. Eisenstein's *Alexander Nevsky* is significant in this respect.

Whereas in the West, the colour white symbolises purity and innocence, the white surcoats of the German knights, the enormous icy surface of Lake Chudskoya, the snow-covered fields are associated with the themes of cruelty, oppression and death, while the colour black, assigned to the Russian soldiers, embodies the positive themes of heroism and patriotism. Which audiences immediately understood.

In another film, a sequence shows a woman inspecting a table laid for dinner and carefully rearranging a vase of flowers. Through reference to the social code, we understand that the mistress of the house is taking charge before the arrival of her guests. But that is not the case. In fact, as she performs this ritual the woman is looking at the flowers with sadness: her husband has had them sent with a note excusing himself. Urgent business has meant that he will not be coming. Now, these flowers remind her of those he used to give her before they were married and that he never missed a single dinner-party before.

As with many other details, such a meaning is decipherable only in the context of previous sequences, i.e. by a code set by events and relevant only to that film, whose originality – like Eisenstein's film – derives from turning the accepted meaning upside down and replacing it with another, exclusive and personal.

But, here as in other examples, what we are seeing are narrative codes, and not codes of language – which are nowhere to be found in significations specific to film.

Analogy and similarity

And yet Christian Metz and other semiologists – Umberto Eco, Emilio Garroni, Dominique Chateau – have been exploring *analogy* (because of the similarity between the object and its image) as a possible basis for a potential codification of film units. Christian Metz writes:

> The notion of analogy is to be treated with care. It is true that for a genuinely cinematic semiology, analogy represents a kind of *stumbling block*: at the precise points where analogy is responsible for film signification (notably, the meaning of every "theme" taken *separately*) all *specifically cinematic* codification fails; which is why, in our view, we must look for film codes on other levels [...]. For general semiology, however, the analogical sections of film signification do not represent a stopping-point; for many things which the film analyst assumes to be "acquired", therefore representing a kind of absolute beginning *from which* the cinematic experience develops, are in their turn the complicated, terminal products of *other* cultural experiences [...]. Among these naturally "extra-cinematic" codes which

nonetheless influence the screen under the guise of analogy, we should point out at least – without the need for a more accurate and complete list – the *iconology* specific to each socio-cultural group producing or enjoying films (the more or less institutionalised modalities for representating objects, the processes for recognising and *identifying* objects in the forms of their visual or acoustic reproduction and, more generally, the collective notions about what an *image* is) and, on the other hand, up to a point, *perception itself*, (visual habits for referencing and constructing forms and shapes, representation of space peculiar to each culture, various auditory structures, etc.). The characteristic of codes of this type is to function, so to speak, in the midst of analogy, to be felt by users to be part of the most ordinary and most natural visual or auditory deciphering process. Contrary to what we thought four years ago [notably in "Le cinéma, langue ou langage?"], it does not seem entirely impossible, nowadays, to suppose that analogy is itself constantly being coded in order to function properly as analogy relative to codes on a higher level – which only begin to exert their influence on the basis of this initial assumption[8].

[compare Michael Taylor's translation:

The concept of analogy must nevertheless be handled with caution. It is true that, for an actual semiotics of the cinema, analogy serves as a kind of stopping block: Wherever analogy takes over filmic signification (that is, notably the meaning of each visual element taken separately), there is a lack of specifically cinematographic codification. That is why I believe filmic codes must be sought on other levels [...]. But, for a general semiotics, the analogous portions of filmic signification would not constitute a point of stopping off; for many things that are assumed to be "acquired" by the film analyst and therefore are a kind of absolute beginning *after which* the cinematographic experience unfolds, are in turn the complex, terminal products of *other* cultural experiences and various organisations whose field of action, being more general, includes a great deal more than the cinema alone. Among the codes that are extracinematographic by nature, but that nevertheless intervene on the screen under cover of analogy, one must point out as a minimum –

without prejudice to more complex and sensitive enumerations –
the *iconology* specific to each sociocultural group producing or
viewing the films (the more or less institutionalised modalities of
object representation, the processes of recognition and *identification* of objects in their visual or auditive "reproduction," and,
more generally, the collective notions of what an image is), and,
on the other hand, up to a certain point, *perception* itself (visual
habits of identification and construction of forms and figures,
the spatial representations peculiar to each culture, various
auditory structures, etc.). Characteristically, codes of this type
function, so to speak, at the heart of analogy and are experienced by viewers as a part of the most ordinary and natural
visual or auditory decipherment.

Contrary to what I believed four years ago (notably in "The
Cinema: Language or Language System?"), it does not seem at
all impossible to me, today, to assume that *analogy is itself coded
without, however, ceasing to function authentically as analogy in
relation to the codes of the superior level* – which are brought into
play only on the basis of this first assumption... (p.111–112)]

This last point is obvious. However, to state, as Metz does, that
"the codes of analogy create a perceptual similarity between signifier and signified", is to see things back to front; in fact, a code does
not create what it codifies any more than a word creates the object
which it describes (if this is a manner of speaking, it is a dangerous
one). Similarity is an effect of consciousness observing the existence of similar features in objects which are then declared to be
analogous.

We may well wonder how or in what this similarity might be
recognised if not the fact that by relating it to the code of analogy
it resembles whatever it is analogous with. But how might this
analogy be recognised if not the fact that there is a similarity,
therefore relating it to the code of similarity? We could continue to
go round in circles (as with contradictions in terms), since the
notion of code explains nothing, means nothing, and codification is
merely a means of grouping, classifying the intuitive data of
experience.

If I am able to distinguish a chestnut tree from a plane tree by
virtue of the code representing the features common to all
chestnut trees, by what code am I able to recognise the chestnut I

climbed as a child, whose specific features are not described in any generalising codification? Obviously, by a sub-code describing its specific characteristics. But, since any chestnut tree, any plane tree, indeed any tree has specific features which make it that particular tree and none other, we might suppose as many sub-codes as there are trees in the world. Which is the same thing as saying that everything which exists is coded. Now, if everything is coded, it is as though nothing were coded and the notion of code instantly disappears. In other words, the term which designates a particular object carries in its meaning the essential characteristics of the designated referent without the need to dress it up in a code.

What is odd is that Metz goes to great lengths to turn the idea of code into an "abstraction", with which he intended to replace the considerably less specious (in my opinion) notions of denotation and connotation. He writes:

> In every film, the codes are both present and absent: present because the system is built on them, absent because the system exists as such only inasmuch as it is different from the message of a code, because it only begins to exist when these codes stop existing in the form of codes, because it is that very moment of growth, of construction-destruction[9].

In other words, the code – at the level of language – is only there to be cancelled or suppressed by the concrete, which means that the concrete is able quite easily to do without it.

If we accept that it is meaningless to refer to grammar or syntax in terms of the cinema, it is even more so to refer to code. However, we should not assume from this a total freedom, a complete absence of structure. There are rules – as we saw with regard to the duplication of time and the introduction of subjective metaphor. But rules entirely relating to logical principles, themselves dependent on the narrative structures involved. The only rules capable of determining the correct interpretation of a film (its comprehension, an understanding of its signifiers) are in fact the rules of logic. Thus, is it due to the fact that we know by experience that things are "either one thing..., or the other", according to the alternatives of the logic of the excluded third [syllogism], that the notions of comparison and simultaneity can be related to alternating montage.

Once again: *anything is possible in the cinema which is justified, which signifies within a given system* – a system, however, of motivated relationships, not unmotivated signs, as with language, the relevant logic being the simple logic of everyday experience, the application of any other being a distant and dubious prospect.

XI

Images and Speech

The sole topic of the preceding chapters has been the image, the basis of film expression. But, towards the end of the 1920s, the cinema added to its resources speech, music and sound effects. Regarded initially as peripheral, the sound elements and verbal messages became gradually integrated into the basic structures, to the extent of forming with the images a more complex, much richer form of expression, even a new formalisation of meaning.

This is the moment to turn our attention to this, having first put it in its historical context. As I noted in my *Aesthetics*[1], the cinema before the talkies was *silent* but never *without sound*. Apart from the fact that speech was unnecessary (or *should not have been necessary*), the odd cries, sounds or even words suggested by the characters' description or behaviour were 'understood' by the audience which had to use its imagination to provide the characters and objects with the sound qualities they might have had in actual reality, and star-struck young girls credited the romantic lead with the sweet-nothings they longed to hear. Since the dialogue was created by each audience member as he or she wished, it is not unreasonable to suppose that this 'imaginary dialogue' was potentially one of the most poetic aspects of a film. On the other hand, silence was meaningless, powerless. One of the benefits of the 'sound-picture' was that it gave a value to silence. The 'weight' of silence has only existed since then, and we know that its expressive power is a not inconsiderable resource.

Going back thirty or so years, we see that the criticisms of the first talkies were precisely those directed against mediocre silent films dressed up in a different form. It is true that a deluge of silly verbosity flooded the screens during the period between 1928 and 1930 (the most verbose films were no more verbose than certain silent films whose verbosity was conveyed through endless subtitles).

I described how Thomas Ince and several others made efforts to keep these to the minimum by giving them an *indicative* role ("in the little town of..."; "eight days later", etc.) and by making sure it was placed between sequences so as not to interrupt the shot continuity by inserting dialogue pared down to its barest essentials.

Most American films between 1912 and 1918 had only the briefest of descriptions. Loane Tucker's *Traffic in Souls*, for instance, a remarkable film for its time (1913), with a running time of more than one hundred minutes, contains only thirty or so title-cards, of the type: "We see Tom searching for, and finding, the traffickers' headquarters", a text which opens the sequence like the title heading of each chapter in a picaresque novel.

Following this path, Louis Delluc in France and Carl Mayer in Germany wrote screenplays where the tight, concise action, reduced to its essentials, did away with the need for redundant explanations, with the drama itself excluding any situations "where people talked". We know that many Expressionist films were without title-cards, in particular those influenced more or less by the ideas of Carl Mayer and the Kammerspiele, such as *Le Rail*, *The Street*, *New Year's Eve*, *The Shadow Puppeteer*, *The Last Laugh*. And, for their part, *Torgus*, *Vanina*, *Variety*, *Waxworks*, even the great epic films *The Nibelungen* and *The Chronicle of the Grey House* contain only the bare minimum. And where title-cards were included, they played a less explanatory and more allusive or poetic role. Thus, in *Nosferatu*, when Huter is left by his driver to find his way by himself to the castle, the title: "As soon as he crossed the bridge, the spirits came to meet him" suggests the crossing of a border, a journey into another world, with no other explanation of the story.

It is obvious that a short title-card has more impact than a piece of heavy rhetoric which ends up longwindedly signifying the same thing but visually. It is better to have: "A year later" than a long sequence of dissolves through the riffling pages of a calendar. Yet, during the twenties, while some directors were trying to eliminate of title-cards, others on the contrary made every effort to include more.

Reaching the "age of reason" – but not yet fully adult – the cinema, always conscious of its own resources, had a crisis in its development when it tried to take on stories, supposedly more profound, whose complexity and profundity were as often as not reduced to the complications of melodrama.

One of the afflictions which plagued the cinema of the twenties was the appointment of "titlers" by the distributors. Employed to write or edit the subtitles, these scribbling nobodies thought they were doing a fine job, "doing their business" wherever they thought fit and naturally believing that it "helped" the film. So, in France, *The Street* was saddled with the following choice phrase: "Prosper Bonassou, noctambule, déambule" [Prosper Bonassou, night-animal, prowls around], following a shot showing a man wandering from gas-light to gas-light. In another, an unhappy lover creeping off into the dusk inevitably invites: "And the black wings of night fold over his gloomy soul". A love-scene: "He brushed her virginal lips with his and they exchanged a kiss into which they poured their souls." One might be forgiven for thinking that the films were there only to justify this verbal diarrhoea...

Apart from the Germans, only the Russian directors were able to find a style suitable for uniting images and text within the same rhythm, the words themselves forming images. In fact, in Dziga Vertov and his verbal interpolations, the images completed an idea suggested by the text, or the text completed a visual proposition. Thus: *He is motionless*: image of Lenin. *He is silent*: image of Lenin. *The crowd is moved*: images of the crowd. *They are silent*, etc.[2] Eisenstein, Turin, Kozintzev, Ermler all successfully followed this method. But the depths of absurdity were plumbed when the letters themselves became animated. "She was frightened", announced a title-card, on which the typography quivered. "Her pain mingled with the rain", declared another, trickling away in the shape of tears or rain-drops.

Concerning an "internal language"

In an essay relatively unknown until now[3], the Russian theorist Boris Eichenbaum argued, as early as 1927, that the silent film, though deprived of speech, was in no way devoid of a linguistic referent. He wrote:

It is always inaccurate to refer to art films as "mute"; as it turns out, it is not so much a matter of "mutism" as of an absence of *audible* speech, a new correlation between speech and object. A correlation, as in the theatre, between mime and gesture accompanying the words may not exist, but the action of words acting as an articulatory mime is retained. The film actor speaks as he is being filmed, and this produces its effect on the screen. [...] Another effect is even more important: *the process of language in the minds of the audience.* For any study of the rules of cinema (especially editing), it is extremely important to recognise that the perception and understanding of film are indissolubly linked to the formation of the interior language which brings together the separate images. The only elements in the cinema perceptible outside the context of this process are "abstruse" ones. To be able to link the images together, the viewer must make a complex cerebral effort, by and large absent in normal usage where words mask or supplant the other means of expression. The viewer must be constantly stringing together the cine-phrases, otherwise he will understand absolutely nothing. It is not without reason that, for some people, the effort of cerebration necessary in the cinema is too great, tiring, unusual or unpleasant. One of the important concerns of the film director is to ensure that the image "reaches" the viewer, i.e. that he is able to guess the meaning of the sequence or, in other words, that he translates it into its interior language. This is how this interior language becomes aligned with the actual construction of the film.

This idea of "interior" or, to put it more precisely, internal language has recently been adopted by various semiologists, in particular Emilio Garroni[4]. Yet, though it is clear that an intellectual effort is needed to understand the meaning of film linkages, this decoding is in our view exactly the same as the "thinking" thought, i.e. the simple consummation of perception, judgment by assimilation, association or distinction.

Certainly, this decoding is organised in the viewer's mind in the form of a "discourse", as a "secondary" film suggested by the first. But this discourse – understood here to mean a logical linkage – is not necessarily linguistic in character or by nature, does not necessarily refer to words, to an internal phonic language, grammaticalised or not. Obviously, that possibility is there and, more often than not, it is employed, since a person generally thinks with words (any social being having learned to name objects as he differentiates them one from the other), but it is a reflex of habit, a learned skill, not an *obligation.*

In fact, this "internal language", though associated with semiotic elements, is not necessarily an "implicit verbal language", as Garroni claims. It may just as easily be *visual*, with the initial, instinctive thought – in no way superficial – working on the *objects* (or the image of objects), on non-verbal formal references and not at all on words. It then becomes the simple logical organisation of mental images on which judgment is based and with which it is established. For "external" language (or language in the proper sense) is only ever the linguistic stratification of the actual forms of thought, the expression of intuitive logic in a discourse organised according to verbal structures arranged and grammaticalised as a consequence.

The child learning to read does not identify different words by referring to the objects named by them, and then discarding them. In everyday language, words are freed from the image of the objects; the thought *has no need of them*. Which is what we mean when we refer to "thinking with words", and the reason why seeing images or objects is related to concepts which are absorbed into verbal structures. Yet, just as the child discards the "associated image" as he starts to master language, so the viewer is able to forget the "associated word" as he finds it easier to decode the film language. Rediscovering the original, intuitive thought, working on the *objects* and freed from the grip of words, the perceptive viewer has no need to form this personal, non-communicative judgment, what might be called an "internal language".

We might add, to be absolutely specific, that the stylistic forms used in the cinema, such as metaphor, are not *borrowed* from the verbal forms in current use, are not, as Eichenbaum and Garroni would have it, "the transposition into a visual representation of an already institutionalised linguistic representation", even though the image might be appropriate and the film metaphor might bear comparison with the verbal metaphor. In fact, the difference between them is to do with the transposition in terms of specific forms or qualities, the *actual structures of thought*.

When Griffith created the first film metaphor, he did not stop to ask how he should go about producing the equivalent of a verbal metaphor. He simply put his images together in such a way as to suggest a relationship experienced at the instinctive level. Having done this, it was a surprise that it should be a metaphor. But though he achieved the equivalent of a linguistic form, he did not *start* from the basis of that form with the notion of creating a possible translation.

It will be argued that, because Griffith's culture was formed by language, this would have led him quite naturally to find a similar device but by different means. Yet this method formalised by words still relates to a way of thinking previous to language.

In other words, neither verbal language nor film language are specific as regards their basic structures, only as regards the formal and formalising elements of the discourse (words, images) and as regards the organisation of these elements. Also, it is pointless to search for a similarity between them in linguistic structures, as though film language were merely a visual transposition. On the contrary, it is to be found *within what makes them essentially what they are,* i.e. within mental structures previous to any explicit form of language, where language – verbal or visual – finds its *implicit* bases through the intuitive formalisation of a series of relationships, differences, similarities, guided (in clear thinking) by the logic of judgment – an impression or interpretation of the logic of reality or what we perceive as such. The ideative mechanisms of the unconscious are sufficient proof of this. But we shall come back to this later on.

The image/text relationship

Thus, the advent of speech and sound provoked a whole series of problems, discussions, arguments and ideas described in the minutest detail by every single history of the cinema – and innumerable articles! – which it would be irrelevant to revisit in the present study.

It would appear that Jacques Feyder was getting near the truth when he wrote: "In the theatre, the situation is created by the words; in the cinema, the words must arise from the situation."

However, it was in Lubitsch's first musical comedies (*Love Parade*) and particularly in his ironic comedies (*Trouble in Paradise*) that the potential of audio-visual signification first began to be realised – the relationship between text and images assuming a new meaning radically different from what was imagined at the time. It was no longer a question of integrating dialogue scenes into as visual an architecture as possible, of ignoring dialogue or cutting it down to the barest essentials, but of creating *signification* through the simple relationship between text and image, i.e. through the contrast, differentiation and contradiction, etc., produced by the juxtaposition of the seen and the heard. It was, in a way, a sort of counterpoint: visual against verbal but, in place of the old-style sound effects capable of producing nothing more than a few vaguely suggested feelings, the relationship assumed a more intellectual quality, with the image-text association creating a new idea in the audience's mind. It was, in the final analysis, the *transposition and extension of the very ground-rules for editing* onto the audio-visual plane: in addition to the idea determined by the succession of two images (or "vertical" montage – following the meaning of the film narrative), there was another idea created out of the direct relationship between the visual and the verbal (or "horizontal" montage), both significations occurring simultaneously[5].

Montage is meant here (and elsewhere in this study) in its most widely accepted sense: meaning determined by relationships (of objects, facts, situations, etc.) either through a direct succession of images or the total space of the field of view, with the visual content constantly referred back to the auditory.

An obvious example will illustrate this more clearly.

In Frank Lloyd's *Cavalcade* (1933), which traces the development of English society from the death of Queen Victoria up to the 1914 War through the story of two families belonging to the English upper classes, one sequence shows us two honeymooners on the deck of a transatlantic liner. The children of two neighbouring families, friends for as long as anyone can remember, they have just realised their dream: to become man and wife. As fashion decreed in high society of the time, they are going to honeymoon by Niagara Falls. A wide shot shows them from the rear on the forward deck of the ship: they move towards the railings. A reverse-angle frames them in close-shot, leaning side by side with the railing coinciding with the bottom frame-line. They look out over the ocean (i.e. the camera) and they exchange a short sequence of dialogue. He asks whether she is happy, whether there is anything he can give her. She is in seventh heaven: 'If I had to die tomorrow', she says, 'I believe life would have given me everything I expected of it'. Obviously, she is speaking figuratively; but, during the conversation, the camera pulls back and reveals, just as the young wife finishes what she is saying, a life-buoy tied to the railing on which we read the name of the ship: 'Titanic'. Then there is a cut to the next shot.

In a different form, this is example of the shock movement backwards we mentioned in another context which suddenly turns the initial meaning of the film upside down and, in this instance, gives a tragic resonance to words with no apparent meaning. A perfect, though perhaps rudimentary and simplistic, example of film language – pure audio-visual signification. A good talkie should be composed exclusively of expressions of this kind. And if we remember the beginning of *Trouble in Paradise*: in Venice, on the Grand Canal, a gondolier is rowing and singing with great conviction at the top of his lungs 'O Sole Mio'. It is raining. To all intents and appearances, he is rowing a pair of bashful lovers. There he is stopping in front of the steps of a magnificent palazzo... But no: it is merely the local dustman on his round, disposing of garbage. The whole film is like this.

The following diagrams will help define more clearly the structure of the talking film. They are not intended to represent a strict rule but to translate schematically a general procedure:

Say we have, on the one hand, a visual continuity A-B-C-D and, on the other, a verbal continuity A'-B'-C'-D' (fig.1). It is clear that:

Shot A is associated with dialogue A'. Each contributes its own special signification and a third signification is generated by their direct relationship: AA' (which we might call the real signification of shot A).

What is more, shot B follows shot A and carries through the logical implications of the primary information of A. A certain meaning results from the A/B relationship but this meaning is corrected by the effect of the A' dialogue. In other words, the A/B relationship is, in fact, an AA'/B relationship, which produces the X signification.

Shot B is, in its turn, associated with dialogue B'. It is visually related to shot C but the signification (BB' plus X) affects C according to the BB'/C relationship. Which produces the Y signification. And so on...

It is clear, however, that, in the A-B-C-D sequence, the shots are *directly* linked together according to the logic of the drama. On the other hand, in the A'-B'-C'-D' sequence, the respective verbal data do not become more closely interrelated. Their meaning is

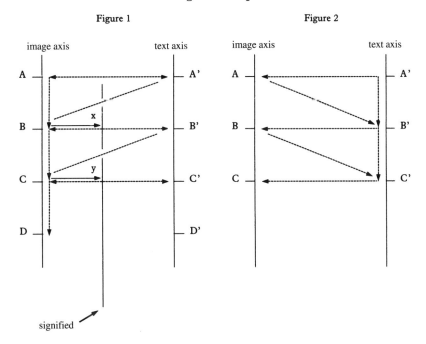

Figure 1

Figure 2

relative to the visual implications. If B' is related to A' in a context different from the visual continuity, it is entirely possible that their relationship is meaningless and that their meaning is defined via B.

In other words, film continuity is based in essence on the visual development which forms the framework, the *structural axis* of the film. This does not mean that the text cannot serve as a hinge, altering or constantly deflecting the continuity, since this is precisely the purpose of its continual interventions. But the logical development and principal significations are based on the development of the images, not on verbal associations.

In filmed theatre or mediocre talkies, the opposite is true. When (as in fig.2) there are shots A and B on the one hand and texts A' and B' on the other, it is obvious that the logical, dramatic, psychological, etc. association develops along the verbal axis: B' follows A' and so on. An image A corresponds with dialogue A' placing the characters and the action in a specific place and time. It places them in a set, on a stage, describing movements, illustrating a situation signified *through words*, offering no – or very little – signification of its own. This is dialogue fleshed out with images. The images may well be pretty enough in themselves; they may provide a pleasant enough spectacle. But it is not what might be called *film expression*.

A good talkie, therefore, is not a film with little or no dialogue (contrary to a long-standing belief). The actual quantity of words has no meaning in this context. A film may have very little dialogue and still be a bad film. And a film with wall-to-wall dialogue may just as easily be outstanding. What counts is not the importance of the text in terms of quantity *but the part it is made to play*.

We should make an immediate distinction, under the general heading of dialogue, between two aspects which, more often than not, are considered as one and the same: "stage" dialogue and "character" dialogue.

In real life, people talk; often, they say nothing, but they talk. It is part of their behaviour pattern: "Hello there. How are you? – Hope it stops raining soon... I've just missed three buses and I'm late as it is... etc." Since it purports to represent life, the cinema must record speech patterns just as it records behaviour patterns. Yet banal conversation is no more relevant than any other noise, unless it sets character or a state of mind. As Merleau-Ponty correctly observes, "the sort of words a character uses and the way he uses them indicates his character more certainly than pages of description." Nonetheless, these conversations, whose psychological importance is crucial, do not get to grips with the characters relative to the drama which involves them. They establish their presence but in no way explain their situation. There can be as much dialogue of this kind in a film without damaging its specifically cinematic qualities for, though it may contribute to an understanding of the characters, it only communicates what they are, not what they think. And it contributes very little towards an understanding of the drama.

Stage dialogue, on the other hand, informs us as to the thoughts, feelings and intentions of the heroes. It is theatrical dialogue. Perfectly acceptable in the cinema, but only insofar as it corresponds with actual reality, i.e. with situations where it is normal for characters to talk to each other, when there is conflict or confrontation. In life, however, people never reveal themselves completely through what they say: there is an essential gap, differing in size according to the individual, between what they say and what they are. There is no such gap in the theatre (at least not of this size) since characters are able to signify themselves only through their words (they have no other choice), as much to justify their actions as to enable the drama to be understood. This is not true of the cinema where a major area of interest is precisely this twilight zone where characters can be *revealed beyond what they say*. The purpose of speech in the cinema is not to add ideas to images. When this occurs, when the information to be understood is conveyed solely through what is said, when the text takes responsibility for the expression and signification of the plot, when what 'engages' the heroes derives exclusively from their speech, then we are dealing with something entirely dissociated from film expression. Indeed, inasmuch as it is art, the cinema has no need to *record significations*, merely create its own.

Obviously, film techniques allow "moments of verbal expression" to be given greater emphasis than any stage-presentation and there is nothing to say that the cinema should not be used to "present" a stage-play. But then it is no longer required to be an art; merely to put itself at the service of some other means of expression, to fix an already completed expression. All that is retained of it are its techniques. However, it is an application with far-reaching consequences. It is no longer "filmed theatre" in the pejorative sense of the word (the camera recording a theatrical event) but *cinematic presentation applied to a stage-play* (with the potential of being greatly enriched by it). Not that the cinema contributes a great deal, since its expression has nothing to do with itself but with the fact that it emphasises, fixes and, more especially, extends the meaning of the verbal expression. Films like *Hamlet* (Grigori Kozintsev), *Henry V* (Laurence Olivier), *Macbeth* (Orson Welles) or *Les Parents terribles* (Jean Cocteau) are ample proof of this. Yet, it is a *means of presentation* and not a *means of expression*. Any art there may be derives from the play.

One may well wonder how a play presented on film is less cinematic than a talkie whose expression depends exclusively on its dialogue. In fact, from that point of view it is not really less cinematic. In one respect, however, it is: a play is conceived and constructed with a view to its representation on a stage whereas a screen-play, even one which is over-dialogued, is conceived to be represented cinematically. Even without visual significations, it is planned at least with a view to a narrative developing freely in space and time, liberated at any rate from the restriction of the stage...

Yet, there is something else which on close examination proves even more important: *the structure of the dialogue.*

In the theatre, everything is organised, prepared and arranged to suit the verbal expression, since this is what contains both the dramatic continuity, its substance and its expression. The play, relying on the words, gathers specific "moments of speech" (uniquely these moments) into a single time and place[6]. In such a way that a play is no more than a series of uninterrupted conversations. The verbal exchanges go back and forth at varying rates according to the type of play, sometimes achieving machine-gun speed. And always witty – or literary. The astonishing thing about the theatre is how clever all the heroes are: clear-thinking minds and golden tongues using polished, tempered and carefully chosen language without pause for thought or choice of words: pure intelligence. However, the source of all this, however cultured and witty, has spent six months thinking about what takes only two hours to deliver on stage. Which means that the actors are "assuming" a text rather than a character. Obviously, they endow their roles with life and verisimilitude but they cannot "live" like cinema actors because their characters and, more especially, the text does not belong to actual reality. The criticisms of overacting, stagey, contrived acting, levelled most frequently against stage-actors can be explained more in terms of the artifice of the text and the needs of the verbal discourse imposed by the stage than by a behavioural or expressive technique which conforms quite easily with the conditions of film. It is odd that no one has noticed – at least to my knowledge – that the actor is always held responsible for what the theatre itself imposes on him[7]. An actor on a stage with nothing to say does not know what to do and strikes a pose. It would be difficult to imagine otherwise for one moment of actual truth would destroy the artifice necessary for the truth of the stage-expression.

It should be obvious that the above is not criticism, merely observation of certain facts. Theatrical truth is *conventionalised* truth, *stylised* reality, a series of artifices enabling us to glimpse an *essential* truth beyond the contrived reality through which it is conveyed. Yet, though these conventions are acceptable (even necessary) on the stage, it is not the same in the cinema where the *realistic* truth is based on a feeling of true reality provided by the representation and setting of concrete reality.

Thus, whether it is all-pervasive or otherwise, film dialogue must provide an impression of life which has been lived, or at least as it might have been lived in the given situation.

It is interesting to tape record conversations with the speakers unaware that they are being recorded. In *Bâtons, Chiffres et Lettres*, Raymond Queneau quotes the observations of the South American novelist and musicologist Alejo Carpentier, with reference to this sort of experiment. He writes:

> The result is something absolutely unrealistic. Conversation has rhythm, movement, a lack of sequence in its ideas with, on the other hand, unusual associations, strange skips of thought, in every way different from the dialogue generally filling the average novel... The result abounds with unexpected revelations on the real laws of spoken style.
>
> I am all the more convinced that dialogue, as used in novels and plays, in no way corresponds with the mechanism of real spoken language (I refer not to words but movement, rhythm, the way we actually argue and quarrel, the way ideas are put together or not). We have gradually become used, since the appearance of the first 'realist novels', to the mechanics of realism, to a kind of conventional stabilisation of speech, which has nothing whatsoever to do with actual speech. In speech, there is something far more alive, out-of-true, out of control, with changes of movement – a logical syntax which has never really been captured.

From which we should expect, for the most part, dialogue improvised by the actors around a given theme or, at least, written dialogue whose content and structure the actors may modify according to their own conception of their characters. Particularly since, in spoken language, as Vendryes points out, phrases tend to divide into two separate halves: morphemes (the syntactical structure) on the one hand and semantemes (the signifying data) on the other. Raymond Queneau observes that: "What you hear on the street is never: '*was it not the Mets who won the World Series last year*' but '*it was the Mets who won the World Series last year, wasn't it?*' [...] Lastly, the future itself is under threat. No one ever says: '*Will you go to the country tomorrow?*' (we prefer the positive form with an interrogative intonation: *You going to the country tomorrow?). I'm going on the midday train* is more usual *than I will go on the midday train.*"

Direct and indirect styles

This section deals with a comparison between film narrative and literary forms, the cinema in our view having a greater capacity in many respects to make psychological analyses.

In fact, the novelist has two forms at his disposal: a direct style, which allows the characters to be described or discovered through what they say, and an indirect style, which enables the author to describe the behaviour of his characters or put himself "inside" his heroes and analyse from within their most secret thoughts. But, moving between the two styles still means moving between one verbal utterance and another, in other words, the reader has constantly to restructure what the text offers him. He has to imagine the situations, the arguments, the reactions for which direct perception would be more involving for being immediate.

A novel is thought out, or imagined. A film, on the other hand, is not thought out; it is perceived. Through the objective representation of objects, the image possesses a liberating power which words do not have. It frees us from reality by giving it to us or, rather, it frees us from the need to imagine it by asking us to discover a *meaning* in it. Moreover, it constantly involves the processes of consciousness (comparisons, judgments, etc.). The consequence in the cinema of imagination is not as in the novel a fictional reality; the point of departure is a perceived reality, which then develops on from that. As Bernard Pingaud observes, time in the cinema "coincides with that of the spectator", whereas in the novel "though the reader can approximate the original appreciation of time, he does not really experience it, except through the proxy of a narrative which shows him only an impression".

The important point is this: the talkie is capable of bringing together all the advantages of literary expression – i.e. the novel – by moving constantly between a verbal and visual style, between description and suggestion, between what is said and what is seen, between actions and thoughts.

Whatever, in a novel, belongs to direct style is translatable in the cinema by dialogue or behaviour. Beyond what is said, it is the way it is said or acted, the acting style.

At the same time, whatever belongs to indirect style is definable as pure visual expression. It is the part played by editing, framing, camera movement, as much as the spatial organisation of the field of view, in association with the action and situation. It is the analysis of behaviour and gesture in an appropriate rhythm.

It is in this sense that the relationship between direct and indirect styles coincides with the relationship between two modes of expression – the visual and the verbal – which act differently on the concept. Whatever appears gradually in a reader's mind during an extended description in a work of literature is directly experienced. Where it takes ten or twenty lines to explain reactions and describe consequences, the image gives them to us instantly. It highlights a gesture, a shudder, the mood of one or the other, it *denounces*, corrects, rectifies, *explains* and fulfils very precisely the role of the novelist in his attitude to his characters. It can examine their frame of mind, define the contrasts between them, use their dialogue to undermine them and, through the relationship between image and dialogue, support or subvert the meaning, altering it continually.

It is plain to see that there are considerably more coordinates offered to a film-maker wanting to draw attention to the psychological dimensions of a character than those available to the novelist. As well as the descriptive image on which it is based, film also includes: analytical dialogue and image, which provides relationships between what is seen and what is heard; interior monologue, which provides relationships between what is said and what is thought; and lastly commentary (which may be that of a character standing outside the action), which provides relationships between commentary, dialogue and interior monologue, related to what the image shows, analyses or suggests. A film is a series of series, overlapping associations and relationships, all referring (potentially at least) to different significations as a collection of indefinitely extended and repeated reflections.

Commentary

As far as commentary in film is concerned, the more unobtrusive, the better. In dramatic films, it most often becomes identified with a particular character's impression of certain events. While the images represent the scenes described, the narrator expresses his point of view in 'voice-over'. This technique makes it possible for scenes with no direct logical connection to be related with verbal associations.

However, when it is a question of an action not involving states of consciousness, the text runs the risk of duplicating what the images are inevitably revealing.

A way of avoiding this redundancy is to off-set (minutely) the image against the sound, so that they do not appear synchronous. A shift of half-a-second is most usually appropriate but, of course, it all depends on the length of the scene, its nature and its importance. It may vary from a half-second to as much as two seconds; but, as a general rule, the commentary must always *follow* the image and not the other way round – since at very least this would be anti-cinematic.

Indeed if the explanation of a fact *precedes* that fact, the meaning we receive from the commentary is essentially verbal. The image then merely fills in the gaps, illustrating what the text has said, not as a commentary but as a *narration* embellished with images. Such is the case with a film like *Le Rideau cramoisi* (Alexandre Astruc) – which I am better qualified than most to assess since I edited it. However hard I argued and tried to explain (we had some battles royal!), Astruc insisted that the text should precede the image. At the time (1952), according to the theories of Bazin, Leenhardt and indeed Astruc himself, the primacy of the text was absolutely sacrosanct. Nowadays, Astruc has stopped liking his film (and, let it be said, it is the best he has made to date): 'It is illustrated literature', he says (in an interview in *Cinéma 62*) – ten years to realise something which was self-evident!

By way of contrast, in a short film made in 1947, *Combourg, visage de pierre* (Jacques de Casenbroot), the film-maker discovers Combourg, its estate and its castle, taking as its inspiration Chateaubriand's famous text which it uses as a commentary. In this film, however, the text follows the images. And since these – very beautiful – images are related throughout to the text and since the perception is *visual*, we *first of all feel* an emotion towards what we see. Yet, even as we feel it, it is directly transferred to our intellect to form a judgment requiring words with which to express itself. And the words are provided for us precisely as we think of them; in other words, our thoughts are moulded into Chateaubriand's actual phrases at the very moment they appear in our minds. What is more, the marvellous prose makes us feel deep down as though we are translating our emotion with the mastery and verbal precision of a Chateaubriand. We feel as he must have felt and, like him, we use words to express what we feel.

Thus, the emotion *precedes* the expression, whereas in *Le Rideau cramoisi*, it is the other way round. Now, an emotion which has *already been signified* loses its power to move. In the cinema, what must have priority is not the signified or the signification but the *continuous passage from the non-signified to the signified, the transition from the emotional to the intellectual through a constantly contingent signification.* As Merleau-Ponty observes:

> Art is fortunate in being able to show how something begins to signify, *not by allusion to previously formed and established ideas but through the time or space arrangement of its elements.* As we have seen, a film signifies in the same way as an object; neither of them appeals to an independent reasoning faculty but to our capacity for deciphering implicitly the world and our fellow men and for coexisting with them[8].

In films with voice-over commentary, usually based on the principle of the "journey-back-to-the-past", the narrator reveals what he knows, but his involvement is only relative. The events he describes are always seen "from the outside". The idea of commentary in the first person happened at about the same time as films where the hero did not appear on the screen; however, whereas films acted in the first person proved impracticable for the reasons we described above, films *thought* in the first person opened up new and boundless horizons. Commentary, assuming the tone and breadth of a kind of self-examination, began to explore a subjective world similar to the world of Proustian analysis.

In fact, the first subjective commentary films (*How Green is my Valley – Brief Encounter*) did not aspire to examinations of any kind. The films merely traced chronologically various facts experienced by the heroes. Once again, it was an objective reality seen from a subjective angle; the narrator testified to his actions rather than to a period in his 'psychic development' and the associated events were set in the past only because the commentary was written in the imperfect or perfect tense.

We had to wait for *Hiroshima, mon amour* (Alain Resnais, 1960) for this hurdle to be overcome. The time experienced by the characters and their memories form the essential elements of this film and its basic subject-matter, though quite important, is treated merely as a starting-point. Instead of describing a character through the eyes of one or more of his fellows, as in *Thomas Garner* or *Citizen Kane*, the film centers itself on the consciousness of a single individual and therefore allows for the kind of self-analysis we have just described.

Mixed up with short dialogue exchanges, the commentary is never explanatory: it translates feelings, states of consciousness. And tautology does not exist, even though occasionally the same thing is being said in both the image and the text, in the sense that it is being understood on different planes. The text is never the verbal equivalent of the images; it echoes them like a kind of interior correspondence, which has the effect of meaning *one thing* while saying *something else*; they complement each other rather than being the same. Dialogue may also be used to extend interior monologue.

It is a fact that the purpose of any film analysis, structuralist or otherwise, devoted to the study of the relationship between images and sounds tend not to take account of the human voice, whose pitch, tone, clarity, though they may not be signifiers in the intellectual sense of the word, have an enormous significance at the level of expression.

A recent study by Michel Chion[9] has filled the gap. Among his other observations, the author notes that:

> Any distinction between visualised voices and acousmatic [translator: "acousmatic" – used to describe a sound which is heard without knowing its origin.] voices is made purely in the mind of the viewer on the evidence of what he sees. Most often, off-screen sound comes from the same real source as other sounds, i.e. from the same loudspeaker.

Yet the attention of the viewer instantly guides these sound emissions (all except music, unless it comes from a visible source, a stereo-system or television set) along the lines of their relationship with the image. Michel Chion adds:

It is not as though there is a body of sounds containing, amongst others, the human voice. There are voices, and then all the rest. In other words, in whatever acoustic background, the human voice structures perception around its own priority[10].

We are in complete agreement. It is clear that, in audiovisual relationships, the most influential association is that between image and text. Sound effects are often very important but, with some honourable exceptions, they only serve as to carry supplementary information. As for music (excluding, obviously, musicals, fantasy films or dream sequences), the argument about what purpose it serves in "realistic" films, i.e. in films whose action is supposed to take place – in the present or not – in the circumstances of everyday reality, could go on endlessly.

It is not that it is without purpose, just that its purpose is different. It has no remit to comment on the image, to paraphrase the visual expression, to support its rhythm – except in exceptional cases. Or to draw attention to its own qualities or meaning. What is true of the text is also true of music: good dialogue should have no meaning, no dialectical logic when it is separated from the images which actually perform that function. Good film music may lose its musically valid structure, provided that, whever it appears, it should have a precise signification *within the film*. Film music is not explanatory or accompaniment; it is *one element of signification* that is all, but from which it draws its force once it is associated with the other elements: images, sound effects and speech. As Roland Manuel points out, "music must surrender its own form if it is to be an ally of the image". Set within a visual context, it must determine the signifying reactions by contrast or specific association.

As well as the emotional or dreamlike atmosphere which it is generally able to contribute in "unrealistic" films, its role in "realistic" films is quite similar to the way it was used in the days of the silent cinema: to provide the audience with the real feeling of time passing, a fictional time relative to which a psychological time could be measured. With the importance difference, that it should be imposed only at certain moments.

XII

Narrative Structures

Christian Metz tells us that what was never *genuinely* anticipated was that the cinema could become above all else a machine for telling stories:

There were one or two hints, right at the very beginning of the cinema, that this would be the direction it would take, but these were insignificant by comparison with how it was to develop later on. The *confluence of cinema and narrativity* represents a crucial moment, which could never have been predicted, but was not accidental either: it is an historical and social moment, a moment of civilisation (to use the sociologist Marcel Mauss's terminology), a moment on which depended the subsequent development of film as a semiological reality.

[...] It was in the need to tell stories that techniques became refined. The pioneers of "cinematic language" – Méliès, Porter, Griffith... – were not interested in "formal" research conducted for its own sake; moreover, they had very little interest (apart from various crude and muddled experiments) in the symbolic, philosophical or human "message" of their films. Men of denotation rather than connotation, their intention above all was to tell stories; they would not be satisfied until they had moulded the analogical and continuous raw material or photographic duplication into the – very basic – articulations of a narrative discourse[1].

[compare with Michael Taylor's translation:

From the very beginnings of the cinematograph there were various indications and statements that suggested such an evolution, but they had no common measure with the magnitude that the narrative phenomenon was to assume. The merging of the cinema and narrativity was a great fact, which was by no means predestined – nor was it strictly fortuitous. It was a historical and social fact, a fact of civilisation (to use a formula dear to the sociologist Marcel Mauss), a fact that in turn conditioned the later evolution of the film as a semiological reality, [...] It so happens that these procedures were perfected in the wake of narrative endeavour. The pioneers of "cinematographic language" – Méliès, Porter, Griffith, couldn't have cared less about "formal research" conducted for its own sake; what is more (except for occasional naive and confused attempts), they cared little about the symbolic, philosophical or human "message" of their films. Men of denotation rather than of connotation, they wanted above all to tell a story; they were not content unless they could subject the continuous, analogical material of photographic duplication to the *articulations* – however rudimentary – of a narrative discourse].

Now, the fact of recounting something is not peculiar to stories or fictions. The most abstract film showing a moving geometric shape is a narration since it describes the moving interplay of lines and shapes, their transformation. To refer to non-narrative cinema is nonsensical; as is a film with no movement in it. A representational picture may be understood at the limit as "recounting something", but only the "showing" part of it. The rapid evolution of the cinema along the lines of story-telling is therefore not the consequence of either destiny or choice but the logical development of its expressive capacities, the scenic framework being incapable of containing any sort of dynamic action requiring space and time to develop or provide an appropriate articulation. The simple difference between, for instance, *L'Arrivée d'un train en gare de La Ciotat* and *L'Arroseur arrosé* (1895) is that the former shows a real event, whereas the latter recounts a little drama but, by the fact that in the cinema recounting is showing, the difference in content does not prevent either or them from being equally narrative. And if "cutting from one image to another" is, as Christian Metz would have it, "cutting from image to language", it is also cutting from representation to narration. As I wrote in the *Aesthetics*:

Without the support of a narrative, visual symbols are meaningless or else become lifeless conventional signs.[...] the literal (denoted) message is a necessary support and no intelligible symbolic (denoted) message could exist without it[2].

There is no attempt here to start listing narrative forms in the cinema, simply to make a distinction between the basic forms of this discourse whose ambiguous interpretations have been the source of endless misunderstandings and arguments. In the interests of greater clarity (if only to make a comparison) and, by the fact that at this level the development of film expression is similar to the development of literary forms, we should refer to the theories of language.

Narrative and discourse (story-telling)

Benveniste makes a distinction in his *Problèmes de linguistique générale* between two different planes of expression: the *story* and the *discourse*, the difference lying essentially in the association between narrator and what he is narrating.

However, to avoid confusion, we shall use the following designations to describe these two modalities: *narrative* and *story-telling*, the term *discourse* being generally understood as covering any form of speaking or verbal expression, i.e. "designating any utterance bigger than a phrase, the phrase having left the sphere of language as a system of signs in order to function as an instrument of communication and signification".

Highlighting this distinction, therefore, Benveniste observed that, at the level of the story – or *narrative* –,

> It is a presentation of facts occurring at a particular moment, without any involvement of the narrator in the story. [...] The events are set out as they happen, as they appear in the perspective of the story. No one speaks in this context; the events seem to speak for themselves[3].

In their apparent objectivity, they assume the weight of reality, such that this weight endows the fiction with a kind of uncontrollable concrete evidence.

In *story-telling*, on the other hand (discourse in Benveniste's terminology), "the speaker takes on the formal apparatus of language and announces his position as speaker"[4]. In other words, the presence of the narrator gives the story an eminently subjective quality. Perceptible in literature, this distinction is even more pronounced in the cinema where the elements of the discourse are objects, concrete realities – the very ones being described – and where any reference to a time, a situation, a narrator present or absent, assumes a realistic dimension unknown in the verbal relationship.

In narrative, even though the storyteller is "absent from the story he is telling", his presence is apparent in the way he tells or describes the story. And yet though this presence is felt aesthetically (form, style), it is cancelled out by the apparent reality of the objects shown. It is true that, though the narrator may bring the events together by arranging them in a convenient order, he can in no sense interfere with their nature or judge them, in short show his hand as a personal view in an objective setting. Whereas in the novel there is an endless shift between the time of the diegesis, which is always in the past (any event has to have been completed in order to be described) and the time of reading, which is always in the present, in the cinema everything relates to the moment of projection, since objects "speak for themselves" only as they show themselves, appear in the film as though they were "in the process of happening". Christian Metz asks himself:

> Is this really so? Is it not more the case that the film image is always in the present? And the film, for its part, always in the past, just like the novel, precisely because, like the novel, it is a story. For the only special characteristic of the novel is to tip everything it names over into what has already taken place; it is a feature common to all stories, i.e. all closed sequences of unrealised events, that these events should be evoked by speech or images[5].

We are in complete agreement, but is he not reimposing yet again the conditions of language, i.e. an exercise in semantics. Film is not an abstract entity; it is a system of images. Though these might be in the present tense, film cannot be. What is in the past is what is *filmed*, the object (or subject) of the narrative and not the film whose particular characteristic is to *tip everything it shows into the present* by the simple fact that it shows it and we can only ever see – perceive – the present. Christian Metz continues:

The steps sequence; rhythmic alternation of various shots, in S.M. Eisenstein's
The Battleship Potemkin, 1925.

It is an indisputable fact that the act of reading consists (essentially) of a "gradual visualisation" [...]. The novel, on the other hand, may be considered in another sense – even though many readers use them to support their own personal narrative – as providing nothing for the imagination, apart from its text (in other words, its signifiers and signifieds).

Plainly, novels only present us with words, but words relating to a concrete reality which has to be imagined if the words are to have meaning. Ideas cannot be generated in a vacuum.

Christian Metz goes on to say that what makes discourse distinct relative to the rest of the world and, by the same token, separates it from the "real" world, is the fact that there needs to be someone to conduct the discourse; on the other hand, it is one of the characteristics of the world not to be uttered by anyone.

Now, film is a form of discourse where the world is (apparently) not uttered by anyone, precisely because it speaks for itself by being *shown*. More precisely, by *allowing itself to be seen* for, though *someone* shows it, though *someone presents* it to be seen, there is no implied intention from an absent speaker or "showman".

The smallest element of film narrative, the "shot", is itself a discourse. Now, when it concerns real or supposedly true events, because it stops being possible to exploit the images without affecting the things they represent, the meaning ascribed to them must in no way violate factual logic. Unless, of course, it is a *story*, i.e. where a story-teller is involved.

Who is speaking?

The most shocking element of *October*, presented as an objective narrative, is when subjective opinion interrupts the present of the film. Confronted by this kind of critical, willfully ironic judgment (the harpists in the Menshevik Congress, the equestrian statue in front of Kornilov, etc.), we can be forgiven for wondering: who is speaking, judging, conducting a discourse about these things?

In fact, Eisenstein makes a judgment of the facts and actions which he orders for dialectic purposes but, for all that, they are still presented within an objectively *present* reality. Now, only events *that have happened* can be judged and separated off as symbols. With the consequence that what Eisenstein does is conceal himself as narrator behind a *present* reality and, *at the same time*, assert himself as commentator in a judgment referring to the past; a judgment, therefore, which cannot be interpreted as his.

In talkies, a commentator can be included as witness to the event or participating in the drama, who transfers everything he comments on into the past. Because the elements – images and speeches – are *separate*, it is possible for the images to follow the representation of reality and the commentary to keep a distance from it. Description and judgment can coexist in the most widely different forms.

On the other hand, commentary is impossible in the silent cinema. And yet it is possible for one of the characters in the drama to act as a commentator, to stand between me, the viewer, and the content of the film, assuming that subjectivity which ordinarily I would be forced to ascribe to someone. In *October*, that someone is missing or totally effaced by the events, which cannot judge themselves and cannot be judged at the moment they actually happen. It is not possible to be both mediate and immediate, present and past – and it is this connection from *past* to *present* which makes these metaphors impossible, whereas a subjective relationship (presented as such) might, to all intents and appearances, have given them the necessary credibility.

As Roger Odin observes:

> The main responsibility of a work of fiction is as much as possible to remove all trace of the subject of the expression. Thus reality will seem to speak for itself and the diegesis will be offered to the audience with all the appearance of the here and now; this is precisely what effect-fiction is[6].

In *story-telling*, on the other hand, where the story-teller is addressing the reader – or viewer – the involvement of this person makes these metaphors not only acceptable, but logical. By putting a sufficient distance in time between the events and the story-teller, the story becomes a kind of *discourse about the world* where facts are exploited as semantic elements for which the logic of the referent ceases to have any great importance.

Had Eisenstein constructed his film as though it were a narration told by an *eyewitness recounting past events*, then any judgment made by this witness, any comparison bringing together separate elements would have been valid because they would not have contradicted the *logic of the discourse* which would have taken the place of the logic of reality.

As we say, commentary in the silent cinema is impossible – apart from the interminable title-cards. But this is only a matter of construction. No one stops to question the strange appearance of a goose, then a naked woman in *A propos de Nice*, because the film announces itself as a satire from the word go. However, it is possible to imagine a discursive structure where the objective conditions of narration and the subjective conditions of story-telling might coexist.

In fact, if instead of a single screen, there were several – Abel Gance's triple screen, for instance – then there would be several frames, several spaces, several potential continuities available to exploit. Then it would possible to imagine an action occurring logically, according to its concrete dramatic content, on the middle screen (the most important) and, on the side screens, supplementary images to exert a symbolic influence on the drama. In these circumstances, metaphorical images at the furthest remove from the diegesis become possible. They are no longer involved *within* the drama but *alongside* it, in counterpoint. The dialectic relationship may be preserved without damaging the factual logic maintained throughout the narrative continuity. It is true that this form is not really used in contemporary cinema, but it is perfectly conceivable.

Be that as it may, in *story-telling*, the story-teller shows himself at the same time as creating a distance in time between him and what he is describing. Present in the film, the events remain inextricably joined to the past.

Such is the case with Sam Wood's film *Our Town*, in which an eyewitness recounts the fortunes of various families in the town, or *Threepenny Opera*, where the action is related by an 'everyman'. Most frequently, however, this form enables a judgment about the world to be made. But, apart from the fact that such a judgment can only be made about *past* events, the objects can no longer be presented as belonging to an objective reality. They become the expression of a thought: the story-teller asserts his identity in what he says through what he shows. Then, and only then, can metaphor be established in an arbitrary way. Offered and assumed by whomever is judging, the meaning stops having to be generated by the implications of the context.

Style of the expression

Making a fiction film, whether concerned with story or discourse, whether narration or narrative, or an alternation, association, overlap of them both (for this hypothetical dichotomy is not exclusive), is both staging something to be stated and constructing the style in which the statement is made, style being, to paraphrase Todorov, "the imprint of the personal statement in the statement". But is there such a thing as statement in the cinema?

During various seminars dealing with this problem, Christian Metz' disciples – Jacques Aumont, Michel Marie, François Jost, Dominique Chateau, Michel Colin – decided, among other matters, on the following: film story-telling cannot continue to be considered merely with the tools used for the study of written story-telling (apparent for some time); the referencing of marks indicating the personal statement, identifying the person making the statement are much more difficult in this context than in language (self-evident); some notions are not literally transposable, which is where the origin of *focalisation* – to which we shall return later on.

Clearly, the personal statement is involved because there is – at the least at the level of the *story-telling* – a commentator, a story-teller, someone making a statement. But this is on the sound-track. The problem lies in the images. And it is apparently pointless to look for the equivalent of assertions or propositional structures which exist only by virtue of the particular syntactical organisation of verbal units. The assertion *Peter is killed* tells us that a specific event is happening or has happened. Now, as Dominique Chateau observes:

> This statement has no equivalent in the cinema at the structural level. Film makes no statement: it merely shows Peter's dead body. His state – blood on his face or chest – and the implications of the context or the dialogue will make us understand that he has been killed, but the image will not tell us this: it will imply it by showing the effects. This shot, considered by itself, cannot be interpreted either as a fact reported by someone else, or as an imaginary fact[7].

True enough. Yet to conclude from this that this shot states no more than is stated by the accidents or incidents of everyday life under the guise of *observation* seems beset by the same habitual confusion between the capabilities of the close-up (showing a single object or an isolated action) and those of other different shots. A distinction which I was at pains to point out: "The close-up of a pistol does not say 'here is a pistol' or 'this is a pistol'; *it merely shows that a pistol is there*". But a wide angle showing various different actions, a medium shot emphasising the different behaviour of two or three characters both betray diversity and simultaneity and thereby act like verbal utterances, though in quite different ways. In these, assertions are replaced by representations, *what is said* by *what is shown*.

An accident cannot be said to "tell itself" as it happens. There is no statement of any sort. And yet, if the accident is filmed from different points of view and the film projected for an audience with no prior knowledge of the event, the impression for them is as though the accident tells itself by being presented in images. By the fact that it is seen (shown) *in a particular order*, it states itself (apparently) in a proposition which gives it a meaning but involves it like the data of a true reality, the narrative (or organising) function being expelled not only from what it shows but from the very act of showing.

So that it is arguable, with justification, that *there is* such a thing as personal statement in the cinema since there is a someone who arranges, stages and puts into images, someone who expresses himself by showing things in a particular way. Except that, instead of speaking, there is *monstration* (to use that dreadful neologism).

And arguable also that *there is no such thing* as personal statement because the fact of making a statement disappears in the imaged data, even though it is through the visible, obvious, frequently aggressive style of the director. A style which, though recognised as personal at the level of judgment, is recorded as an objective reality at the level of the percept.

In the same study, Dominique Chateau wonders whether "it is possible to link together any two shots in any order". It would not appear so, even though the basic meaning is governed entirely by the current of meaning in which these shots are involved. There is a well-known psychological test whereby ten people are each shown identical series of ten or twenty photographs and asked to assemble them into an order so that they tell a story. Almost always it turns out that there are as many assemblies – stories – as there are subjects.

However, this becomes logically impossible beyond a certain number. It is not that the end result is nonsense (unless the effect is deliberate, as is the case with verbal expression), but that no signification is produced, because the juxtaposed frames become like two alien bodies laid side by side.

The phrases *un grand homme* and *un homme grand* have different meanings [translator's note: in translation, the nuance of the position of the adjective *grand* in the two phrases is lost because in English the adjective always precedes the noun which it qualifies.] Similarly, two shots reversed in order may produce a contrary meaning. For instance, we have:

A. A wide-angle representing a square into which a couple walks, crosses and walks towards the camera, leaving frame on the left.

B. Seen from the rear, the same couple climbing up a flight of steps (as, for instance, from Montmartre to Ménilmontant).

If the order is from A to B, the square is at the bottom of the steps, which the couple then climbs having already crossed the square. On the other hand, if the order is from B to A, the square is at the top of the steps because the couple climb the steps to reach it. The inversion is only topographical, but topography has a definite meaning...

Moreover, in an article on "Narratologie", François Jost asks the questions whether it is possible to know "on the one hand how the image and/or sound signify. And, on the other, how the film tells its story"[8]. In fact, the two questions cannot be compared. Yet, by doing so, Jost poses the problem as would every single critic whose method is to analyse linguistic or literary forms, whose first concern is to ask how syntactical forms signify and *then* examine how the textual organisation operates. Now, in the cinema where the forms of editing – the signifying structures – provide a *given* signification (the syntagmatic organisation merely providing a superficial model), it is by examining how the film *tells its story* that we are led to understand how the images *signify* and no grammar ever devised is capable of ratifying their different modalities. Which leads us to wonder *why* images signify – a problem seldom explored with reference to language where the signs are unmotivated and the semantic structures governed by syntax; which is not the case with images...

Consequence and consecutiveness

Meanwhile, still on the subject of "how", one can say that, though I see the film – look at it, perceive it – as I do objects in everyday life, I *understand it* as a discourse. A discourse whose continuity is partly founded – at the level of understanding – on the idea of causality.

Roland Barthes, in his "Introduction à l'analyse structurale des récits", points out that:

> The spring for narrative activity is the confusion between consecutiveness and consequence, what comes *after* being read in the story as *caused* by[9].

An argument I had developed myself three years earlier, pointing out that:

> Once there is a potential logical relationship between two successive terms, this immediately generates in the audience's mind an idea of causality. In other words, B is understood as the consequence of A, even if this is only temporarily valid [...]. Just as in reality objects following each other are largely self-generating (*apparently*) in events presented successively by film, i.e. in shot-relationships, our minds look for the causal link. They do so because they recognise – *think* they recognise or *want* to recognise – the image of the organising patterns created by the causal links[10].

If it is true, as Noguez suggests, that this definition of narrative "is by and large accepted nowadays", I had no sense that I was making a sensational discovery when I pointed out this psychological mechanism, which I imagined everyone had known about for years. However, Michèle Lagny, Marie-Claire Ropars and Pierre Sorlin wonder:

> What are the special social agents which carry the narrative, suspend it or divert it? On whom does the initiative of the action, the allocation of personal vision or speech depend. In short, who has the right to impose his subjectivity, to offer the audience the illusion of a subject worthy of disclosure?[11]

Focaliser and focalised

We saw how, in narration, the image representing the point of view in a narrative does not have a place in the diegetic space. Its placing can only be apparent through successive shots themselves placed relative to each other in respect of the narrative flow. The image is personalised only to the extent that it is identified with the look of someone standing outside the field of view and presented as "looking at someone or something".

This so-called *subjective* shot, used from *Variety* (1925) onwards, and itself the subject of much theorising between 1945 and 1950, has been reinvented by various semiologists – or semioticians – including Gérard Genette, Tzvetan Todorov and Mieke Bal – but at a purely literary level. Interested by the problem of the locutor (who is seeing? who is speaking?), Gérard Genette suggested the term *focalisation* to describe (or characterise) the point of view of the narrator or one of the participants[12]. At which point, the film semioticians joined in, as though they were discovering new ideas applied from linguistics. François Jost, meanwhile, in an attempt to sidestep the resulting confusion, coined the term *ocularisation* to describe the "relationship between what the camera shows and what the character is supposed to see[13]".

In fact, the term "focalisation" has meaning in the cinema only in the sense that it describes the subjective shot ascribed to the vision of character X... Otherwise it is redundant, since all images depend on the focalisation of a predetermined optical system.

Thus, to say that "each shot taken separately relies on focalisation" and that, "since the filmed object always exists in the context of being external, it is always *placed relative to the focaliser as well as relative to the objects with which it coexists in the filmed space*[14]", is a virtual definition of the framing and field of view encompassed by the camera, i.e. the actual shot, without changing anything. Even taking for granted the "various modalities of diegetisation in the focaliser", focalisation – becoming synonymous thereby both with shot and representation (focaliser/focalised) – may be understood as either *exterior* (objective, impersonal, external to character X...) or *interior* ("in place of", or "with").

Now, whether the camera is "in place of X" or "with X"; whether X is – or remains – included within or excluded from the field of view, it does not make the vision any the more "interior". It merely means that it is *visibly* related to what X sees. It is therefore simpler – and more useful – to refer to the shot as subjective; especially since, though it is vitally important to make a distinction, in *written* narrative, between focaliser and focalised, to describe *who* is looking and *who* (or what) is seen, in a film the focaliser is objectively placed relative to the focaliser, otherwise referring to subjective shots is meaningless.

Furthermore, Michèle Lagny and her colleagues present, via this concept of focalisation, an analysis of interior monologue which they compare, at the auditory level, with a subjective image, it being clear that "a film may show what someone is seeing and at the same time tell what he is thinking".

For his part Michel Colin attempts to impose a typological value on panning or tracking shots according to whether they move from left to right or right to left. Taking a concrete example from *The Last Train to Gun Hill*, he suggests that the left to right pan has the purpose of moving things forward dynamically, whereas a right to left pan has, by contrast, the purpose of binding them together". This with reference to the structural difference between statements such as *Wren built St. Pauls* and *St. Pauls was built by Wren*. In the first phrase, he says, the subject *Wren* is not really affected by the influential dynamic bearing on the term *St. Pauls* from its position on the right. On the other hand, in the passive phrase, *Wren* is hugely affected by the influential dynamic (also placed on the right)[15]. Now, this difference is made apparent by the fact that *monument* on the one hand, and *Wren* on the other are the complements of an assertion and not at all because they are "in the position of a rheme". They are simply a response to the implicit question: *What has Wren built?* *St Pauls*; *St Pauls was built by whom?* *Wren*. This derives from elementary grammar and not structural linguistics. Whatever the case, shots are not constructed like phrases. The signification of a tracking or panning shot is certainly the function of style and method, but it has essentially to do with the nature of the filmed events. There is no rule here which has the force of law.

XIII

Symbols and Metaphors

We know that all objects become symbols when they assume a meaning not their own. Thus, in the cinema, from the moment concrete objects are employed as signs, they become (close-up or not) *symbolic signs*. As we have just noted, sign and symbol are used at this level to describe the same signifying unit. And yet, the same objects in the same film, even in the same sequence, may or may not possess this quality – as is evident in the following sequence from *M*. Through the angled glass of an armourer's shop-window, Peter Lorre watches a young girl coming out of school towards him. To be able to follow her without drawing attention to himself, he crosses the road (leaving shot). Continuing her journey, the girl walks past a bookshop window behind which we see: a cardboard arrow flashing on and off and two discs revolving in opposite directions, one making concentric and the other eccentric circles[1]. The girl gazes at them absent-mindedly. For us, as for her, these are advertising gimmicks. Now, a the girl runs into the arms of the mother who has come to collect her, the camera reframes onto "M", Peter Lorre. Seeing that his quarry is about to elude him, the man, puffing and panting, suddenly crosses the road and regains his breath in a nearby corner of the shop. The objects in the shop-window (which fill the screen almost entirely, Peter Lorre being on the extreme right) immediately take on an unexpected symbolic quality: the concentric circle represents the obsessional focus of the sadist, the eccentric circle his insanity, the breakdown of his mind, and the arrow, the incessant hammering of his obsession. This is achieved because he is present and a process of transfer relates *what we already know of him* to these objects. In front of the little girl they have no meaning; in front of Peter Lorre they assume an enormous significance. Of course, we credit them with it, but only because the context allows us to do it. Even so, these images only symbolise what they signify. They are as much part of the form of the statement as of what is being stated. The symbol, on the other hand – or rather the *symbolic expression* – involves the substance of the content or its temporary meaning. It is dependent on the many meanings inferred from the relationship of a certain form of the content with a certain form of representation, from a transfer of meaning, from being diverted into conjecture.

However, preexisting this narrative symbolism, preexisting even the quality generally assigned to the close-up as a sign, an image seems to possess an inherent quality as a symbol.

As I have just pointed out, no image is a copy of reality, since the process of filming is already a formalisation (angle, framing, size of shot, etc.) of a reality literally 'absorbed' by a duplicate which is at the same time a kind of symbolic representation. Objects become in it the symbols of what they are in a representation concealing, far beyond superficial similarity, a truth which they themselves are incapable of expressing. *Reproduction is richer in meaning than the reproduced object.*

Thus, beyond this direct symbolisation – or implicit mediation – which is merely the basic connotation of the denoted – there is the *symbolic expression of objects or forms*, sometimes produced by the framing, as in the celebrated example in *Broken Lullaby*. One Sunday, in a little Westphalian village a few months after the 14–18 War, onlookers are watching the march past of the "steel helmets". The camera, at waist-level, tracks sideways along a row of spectators, but from behind as though trying to slip through to the front. Suddenly it sees a gap left by the missing limb of a one-legged man and composes an image framed in such a way that we see the regiment, with the band leading, march past between the good leg and the crutch, under the top the stump amputated at the thigh.

This unusual framing, whose purpose is obviously cruelly ironic, is, at first sight, as 'contrived' as the harpists' sequence in *October*. Yet, the camera reframes and immediately shows us a legless cripple – another war victim – who, taking advantage of the crowd to sell his shoe-laces and ribbons, darts a look fondly past the soldier's leg towards the street, while the sounds of the marching, the music and the shouts of the crowd form the acoustic background to the sequence. Artifice is instantly replaced by documentary truth...

Justification of the symbolic sign

There would have been no need for this kind of justification had the story been subjective (unless the narrator had beeen the legless cripple), but in narrative the symbolic functions must always be carefully integrated into the concrete reality, *committed* by the events, as in Lubitsch's film, and not applied arbitrarily to them, as, for instance, in *New Year's Eve*. In Lupu Pick's film, the compressed, tense action is constantly intercut with shots of waves crashing violently onto a beach. But this all takes place in Berlin. So what are these waves doing in the cabaret – which is the setting of a drama not told from anybody's point of view – except to create a symbolism telegraphed by the director?

I have already criticised the end of *October* where Eisenstein contrasts the butchery of the strikers with shots of cattle being slaughtered in an abattoir. The arbitrary nature of the contrast is obvious because the action takes place in a metal foundry; but because this foundry is in a big city and there is an abattoir nearby, the parallel is acceptable. In Lupu Pick's film it is not. That is to say, it is no longer acceptable, bearing in mind that this film, produced in 1923 was one of the first, along with Eisenstein's, to create symbolic comparisons based on montage at a time when symbols were still being imposed on descriptive shots through silly superimpositions.

When, in *Earth*, Dovzhenko shows us a woman in labour just as the funeral of the young Kolkosian is taking place, this event is presented as pure coincidence, with the two events not confused by alternating montage. We might read a symbolic signification into this association but the film does not state it expressly (though of course it implies it). According to Eisenstein, Dovzhenko should have contrasted with the burial scenes a shot showing the pregnant woman standing *isolated* in the countryside watching the funeral procession pass by. Then, as he says, the image would have been associated with the idea of fertility by becoming its sign, its emotional equivalent.

Concerns of this kind are no longer current in contemporary cinema. The preference would be to show *in the same frame* the funeral procession and the pregnant woman with the latter placed *in the foreground*. The symbolism of objects may be used without necessarily isolating them to create a kind of temporary abstraction. There are countless examples. Using one from Eisenstein himself, there is the sequence in *The General Line* where the peasant woman goes to borrow the Kulak's horse. It is midday. The fat, wheezy Kulak is stretched out having a nap. Beside him there is a large bucket full of beer; in the bucket, a ladle. Marfa is seen from the back; she appears to be asking a question. The half-asleep Kulak sits up, ladles some beer down his throat, replaces the ladle and goes back to sleep. Marfa is motionless. Then we see (as she sees) the ladle slowly filling and swaying to the bottom of the bucket – an image of refusal, misery, lethargy. Marfa's shoulders involuntarily follow the movement of the falling ladle, then she lowers her head, turns and leaves...

We should also mention the 'procession for the rain' and, from among many other films, a number of sequences from *Citizen Kane*. In particular, the electric light-bulb flickering off as Susan sings off-key; Kane's shadow gradually covering Susan as he approaches her, apparently blotting her out under his domination.

We know that this film was one of the first to show an object in close-up without isolating it, using deep-focus. The object here *does not so much imply* the idea of poisoning, it *provides the evidence of it*. It becomes the symbol of an action rather than an idea. At the same time as being in control of the symbolic signification, the event is captured in its documentary reality, *its concrete manifestation*.

Obviously, up to now we have been concerned with the different aspects of the symbolic sign rather than the symbolism of the content, which may revolve around natural elements through a transfer of meaning based on emotional reactions: the mournfulness of a landscape, the loneliness of icy wastes, the violence of the ocean, etc.; occasionally through a Freudian transfer, but whose meaning often leads to rather dubious interpretations.

Symbolism of form

In this respect, the symbolism of form is more direct, depending neither on narrative structures, nor on editing (hardly) but on pictorial, plastic or architectural connotations based, as with the symbolism of objects, on emotional reactions; yet intellectualised, codified by a whole esoteric tradition: a symbolism in which the dynamism of vertical lines, the softness of curves, the precision of straight, broken, horizontal or diagonal lines act like appeals to the unconscious, to the imagination, to the indeterminate, and which Expressionism exploited in many different ways.

It appears that the strange fascination of the genre is due to the fact that *the form of the expression is none other than the form of the content*, according to a formula unique in the cinema. Whereas the close-up signifies through concrete objects "being turned into relative abstractions", Expressionism – which is essentially concerned with set-design – signifies through the formalisation of an idea. The (considerable) difference is that signification develops from a stylisation existing prior to the filming process. Objects are shown through a *decoded*, directed reality. Not according to a meaning belonging to a represented world beyond its representation, but to the decorative interpretation drawing from ideological, metaphysical or psychoanalytical areas for its meaning. There are countless examples. Among others, there is the staircase/steps symbolism, which is fairly constant in all the Expressionist directors' work, but in particular in Fritz Lang where the staircase

Symbolism of form: the street in Henrik Galeen's
The Student of Prague, 1926.

(always rectangular) expresses an upward movement towards an ideal (*Der Mude Tod* [*Destiny*], *Nibelungen*) at the same time as symbolising the accession to power, the desire for power, whereas the spiral staircase (in the form of a whorl), turning back on itself, as in *The Golem* (by Galeen and Wegener), has a disturbing significance. The symbolism of the underground cave, representing the maternal belly, the cradle of the foetus, the place where aspirations and the destiny of the world are played out.

Often morbid and despairing, Expressionist drama is registered within the actual settings: angular shapes, shakey structures, vaulted ceilings, melancholy vistas, stagnant pools, etc.[2] This is not the place to analyse their meaning (a whole book is required), merely to point out that, if Expressionism is to some extent codified, it is only in respect of a meaning established according to the rituals of a primordial *mimesis* – although the glimpses of intuitive meanings (which we shall come back to later on) are, in my view, much more convincing. Here, as elsewhere, there are no *a priori* rules.

Staircase symbolism: *Metropolis*, by Fritz Lang, 1926, and *Nibelungen*, by Fritz Lang, 1924.

Though a good many films are still permeated with it, Expressionism is out of fashion. It is unlikely that filmmakers will ever return to such blatantly obvious symbolism, but, however subtly it is used, it is still there. It is simply left to the personal interpretation of each individual and arises from natural objects rather than forms. This is how the last few images in *Incompreso* (Luigi Comencini, 1967) – those of the lake in which the child drowns – may be understood as symbolising the image of the mother (dying several years earlier) whose infinite tenderness shrouds the tiny corpse. However, there is nothing forced in this.

I choose not to include here all the symbolism implied by the motivations of the drama, by the themes for which the film is very often merely a painstaking illustration. Father fixation, oedipal obsession, castration symbolism and other phallic complexes or paranoid situations can all be easily expressed on film, provided actions or events are allowed to develop which, as in reality, do not seem to have been created for the purpose of defining them.

More precisely, I believe that there is more genuine – but implicit – psychoanalytical truth in Buñuel's *Las Hurdes* than even *That Obscure Object of Desire*. But the fact that the symbolism is

implicit may have opened the door to all kinds of possible crazy interpretations. And there are critics who have done just that. . .

There is, however, a sort of "accidental" symbolism which is no less interpretative and which depends on the circumstances of filming and on serendipity, for the image is always of a "moment", as it is an aspect of the world.

Let us imagine a scene in which a couple have a row during a day out. For various reasons the director has chosen to film at the seaside. It has been raining. Low tide has left the beach uncovered but, because of the weather, it is deserted. The man moves away into the distance. The image showing him tiny on this deserted beach (whose size may be emphasised by the framing) immediately carries with it the idea of loneliness, abandon.

Or perhaps the scene takes place out in the countryside, on the edge of a wood, with the sun beating down? In this context, the forest into which the man runs seems to swallow him up, absorb him. And the idea of oppression, suffocation is instantly created. It is the same event, the same dialogue and yet the scene assumes a

Symbolism of light and shade: Benjamin Christiansen's *Witchcraft through the Ages*, 1921; John Ford's *The Long Voyage Home*, 1940.

totally different signification. In fact it is no longer the same scene, for what is important is not so much the row reduced to its essential argument, but what it signifies, what it gives the audience to think about.

Now, instead of letting his character disappear amongst the trees, the director chooses to have him stride away across fields. And intends to shoot the scene at midday, with the intention that the harsh sunlight, the sharp contrast between light and shade will express the violence of the row, whatever the words spoken. But unforeseen circumstances delay shooting – the camera jams or tape-recorder breaks down. Hours go by while a replacement is sent for. But the scene has to be shot on that day at all cost. When finally everything is ready, it is past four o'clock. The sun is already setting, the shadows are lengthening and the weather is turning, with heavy storm clouds on the horizon. The sky is dark. But the director decides to shoot in any case. The man strides away up a little winding path and disappears across the fields.

And it is no surprise to find, on the image, the stormy atmosphere, the dull light, the heavy sky reflecting, in symbolic counterpoint, the feelings which tear the hero apart. The critics are

bound to find some sort of symbol in it. The director might deny it: he never intended it. But it is *there*; the film shows it. And the critics are right.

What one may conclude from this is that many significations are fortuitous, subject to the vagaries of chance and uncontrollable nature. So much so that those filmmakers who take greatest care to control the plastic significations very often overlook that "moment of things", which is sometimes more significant even than the framing.

Be that as it may, symbols assume their meaning only in respect of the events which they use as anchor-points enabling them to be interpreted. It is obvious that the literal message – narration or narrative – is a necessary subject and that no intelligible symbolism can exist without it.

It will be argued that, if objects and the shape of objects have symbolic meaning, it is only because of particular cultural traditions, and therefore, a particular code. That may be so. But, once again, this only concerns what is filmed and, once again, the notion of code seems to me misplaced. Cultural traditions, as with social traditions, are not everywhere the same. Symbolic expressions are not laws unto themselves. They presuppose a margin of freedom, personal interpretation which the rigidity of a code cannot encompass. Without going so far as ideologies, two contradictory critical stances are sometimes all that is needed. And the civil code is the same for everybody.

Having examined the symbolism of films and images, all that remains is for us to consider the potential symbolism of the film effect at the level of the narrative (rather than narration).

Symbolism and psychoanalysis

I observed twenty years ago in my *Aesthetics* that the spectator in the cinema is closer to being a *voyeur* than a spectator because of the fact that in its realistic objectivity the filmed event is presented as though it had been made for the person looking at it, just like an accident happening in front of a chance passerby. Of course, I was using the word *voyeur* in the sense of *witness*, not the narrow keyhole interpretation used by psychoanalysts. Clearly, the passerby watching, moving closer, and asking questions is satisfying a curiosity which is not always unconnected with a suppressed desire or some other subconscious manifestation – but without there being any libidinous element involved, any more than for the spectator who *deliberately* chooses to go to the cinema in the desire to see a film. And yet, by identifying the notion of voyeur with that of a child watching his parents being intimate (as though this were a common event), certain psychoanalysts have gone as far as to conclude that "the film signifier has an oedipal quality", a conclusion which effectively reduces signification to the level of an unequivocal primary process in which the image – or secondary process – merely performs a registering function; or relates everything to purely sexual impulses and turns all symbolism into the unconscious transfer of desire.

We intend to come back to the idea of the *snare* and other notions which constantly arise but, through the symbolism of reflections, various critics have continually referred to Lacan and the "the mirror stage" by invoking the affective relationships between audience and film. It is clear that the spectator projects onto the motivations of the drama a fiction providing a more or less dreamlike resonance. Yet, if the spectator recognises himself in the film (though he is not registered on the screen as he would be in a mirror) it is doubtless because, to a certain extent, he rediscovers in it his own experience of things. However, there does not seem any need to refer to a stage crossed by the spectator nor to use the spectator's repressed impulses as a basis for turning the cinema into a "symbolic scene". The harder it is to justify "the mirror stage", the more shakey its foundations.

"The moment at which the child (at 6 to 18 months) perceives his own image and the image of a fellow human being – the mother holding him, for instance – is fundamental in the development of the Self", writes Jacques Lacan, for whom the primary distinction between *self* and *other* is founded on *identification with an image*. However, though it seems obvious that he should discover his physical individuality through seeing himself in a mirror, this is not inevitable: *he needs a mirror*. But, mirrors in any number have only existed since the XIXth. Century and then only in the middle classes. We can be forgiven for wondering how the "mirror stage" could have existed in working class children at a time when mirrors, even small ones, were rare and how it would operate nowadays in mudhuts, igloos and slums. The relationship between subject and object, self and non-self is no less apparent.

The mirror stage makes it easier to be conscious of the *self*, but it is not essential. Unless the proposition is that in primitive societies where there are no mirrors this consciousness does not exist – which would be strange, especially since Lacan argues that the main basis for symbolic transfers, slippages of meaning and other metaphorical expressions is this dual relationship. But, if we look at the anthropological work of Lévi Strauss, Lévy Bruhl, Durkheim and others, those who express themselves (or are expressed) in a fundamentally symbolic way are precisely people in primitive societies.

The mysteries of the expression to which the cinema constantly leads us may well lie in the unconscious, the collective unconscious which is closer, in my view, to Jung's or Cassirer's ideas than Lacan's hypotheses, but any further investigation would divert us from the more general considerations of this present study.

Metaphor and metonymy

In an article in *Les Cahiers du cinéma*, Roland Barthes, referring to Jakobson's rhetorical models, argued that the cinema is a *metonymical* rather than a metaphorical art[3]. To which I would reply, also referring to Jakobson, that the cinema is an *essentially metaphorical art*, although the metaphor almost always catches us unawares.

The contradiction is quite obvious and deserves further comment in that it implies a necessary distinction between *metaphor* and *metaphorical expression*.

Generally speaking, metaphor implies an analogical substitution whereas metonymy signifies through the contiguous relationship between an actual term and a represented term. A comparison such as: the piece of paper is flat *like* a tree leaf eventually leads to an eclipse, first of "like" and then the term of comparison, which eventually replaces what it is being compared with. Which is how we arrive at: *a leaf of paper*. However, once formed like this, the metaphor very quickly loses its evocative power and becomes a kind of lexicalised syntagma, a unit of signification which no longer has a denotative value. The poetic or connoted meaning has totally disappeared. Interpreted in this sense, i.e. in its lexical sense, the metaphor becomes "extinct".

Metaphorical expression, on the other hand, which is productive of meaning and is not the fixed result of an acquired meaning, is always based on metonymy. In the expression the *crowds are flocking*, there is a slippage of meaning, a transfer of attribution from the idea of sheep flocking to the crowd, but in no way a substitution of one term with another. The same is true of poetic images. When Apollinaire writes *Soleil, cou coupé* [Sun, slit throat] by comparing (or associating) the setting sun with a cut throat pouring blood, or when Valéry suggests *Été, roche d'air pur* [Summer, rock of pure air] to imply a solid weight in the absence of matter in the sky-blue clarity of the midday sun, these are expressions beyond paradigmatic substitution, connotations produced by a contiguous structure.

The same is true of film metaphors. Jakobson strangely contradicts himself when he quotes, as an example of "acquired" metaphor, the famous opening in *Modern Times* where sheep are shown jostling each other to jump over a hurdle and, in the next shot, people jostling each other outside a subway station[4]. These two shots, which are perfectly juxtaposed in time one after the other, form a very precise metonymy (according to the definition he gives). Of course, the meaning of one is related to the other as in the poetic images quoted above, but, though it is clearly a metaphorical expression, it is not a metaphor like a *rainbow* or a *wingnut*.

Film does not establish its significations with metaphors. It *builds* them by contrasting facts and actions in juxtapositions, created most often in editing and whose connotations always have to be deciphered. The metaphor is not *presented*; it only exists as such (its meaning) in the mind of the audience.

In language, genuine or lexicalised metaphors only exist because words deal with concepts. Images deal with objects, however, with concrete facts which cannot take each other's place, but can only undergo a change of meaning. Thus, every metaphor presented as such in a film appears as alien, outside the action. It is most usually a concept objectified into something, such as the calendar whose pages turn to indicate the passage of time, instead of the concept being produced by the relationship of objects – objects which thereby have a preestablished meaning laid on them before being involved in the action, the idea being *stuck* on instead of being *implied*. It is, if you like, what happens when you illustrate an idea or try to put a literary formula into pictures.

Synecdoche, sometimes considered as a metaphor, is also a metonymical device enabling an idea or object to be indicated by a term
whose meaning includes that of the original term or is included in
it. The singular replaces the plural, the type the species, the
abstract the concrete – or the other way round. Most often the
part takes the place of the whole: a sail for the ship, a palm leaf for
the tree. This trope is familiar in the cinema where metonymical
juxtaposition becomes changed into metaphor without the
syntagma (this contiguous form) becoming paradigmatic (integrated as a fixed sign, like a lexeme, following a substitution of
meaning). This is the case with the pincenez in *Potemkin*, the
drowned body in *Païsa*, the ball in *M*, etc. Clearly, here as in
other examples, the connoted meaning is objectified into an object,
which performs the function of a sign; but this objectification
depends on the connotation: it does not precede it or present it
ready-made. The object/sign can only ever exist in terms of its
context, indeed in terms of the film in general; and never as a
function of language.

The major difference between literary and film synecdoche is
that the former is most often based on generalisable semantics
whereas the latter is always contingent. The part to the whole relationship is accidental because film connotation is open to all
possible significations (though these might have not direct or
indirect association with what the image presents). Through
simple synecdoche, the image of the pincenez symbolically
signifies the "absence" of Doctor Smirnov and, by extension, the
downfall of the ruling class which he represents. Now, however
you look at it, the downfall of a ruling class is not an attribute of a
pincenez. This idea can only be suggested within the framework of
The Battleship Potemkin. It is implied by a whole series of associations within the narrative flow of this particular film.

Moreover, in certain metaphorical expressions based on
comparative association, slippage of meaning or inclusion does not
exist, only an exchange of signification where one borrows from
the other. This is the case with the famous end sequence in
Mother where we see, first together and then one after the other,
strikers marching along the embankment and the Neva carrying
pack-ice, and the image of the breaking ice-flows symbolises the
popular uprising. But the world of the "river breaking through its
icy girdle" becomes a metaphorical expression of revolt only

because the revolt is actually occurring and its meaning, immediately transferred to the images of ice, turns the breaking ice-flows into the symbol of something of which the uprising itself is only one single representation: the anger of the people, the idea of "revolution under way". The signified is assured in the signifier by giving it the power to signify, that is by endowing it with its own significations.

Thus, it is clearly possible, under particular circumstances, to agree with Barthes that the cinema is a metonymical rather than metaphorical art, though essentially made up of metaphorical expressions...

The lexicalised metaphors of everyday language never grow old because they are already just clichéd and commonplace units of signification, lexemes – or monemes – like all other words. Metaphorical expressions, on the other hand, do become tired and "clichéd". Which *ought never* to happen in the cinema where the use of fixed signs is strictly taboo, but which does happen whenever an "acquired" metaphor is stuck onto a syntagmatic meaning, as with the example of the calendar quoted above. The difficulty is to ensure that the metaphorical expression is original but that it also preserves its naturalness, i.e. its *objective basis*; that it should flow from documentary facts, from the truth of things, for, even in the most far-fetched "fantasy" film, the cinema exploits concrete reality and the logic appropriate to the chosen style.

The "literary" image

This brings us on to the literary concept "put into pictures", as opposed to a film concept, as is the case with shots with endless dialogue. But, before we go any further, we should define our terms.

The literary concept *put into pictures* has nothing in common with the adaptation of a literary work which on screen may have a purely filmic expression. Moreover, a shot with endless dialogue may not necessarily be overlong or one in which there is too much talking. It is vital that we should not mistake one thing for another.

What I mean by literary concept is a symbolic, metaphorical or other concept whose meaning is abstract, whose signification is provided by words and which is applied to the cinema through a concrete representation in such a way that it signifies with *what has already been signified* instead of exploiting specific resources.

As an example I would quote, from painting, Proudhon's canvas *La Justice et la Vengeance poursuivant le Crime*. We see two women in blouses in the open air, one armed with a sword representing vengeance and the other carrying a torch representing justice, both of them chasing Cain dressed in animal skins. The word is beautifully executed, which does not stop from being a dreadful picture. In fact, all the painter is doing is illustrate ideas through a concrete representation, rather than suggesting feelings through the interplay of pictorial qualities. And, instead of expressing the concept, the formalisation makes it look ridiculous.

There are many examples of these ideas "put into pictures" (which, in painting, represented the great days of "pompierism") in the best films, even the most esoteric. Without wishing to be dog-in-the-manger, I mentioned some time ago that *Un Chien andalou* drew on a literary surrealism *applied* to the cinema, instead of a surrealism of the cinema. With the exception, let it be said, of the opening image. The eye cut by a razor as a cloud

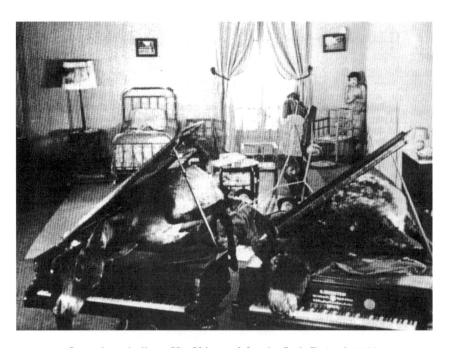

Surreal symbolism: *Un Chien andalou*, by Luis Buñuel, 1928.

passes across the sun, cutting it in two is a purely visual association of ideas, worthy of the Apollinaire verbal image: *Soleil, cou
coupé*, not to mention the whole freudian-masochistic symbolism.
But the image of Pierre Batcheff dragging a piano behind him
(symbolic of the bourgeois good life) on which two priests are
lying (symbolic of religious taboos and clericism) alongside a
haunch of blood-dripping beef (symbolic of overindulgence and
consumption) is nothing more than the illustration of surrealist
symbolism in its essence but literary in its conception and expression. It is not far removed from Proudhon's painting. The signification is introduced into the film, not created by it. If a surrealism
of the cinema is required, one has only to turn to slapstick
comedy: Buster Keaton, Harry Langdon, the Marx brothers,
Chaplin very often and even Laurel and Hardy. Slapstick is always
surreal, particularly when it is filmic. . .

To quote a French film, I believe that the scene of the boot
unbuttoning in Pierre Étaix' *Yoyo* (a gag worthy of the best of
Chaplin) has a more obvious visual surrealism than even *L'Âge
d'or*. Obviously, it lacks the ideology of the latter and the whole
iconoclastic mechanism which gives Buñuel's film its quality. But
I am looking at this purely from the point of view of expression,
considering the signifier/signified relationship, and not the idea
being expressed.

"Overlong" shots

As far as overlong shots are concerned, it is fun (in a manner of
speaking) to follow all those pedantic debates about whether shots
should be long or short, whether they should be fixed or should
move, whether they should or should not composed in depth;
where close-ups or medium shots are discussed as though they had
independent values, were signs established, codified and controlled
by a set of generative laws as might be found in grammar or
syntax. It is all too easily forgotten that the cinema is an art of the
concrete, that the image is an image of something, that it presents
facts and actions, that, apart from what separates them in terms of
size, the quality and meaning of close-ups and medium shots
derive entirely from their contents. It is all contained in the way
things are presented, assembled, given meaning; but this formalisation depends on what is being formalised.

Whether it is a tracking-shot or, as is most often the case, a fixed shot, a shot is long only if is felt to be "too long", i.e. that its duration extends beyond the time necessary for its content to be expressed in its entirety. The former depends, therefore, on the latter, on the dynamic or static quality of what is represented.

In the interests of simplification I offer two examples: take, for instance, a fixed shot, framed in a wide-angle, showing two people sitting in a room chatting to each other. As with every other image, this shot is instantly perceived in its totality. It is given sufficient time to be decoded, analysed; that is, for the details, framing, organisation of the field of view, the many associations and meanings arising from this, to be appreciated. All of which, with rare exceptions, can be contained within a minute at most. If the duration of the shot extends beyond this, because the image has exhausted its meaning, the couple carrying on their conversation have nothing more to tell me. All that is left is the verbal signified for which it has become merely a vehicle. It shows me a couple talking to each other – which it has already done – and lets me hear dialogue which I could understand just as easily with my eyes closed. Even if the behaviour of the speakers is such that I can learn about their characters, the gestural signified remains totally secondary because the characters are not active.

Let us now look at a film, no less "verbose", whose shots (though they are many and varied) are rather long: *Scenes from a Marriage*, consisting of a long duologue between an aging husband and wife. This is certainly not one of Bergman's best films, but all the shots – which are fixed – are relatively close: medium shots, mid-shots, close shots. The result is that, as the couple talk to each other in conversation, we receive the full value of the glances, the lip-twitches, the eyelid flickers, the thousand and one tiny imperceptible reactions which play over the characters' faces and which give what they say a dimension and resonance informing us about their state of mind and act as probes into an analysis of their character, their psyche, the microscopic examination of their feelings. There is a constant association between what is seen and what is heard, the one prompting, altering, correcting the other. Because the verbal signified is the primary meaning, this is clearly not pure cinema; however, it does convey film expression. Text and image, continually interwoven, take precedence in turn. Recorded seven metres from the camera making it impossible to obtain any visual signified, the film would be nothing more than recorded dialogue. Which is where the difference lies. Of course, in a connected sense, *Autumn Sonata* has a totally different value. Which is as far as we can go.

Another consideration is the supposed translation of "real time" to which a host of extremely boring films owe their existence.

It is odd to realise how much the exponents of this type of film forget that time is only felt or experienced via the facts and actions through which we live. It cannot be expressed except by means of these actions, even though, through the attention we give them, they destroy the notion of time which they involve. The perception of time – its control, measure, weight – disappears as it is experienced. Clocks provide an objective account, but the impression of duration only exists relative to experienced feelings. Hours spent in pleasure seem to last only a few minutes. As the popular expression has it, "time flies when you're enjoying yourself". On the other hand, time spent waiting seems interminable. We feel "in ourselves" the time passing because our attention is occupied by nothing – nothing concrete or immediate. In other words, only boredom allows us to feel the weight of time passing.

It is easy to show people being bored. The most intelligent or subtle films suggest this or signify it from the outside. However, the films I mean which intend us to feel "time passing" can only do so by making us share the feelings of their characters, i.e. by showing us images of the hero staring vacantly into space, bored stiff and boring us stiff with his boredom.

Obviously, I am referring, not to what is called "dead time" (which is often meaningful, frequently more so than moments of high drama), but to those "empty moments" which stretch interminably through films trying to make us feel deadly voids which nothing can fill. Is this an admission of impotence or a pretension even more pointless than what it presents? Realism, even psychological realism, is not a transfer process. Otherwise, why not show us a hour going by and in a single shot, fixed (as might be expected), a man sitting bored on a park-bench? And on the sixtieth minute a girl coming to meet him. It might be the beginning of a quite different film. But it would be no more interesting; we would have no greater feeling of the "weight of time passing..."

Deconstruction and dedramatisation

Moving on to another point, we feel justified in asking those who for the last few years have been endlessly using the word *deconstruction* what they can possibly mean by, or infer from it.

There was obviously an attempt to stand against the classical narrative forms, conventional story-telling, the linearity of drama, and to replace preestablished structures with a narrative freely exploiting time and space. All of which was valid enough but, far from being 'deconstructed', required instead a far more complex organisation. But this complexity required a precision already inherent in the classical forms. Dependent on the circumstances of the drama or the psychological situations, it frequently became more flexible, more relevant even, but more difficult to realise, because its apparent freedoms laid it open to every available possibility. Which would be sufficient justification of the term when, in this instance, construction is more important than anywhere else.

When the Anglo-American novelists of the twenties (Faulkner, Dos Passos, Aldous Huxley, Virginia Woolf, not to mention James Joyce) reinvented the structures of the novel by making widespread use of a-chronological narratives, not one of them would have thought in terms of deconstruction. On the contrary, what could be more "constructed" than *Light in August, Manhattan Transfer, Point Counter Point* or *To the Lighthouse*?

Thus, dedramatisation seems to me easier to justify, from the moment a *narrative development governed by rules is replaced by one governed by facts*. In place of the rigidity of a restrictive grand design, we can refer to a drama obeying the currents, impulses, contradictions which form, control and alter it; but it is obvious that the circumstances and associations of such a drama have to be anticipated in order for the film to be made in the first place. Thus it could never be a matter of making a film without a preconceived idea or plan, but of ensuring that this preplanning does not paralyse the action, make living qualities stiff and stilted, that the general effect is *as though* the filmmaker had accidentally captured the events, as though he had snatched them from life itself.

It is not a matter of "staging" a preestablished story, but of creating situations, bringing characters into conflict, revealing perspective, in short of moulding events which, as they unfold, "become organised into a story": *it is a matter of deciphering reality rather than presenting a reality already deciphered*. Not situations to exploit a character, but characters to exploit a situation. Facts and actions developing together or in conflict through a choice, an impulse, free will, with an ever-present ambiguity, and not the slavish execution of an obviously preconceived plan. From this starting-point, film ceases to present a world in images; *it forms itself into a world in the image of reality*.

Such, generally speaking, are the intentions and directions of modern cinema – the best of it, at least. Yet this treatment of narrative, this construction of a form which delivers its own content while keeping control a narrative logic based on the circumstances, moment, places, characters, is the most difficult balancing act of all.

As I have indicated, only a very few have been entirely successful thus far, since the impression given by narrative structures frequently seems so arbitrary that they are more easily justified by the contrivances of a story constructed in the normal classical manner.

For it is obvious that this manner of telling a story by jumping around in time and space, present and past, reality and fiction and where the memory process carries as such weight as the action taking place is acceptable only when it is justified. For the rare masterpiece, how many films are there which are effectively deconstructed, i.e. poorly constructed?

In the belief that they are renewing forms of expression by adopting an "anything goes" policy, the latest filmmakers believe they are "copping out" if they follow a linear development. Playing with time, discontinuous montage requires the greatest amount of clarity but the minimum justification.

There is nothing more lucid or comprehensible than, for instance, *Cria Cuervos*, made despite a number of interruptions, not to mention *Lenny*, *Providence*, and many other similar films. On the other hand, in Paul Vecchiali's *Femmes, Femmes*, an otherwise quite linear film, where two actresses past their prime behave in a manner to make a ten year old blush, the director interpolates various flash-frames showing photographs of film-stars. The allusion is obvious. But these inserts interrupt the narrative flow at moments where neither of the two women is given the (dramatic or psychological) context in which to think about stars whose success they might envy. The effect is gratuitous. Is it that the director was attempting to assert his free will? If this were so, his implicit presence behind the puppets whose string he is pulling is illogical – in terms of the narration – whereas in a subjective narrative it might have been acceptable.

The last problem associated with the different forms of narration is *verisimilitude* [*plausibility* in Michael Taylor's translation of Metz]. A problem of content rather than form, but one which depends on the latter. Since Christian Metz has proved the point, it would seem simpler and fairer to refer the reader to him rather than simply go over the same ground[5]. Except to say that if verisimilitude is something associated with the cultural ideological attitude of an audience to a particular genre, then credibility – the credible – is something else deriving from possibility or impossibility, sense or nonsense, i.e. from the logic of things – which we shall examine further on.

XIV

Rhythm

As I have previously stated, because of their fixation on the linguistic parallels in film, semioticians have not paid the slightest attention to rhythm (rhythmic structures) which notwithstanding plays a vital role in literature, beyond the mere parading of metaphors, at the level of verse and poetic forms.

During the twenties, once the principles of editing and the basic rhythmic forms had been properly established, the main body of experimentation into the relationship of time between shots was undertaken by two schools of cinema: the Soviet school which, with Kuleshov as the guiding-light, attempted to promote symbols and image-ideas; and the French school which, with Abel Gance leading it, became committed to the notion of pure visual rhythm and signification relative to the time-value of the images.

In this respect, Abel Gance's *La Roue* marks a decisive turning-point in the development of the cinema. Taking Griffith's discoveries and metric montage a stage further, this film introduced in certain sequences (the runaway train and the death of Norma-Compound, etc.) an accelerated rhythmic form produced by a montage of shots becoming progressively shorter and shorter. The brevity of the shots and the pace of the tempo made it easier to accept the rhythmic possibilities of film and, from then on, the number of theories and hypotheses proliferated and brought into being a movement later described as "avant-garde" simply because its sole purpose was that of experimentation. As Jean Epstein recalls,

It was the most significant period in the general development of the French cinema and the most productive in terms of new techniques added to this new means of expression, the most fruitful in terms of technical and theoretical discoveries which, to this day, remain a source of instruction and which were to plot of the course of the evolution of the talkie. The first golden age of cinema in France during which it suddenly became aware of its own resources, conscious of its own character, its own will and its capacity for becoming an independent art-form[1].

For this reason, the problem had to be approached and studied on its own terms. The relationship between short scenes and larger general scenes most clearly apparent in terms of the andantes and crescendos of Griffith's films and particularly well illustrated in Abel Gance's *La Roue*, reveal affinities between the cinema and music. The analogy is well documented. Émile Vuillermoz, the music critic, wrote as early as 1919:

> Composition in the cinema is without a doubt subject to the confined laws of musical composition. A film is written and orchestrated like a symphony. The "phrases" of light have a rhythm of their own[2].

The "word had become flesh". While Louis Delluc, who was to some extent the leader of the French movement to renovate the art of the cinema, was declaring that: "We must create a cinema which owes nothing to the theatre, or to literature, but depends exclusively on the quality of its moving pictures", critics and film-makers, looking to music as the source of visual rhythm, were declaring for their part:
Léon Moussinac:

> If we attempt to study cinegraphic rhythm, we can see that it has an obvious counterpart in musical rhythm [...]. It is also why the cinegraphic poem as I see it will be closely related to the symphonic poem, the images being to the eye what the musical sounds are to the ear [...] the subject matter will no longer be the main feature of the film; it will be the general theme or even better the visual theme. [...] And we shall say: it is from rhythm that the cinegraphic work of art derives its order – without which it could never hope to be a work of art[3].

Abel Gance:

> There are two kinds of music – the music of sound and the music of light (I mean the cinema); and the latter is higher up

the scale of vibration than the former. Does this not mean that it can act on our senses with the same power and subtlety?[4]

Germaine Dulac:

Only music is capable of stimulating the same sort of impression as the cinema and we are able, in the light of the sensations which it offers us, to understand those which the cinema of the future will offer us. The cinema does not have any clearly defined boundaries; which might lead us to conclude, in the light of known facts, that the visual idea, a theme dear to all film-makers, is inspired by musical technique far more than any other technique or ideal.

Music which provides us with that special transcendence of human emotion, which records the manifold states of our souls, is predicated on the movement of sounds, just as our art is predicated on the movement of images. Which helps us understand what the visual idea is, the artistic development of a new form of sensitivity.

The "pure" film we all dream of making is a visual symphony of rhythmic images which the feeling of the artist alone coordinates and projects onto the screen[5].

Fernand Léger:

The future of the cinema, like that of painting, lies in the interest with which it can endow objects, fragments of objects or totally imaginary fantasies.

Where painting goes wrong is in the subject-matter.

Where cinema goes wrong is in the script.

Freed from this dead weight, the cinema can become a huge microscope revealing things which have never been seen or felt[6].

To dispense with the script – in other words, story and anecdote – and turn the cinema into visual music (self-expression in terms of a self-significant rhythm) was the aim of a whole generation of artists and experimenters in the period between 1920 and 1925.

Yet this search for pure rhythm, for an expression which would be for the eye what music was for the ear was not just the effect of

Abel Gance's film or Émile Vuillermoz' ideas, nor of aesthetes' desperate to free the cinema from its theatrical yoke.

The movement, developing all over Europe, was urged on in particular by painters – notably Vicking Eggeling, Walter Ruttman and Hans Richter in Germany; Fernand Léger, Marcel Duchamp, Man Ray and Picabia in France. However, the first of these was undoubtedly Léopold Survage[7]. Guillaume Apollinaire who staged an exhibition of this painter's work in 1917 went so far as to say that Survage had "invented the new art of painting in movement." Coloured rhythm, as he called it, "was on the point of being shown to the public via the cinema – that tremendous propaganda weapon – when war interrupted his plans." Survage had published in Apollinaire's revue *Soirées de Paris*, in the July–August 1914 issue, a statement which defines the originality of his discoveries[8]. We should not linger over this although it does lead to abstract films and a parallel cinema which continues to develop. But, because rhythm is above all a *musical* structure, it is important to set out various basic definitions.

Rhythm and proportion

It was E. d'Eichtal who formulated the simplest and most broadly based definition: "rhythm is in time what symmetry is in space." Also Vincent d'Indy (whose definition is really only an echo of d'Eichtal's admirably clear and precise formulation): "rhythm is order and proportion in space and time."

Yet we must agree with Pius Servien in pointing out that rhythm is *perceived periodicity* and in using the term symmetry in the sense of "commodulation" or harmonic proportion. With the effect that, though in the words of Matila Ghyka in his *Essai sur le rythme* "the Vitruvian theory of proportion and eurhythmics is now no more than a transcription into space of the Pythagorian theory of harmony or musical intervals as can be seen in the *Timaeus*", we may alter E. d'Eichtal's definition and say that – within certain limitations – commodulation is in space what rhythm is in time.

Whatever it may be, rhythm, as Herbert Spencer puts it, "occurs wherever there is a conflict of irreconcilable forces." This being so, if, as Gaston Bachelard assures us[9], "there is a functional need for the contradictory interplay of functions", then rhythm is a kind of dialectic of time rather than a continuity whose intermittent variations distort for us the normal flow of time. In fact, it develops according to a pattern of alternating tension and rest – the expression merely of a constantly renewable conflict.

Moreover, if rhythm is rhythm only insofar as it is perceived, its framework is inevitably the limits of our sensory capacities. In other words, the complex of relationships constituting rhythm must be perceived as a "whole" to which each of its parts can be directly related. And this is possible only inasmuch as our memory is capable of doing this, by involving a process of "persistence of image" (auditory and visual), similar, as an effect of consciousness, to retinal persistence at the physiological level. As Paul Souriau writes:

> Auditory sensations have a detectable duration independent of the physical impression. When I hear a sudden crack, the crack continues to sound in my ears a long while after the vibrations in the air have stopped, and when even the sensation has gone, I can still feel it in my consciousness like an ideal resonance, like an image following the sound, that lasts even longer[10].

Thus rhythm can be perceived only insofar as it is governed by our consciousness. Only relationships of time of the order of seconds or fractions of seconds relating to a whole lasting as much as thirty seconds can be perceived as rhythm. Obviously, each rhythmic period may also be rhythmically related to subsequent periods in the film, poem or melody but the actual rhythm of the whole work – the sum-total of all these relationships – can never be perceived as such. It can only be understood as a rhythmic lapse of time, i.e. as the overall curve of a modulation gradually followed through its various perceptual effects accepted as rhythmic. For, though our perception may "retain" a duration of less than a minute and grasp the relationship of these interrelated parts, it is utterly incapable of performing the same task for the work as a whole. Thus the notion of rhythm cannot be accepted as anything but an intellectual process which reconstructs mentally the perceived relationships in order to abstract an approximate general "idea".

By the same token, we can speak only metaphorically of, for instance, the "rhythm of the seasons". The seasons do indeed manifest a rhythm, from the intellectual point of view and "relative to the Cosmos", but it is a rhythm in which we are also involved, dominating us – the effect of which being that we are incapable of recognising it as such except in terms of an abstract concept (one, moreover, which is entirely anthropocentric).

The ancient Greeks – Pythagoras and Plato – proposed the human body as the ideal model for eurhythmics. And it is true, as Matila Ghyka indicates, that the "two psycho-physiological cadences of life (heart-beat and breathing) do provide us with, on the one hand, the basic notion of 'measure' (the normal pulse-rate of the human heart = 80 beats per minute), of order and the relative notions of 'fast' and 'slow' and, on the other, through the rhythm of breathing (a perfect rhythmic phenomenon with its tension, release and rest), the reflection and accompaniment of the waves of emotion of which the rhythms of verse and music are the sound-expression[11]."

As Ludwig Klages has said, "rhythm is a commonplace phenomenon of life, to which every living creature, including man, subscribes. Measure is a human fabrication. Rhythm can appear in its most perfect form in the complete absence of measure – on the other hand, measure can only exist relative to rhythm[12]."

Measure is nothing more than a practical convenience. It is the process of ordering rhythm intellectually, a means of observing it, of giving it a fixed framework within which and by reference to which it may promote its expressive mobility. Thus measure regulates rhythm without however submitting it to an autocratic rule for fear of harming its spontaneity. Indeed rhythm is by no means subject to measure; rather the reverse is true, rhythm using measure as a point of reference in its free development.

Be this as it may, measure, originally used to regulate rhythmic flow without circumscribing it within a narrow framework, allowing the stresses to fall on a particular measured phrase, finally came to control rhythm itself. The divisions of rhythm had to coincide with the divisions of measure and the stresses had to fall on the "down-beats" (or strong beats). In this way, rhythm became subordinate to measure – which explains the pervasive confusion of the two.

Cadence is nothing more than the "index" of rhythm, that is, of recurrent patterns or stresses. Of course, cadence is not rhythm but it supports rhythm in that its equal beats must be regulated according to certain relationships and certain laws. A total irregularity of cadence would mean that there would be no rhythm strictly speaking. Moreover, the repetition of uniform beats (but with variable tonality and pitch) is a sure means of inducing hypnosis or hallucination (oriental music, voodoo, etc.).

Metrics is the notation of the natural measures of rhythm, as distinct from the proportional measure of time. It is the arithmetic expression of periodicity. Notation of this kind does not claim to record the whole expressivity of rhythm (for instance, it cannot take account of the relationships of sound-quality, pitch and tonality); it transcribes its basic feature – measured periodicity. It measures cadences, i.e. proportions in time.

Mathis Lussy has said: "Remove the intonation, i.e. the different pitches of the sounds, from a page of music, write down all the notes and rests on a single line of the score and what you have is the rhythmic design, the skeleton of the music, its bone-structure." This design, this notation, is what I call *metrics*, a notation which can be expressed in seconds or factions of seconds relating either to the measured bars or to the basic phrase. Interpreted in this sense, metrics is of no practical use of music – and this is why it is confused with the metronomic units governing the bar. This is how it has been interpreted in this study – our interpretation being directly adaptable to film rhythm in the same way as to verse rhythm.

We should bear in mind that we are not referring to linear representation – graph or sine-curve – like those dreamt up by Étienne Souriau which are a kind of graphic transcription of the qualities of a piece of music, an "approximation" rather than a metric system[13].

To sum up, we are of Matila Ghyka's opinion that "rhythm derives from the action of proportion on cadence." Yet it is not equal to the sum of its parts. It is not the simple addition of related times or related pitches; it is the effect of such an addition. A synthesis, not an aggregate. And, by the same token, metrical analysis can only take account of the rhythmic diagram – not rhythm itself.

Just as the criterion of good musical rhythm is that it should flow continuously (albeit intermittently) developing beyond the discontinuity of the measure yet dependent on it, the criterion of good film rhythm is that it should be a modulation whose uniform progression and uninterrupted continuity transcend the fragmentation and discontinuity of the shots, while at the same time dependent on them.

As we shall see further on, all we can ever really perceive are relationships, differences and discontinuity. Thus pure continuity could never constitute rhythm. *Rhythm is a development whose continuity is guaranteed and defined by the discontinuity which makes it apparent.* It is the harmonious development of a series of self-generating beats whose very quality as beats is based on a difference of time.

Verse rhythms

Clearly, the rhythm of verse is easier to reproduce, if only in terms of what makes it rhythm, the word having a concrete and relative permanence. Because metres have a fixed structure, cadences allow only a limited number of variations. Yet, this does not alter the fact that, though it is possible to translate, with arithmetic notation, the intervals between various stresses, it is practically impossible to do the same for relationships of pitch and alliteration (which are not subject to any formal laws beyond their own verbal content. The modulation of the verse is exclusively dependent upon a very general rule, alien to all specific forms of versification.

Moreover, *verses are not made of words, but syllables.* Words have meaning which they retain (alterable according to context), but syllables – which have no intrinsic signification, are the musical and suggestive substance of the poem. They add the constant mobility of pitch to the uniformity of metre and tone of the structure.

And it is the relationships of pitch, modulating and colouring the strong and weak beats with their infinite variety, emphasising the stresses with their intensity, which are what actually comprise rhythm (metre being responsible for cadence). There is an amalgamation or superimposition of the periodicity – symmetrical or asymmetrical – of stresses, distributed according to certain rules, and the more or less regular periodicity of the pitch, sometimes falling on the weak beats, sometimes on the strong beats and performing, in the development of the poem, a role similar to that of intervals in music. Though they only become apparent in the verbal continuity, the harmonies of the verse are nonetheless harmonies in the strict sense. They determine the melodic development of the poem and only the stresses are subject to inflexible rules. Under the heading "periodicity" is included the recurrence of various sounds or meanings (images, concepts, etc.), but if, as Pius Servien says, "a rhythm can be broken down into tonic and arithmetic rhymes of pitch and duration", then rhythm can be said to encompass everything. In other words, rhythm is what is produced when all these elements act and react relative to each other. Pius Servien notes,

> The greatest difference between musical rhythm and the rhythm of verse lies in the diametrically opposite role that pitch plays in each. Nothing changes if the pitch is changed in a musical theme, whereas, with words, pitch is of the utmost importance[14].

In Verhaeren's verse, "Voici le vent cornant novembre" [tr. literally: 'Here comes the wind heralding November'], "the image," Matila Ghyka writes, "is almost swallowed up by the sounds." He is right if he means the intellectual image, but the interplay of the sounds superimposed onto the intellectual image itself creates a new image (which we have called the verbal image). No longer is the idea suggested by the association of the words "vent" and "novembre" of primary importance – it is the wind itself which we hear whistling through the words describing it (though obviously never purely imitative).

An analysis of the tonic rhythms in Chateaubriand's line "Le dé*sert* dérou*lait* mainte*nant* devant *nous* ses soli*tudes* démesu*rées*" [translator's note. literally: 'The desert now unfolded before us its endless wilderness'], merely by placing the accent (which changes from the third syllable in the first words to the fourth and then the fifth), Chateaubriand prolongs the rhythm and slows it down as he translates into rhythmic terms (i.e. perceived stresses) the endless vistas of wilderness which he is describing.

We clearly see that the translation of an idea or impression into perceptible form is not merely an effect of sonority but also of stress, in other words, verbal plasticity.

In reality, the poetic image is much more a form of style than an image, the latter being a mental creation. Whenever any image is reflected onto the plane of language it becomes a *form*. René Waltz points out that:

> When an idea is reduced to itself it never extends beyond its own content: the most complex idea is simpler than even the simplest of images. The image, on the other hand, even stripped to its bare essentials, is synthetic by nature. It groups around the object, or its concept, circumstantial or additional notions which become amalgamated with it, forming, on a psychic level, a kind of fictional, more or less heteroclite unit[15].

And yet, even when it presupposes an intellectual "movement", the formation of an idea, the creation of a strange and unexpected association, the poetic image is remarkably *static*. Only rhythm is *dynamic*. The image is part of painting; rhythm is part of music.

The music of images and "pure cinema"

But, of course, our interest here lies in cinematic rhythm. Consequently, we shall not take this short conspectus over the rhythms of music and poetry any further, except to say that the experiments, begun in 1923 following *La Roue*, in the direction of so-called "pure cinema" led to many criticisms and controversy. Henri Fescourt, a director educated initially at the Schola Cantorum, had this to say:

> We believe in the possibility of a kind of cinema connected to music through its rules. However, we also believe that there is a misunderstanding nowadays about the type of experimentation we should undertake.
>
> Rhythm, composition, melody are *modalities*. To what should they be applied? What *material* can the cinema offer with regard to the strict ordering of musical sounds? Line up a hat, a book, an inkwell or even just shapes: squares, circles, spirals. Is it possible to create spontaneous harmonies from these: *Do, do, so, mi*? When these harmonic elements are discovered – which they surely will be – we will be able to talk of "music for the eye". Until then, we must have the courage not to subject the anarchy of "total cinema" to the tender mercies of an art so strictly regimented as music[16].

Émile Vuillermoz contributed the following in 1927:

There are basic, exceptionally close relationships between the art of assembling sounds and the art of assembling measures of light. The two techniques are strictly similar. We should not be too surprised that they should both depend on the same theoretical postulates and on the same physiological reactions of our organs to the phenomena of movement. As a matter of fact, the optic and auditory nerves have the same capacities for recording wave-patterns.

Thus, in the composition of a film we find the same laws as those governing the composition of a symphony. This is no figure of speech, it is a tangible reality. A well composed film instinctively obeys the most classical criteria from academic treatises on composition. A cinegrapher [sic] must know how to write melodies for the eye on the screen, expressed in a suitable movement with appropriate punctuations and necessary cadences. He must control the balance of his developments, know how much time to devote to a particular embellishment without compromising for the audience what might be called the tonal feeling of his composition.

[...] This arrangement and alternation of movement is what is generally termed rhythm in the cinema. Which means that, by extension, it has a rather different meaning from what it has in music. Yet it is easy to understand the parallel being drawn. Certain sequences in Abel Gance's *La Roue* are constructed in a rhythm similar to symphonic *allegri*. A director like Griffith brings to all his compositions an extraordinarily infallible musical instinct. In *Intolerance*, he appears to have edited his film under the guidance of a teacher of counterpoint. He introduces his four themes one after the other, develops them, divides them up, creates variations on them, explores a rigid counterpoint of images, then speeding up the movement and repetition of the themes, he gradually tightens up each of the entries until he produces the final stretto, consistent with the most rigorous commandments of classical fugue[17].

We must establish common ground between these equally valid but contradictory view-points. It is abundantly clear that there is a close association between film and musical rhythm, that the same laws governing the composition of a symphony also apply in the composition of a film. However, this only takes account of the rhythmic structures, that is any relationships measurable with a chronometer or "unitary measurement" of film (a second, or 24 frames or 0 m 45), not those relationships which are *felt* or perceived as rhythm.

Vuillermoz says: "As a matter of fact, the optic and auditory nerves have the same capacities for recording wave-patterns". His error, shared by a great many film-makers, is the source of the enormous confusion which exists with regard to the rhythmic capabilities of film from which the theories of the "avant-garde" and the experiments described above derive.

Nevertheless, Moussinac was already observing that:

> Though our eyes can appreciate the difference between colours and between shapes and between relative distances in perspective, they cannot appreciate rhythmic developments in the movements they perceive – they cannot see movement in movement. [...] If musical adaptation currently seems to us necessary most of the time, it is because we do not perceive rhythm in film or (when it does exist) do not perceive it very well and because (an effect of the movement in the images creating rhythm) in order to please ourselves we try to find it in music.

But he adds:

> Why are our eyes always less sensitive to rhythm in the cinema than our ears? One supposes that it is mainly a question of education[17].

Of course it is a question of education. Yet there is a threshold of perception which our eyes cannot cross which means that subtle relationships of time are totally alien. Whereas our ears can pick up differences of time of as little as a tenth-of-a-second and wave-patterns of pitch and tonality of as little as a comma (81/80) [tr. a minute interval or difference of pitch], our eyes cannot perceive relationships of any less than a fifth of the duration of a relatively short shot. And though our minds are able to discern a certain difference in time between relatively long shots or between successive sequences, they remain incapable of evaluating it in any precise sense – unless the difference is very marked as, for example, when the time of a shot is doubled or tripled – in other words, clumsily. And where our ears are able to perceive effortlessly as many as twenty different notes or beats every second, our eyes can tolerate only with difficulty and for a short period of time image-sequences of a sixth-of-a-second.

As Ernest Meumann points out: "in experiments conducted to measure the relative sensitivity of the senses in estimating time, sight proved to be the most obtuse." And David Katz is able to state that "in no area of the senses is there such acuity as in the area of acoustics" only because the ear is the organ of rhythm par excellence. It is designed to perceive, not only relationships of sound, but relationships of time. And though it cannot perceive space, it is at least able to perceive spatial "dimension" through relationships of pitch and, particularly, sound-direction.

The eye, on the other hand, is designed to perceive space and spatial relationships. It is the organ of proportion par excellence. If it perceives relationships in time, these are always subject to the requirements of a certain framing. In other words, it is by referring to spatial data that the eye is able to evaluate the relative duration of objects. It cannot confer any meaning on these time-relationships though, because of their structure, movement or intensity, the represented objects *already* have a certain meaning conferred on them *a priori* by the space in which they are found.

To return to Ruttmann's or Vicking Eggeling's experiments, it is clear that the eye is able to perceive relative durations from shot to shot because the relevant geometrical shapes become altered within these durations and because the relationships of time are always clearly marked. Yet what is most significant is that these relationships in themselves convey absolutely nothing. They do not provoke any feelings, or any specific states of mind. For instance, if we stretch a spiral for two seconds and distort a cube or diamond for three seconds, this relationship has no external justification. There might just as easily be three seconds of spiral and two seconds of cube or they might follow each other in reverse order. I have performed the experiment many times over with my students at the Institut des Hautes Études Cinématographiques (I.D.H.E.C) or before audiences at cinema-clubs; a film is projected right side up, then backwards, in other words, putting the last image at the beginning of the sequence: the result is exactly the same. These pure movements are not without a certain decorative value but, in whatever order they follow one another, the relationships which bind them together are shown to be absolutely gratuitous. We can perceive a certain rhythm; in other words, we are perfectly aware of a relationship of proportion between successive shots, between relative durations of moving shapes but this relationship in no way gives rise to any particular emotion since simple visual pleasure clearly cannot be described as emotion (and, beside, it is a pleasure which is the same whatever order the shots follow one another). The reversibility of this "rhythm" is proof of its lack of signification, its emptiness: the absence of potentiality and non-determinism. It is inconceivable that any feeling of actual duration (or indeed any measure of time) should be communicated via these abstract durations, devoid of any deep emotional qualities.

Although two chords placed in a particular temporal relationship already contain an emotional content by virtue of the simple relationship of pitch and tone (since all sound-matter has intrinsic signification as well as signification in terms of its rhythm), the relationship of abstract forms or sketches still appears aimless.

Thus it is established that visual rhythm becomes deprived of the power to move and signify from the moment the forms for which it provides the rhythm become deprived of objective signification and primary emotional force. The mobility of an abstract sketch is an intellectual emotion devoid of direction and effective power. It is a "catalyst" incapable (even "potentially") of creating emotion since the potential of the movement is contained in the gratuitousness of its design. In brief, visual rhythm contributes nothing in itself. It creates nothing. In other words, "pure" rhythm does not exist in the cinema any more than it does in literature. Only in music does pure rhythm exist and there it is the music itself.

Thus it is a trap for the unwary (albeit an attractive one) to consider our visual perception of film in the same terms as our auditory perception of music – for the two reasons we have just described: the inability of our eyes to appreciate even moderately subtle relationships between shots; and, secondly, the lack of expressivity of these relationships considered for what they are[19].

Provided they serve merely to indicate these limitations, the efforts of the "avant-garde" will not have been in vain.

Film rhythm

Though film is presented primarily as an objective reality organised within a certain space, it is in time that it achieves its most direct expression, its most obvious signification. "Time passing" in the cinema is not produced, as in music, by rhythmic form but by events being followed through in sequence. It is a time experienced by characters objectively presented to us, not a sequence of time formulated and conditioned by pure rhythm. However, though this sequence of time may not be produced by the rhythm, at least it develops within a rhythmic form conditioned and justified by the dramatic reality whose constant development it is continually altering.

Endowed with a materiality, a weight, a density which ensures the concrete existence of figures and objects, their static (or spatial) quality is in inevitable conflict with their accompanying movement. Thus, to all intents and appearances, film rhythm is not free, whereas musical rhythm (the rhythm of sounds with no concrete reality to further and, therefore, no static qualities) has no other referent than its formal needs. And yet (to state it more clearly), this referent has itself to be referred to an established body of physical laws: interval relationships, correct or incorrect harmonies, tonal requirements and many others beside – with the effect that the "free" rhythm of music is, in fact, restricted. On the other hand, film rhythm, subject to the constrictive weight of spatiality, to everything which rhythm entails, is not subject – as far as the objective description of material objects is concerned – to any formal law or externally imposed rules.

Film rhythm is linear. It is the rhythm of narrative, whose continuous flow never repeats itself. Since its content is continually moving and changing, its patterns take as reference a certain representational form rather than the represented data. The same movement intensity is produced by different movements, the same time-sequence by different actions, the same framing by contents without direct associations. As we have said, it is the free and "continuous" rhythm of rhythmic prose, never imposing a metric system on its cyclical forms but rather allowing its own requirements to dictate its terms of reference. The infinitely variable terms of these forms render visual rhythm virtually indefinable.

Whereas music deals with the same qualities reinterpreted in *different* forms, the cinema is exclusively concerned with *similar* qualities recognised in *dissimilar* forms. And, for this reason, we cannot speak of the cinema in terms of good or bad rhythm (if rhythm is to be understood as conforming or otherwise to certain rules or fixed forms). The principles of visual rhythm do not transcend (even potentially) all their applications but are inherent within each of them. Rhythm exists by reason of what has to be put into rhythm. It can therefore only be judged in its applications, not as a body of so-called absolute standards. Yet, at the same time, one or two genres quite consciously involve the use of a specific rhythm. Clearly, a psychological film does not have the same rhythm as, say, an epic; it would be foolish to think otherwise.

Because film rhythm is experienced primarily by virtue of the effect of editing, it is easy to conclude that it is its natural consequence. Which is justified in a certain sense but completely mistaken if by this we mean creation in its entirety. This misinterpretation gave rise to a number of films between 1922 and 1926 which claimed to be rhythmic because they presented an action broken down into an infinite number of silly little bits – confusing rhythm with speed and assuming rhythm to be a simple matter of metrics.

In fact, editing (beside the fact that it allows the film to be structured) gives the film-maker the opportunity to define the temporal proportions of shots and sequences, i.e. their relative lengths. But rhythm is not made up of simple relationships of duration. A film is not rhythmic because someone has decided arbitrarily to edit a series of shots according to a predetermined metric pattern. Rhythm has more to do with relationships of intensity – but relationships of intensity contained within relationships of duration.

The intensity of a shot depends on the amount of movement (physical, dramatic or psychological) contained in it and on the length of time it lasts. Indeed, two shots of the same length, that is the same actual duration, may provide a *greater* or *lesser* impression of duration depending on the dynamics of their content and their aesthetic characteristics (framing, composition).

For the same action (a battle, for instance, such as the Battle on the Ice in *Alexander Nevsky*), a long-shot contains more movement than a close-shot. Yet this movement may be more intensely communicated through a medium-shot. Consequently, though a long-shot might be the same length, it will give the impression of being longer because it is less intense. However, if, by reason of the number of varied movements it contains, it demands a greater degree of attention and, therefore, a longer perception time, then it will appear shorter.

Since the important factor in rhythm is not actual duration itself but the *impression of duration*, it is this quality and it alone, not a predetermined metric length, which serves as a referent. Generally speaking (but without laying down hard-and-fast rules because of the infinite number of variables involved), we may say that, *for a given length of film*, a dynamic long-shot appears shorter than a dynamic close-shot; but a dynamic close-shot appears shorter than a static long-shot which also appears shorter than a static close-shot. In other words, the more dynamic the content and the wider the framing, the shorter the shot appears; the more static the content and narrower the framing, the longer the shot appears.

If we wished to create an impression of equivalent duration with these shots, we would have to give (for instance): 20 secs to the dynamic long-shot; 14 to the dynamic close-shot; 10 to the static long-shot and 6 to the static close-shot. We would not, of course, be creating equal durations but rather durations *proportional* to the interest and signification of the content. It is this interest and it alone which can and must determine the shot-relationships, calculated *in terms of the impression of duration which they produce and not by virtue of their metric length*.

Since we cannot be absolutely sure of the impression we are likely to obtain (because of the many constantly variable factors involved) it is only *a posteriori*, i.e. at the editing-stage with the image on the editing-bench, that we can judge it at all accurately. From which we might deduce that it is in fact at the editing-stage that the rhythm of the film is *laid down* (even though, strictly speaking, it is not creation but adjustment).

In other words, film rhythm is never an abstract structure controlled by formal laws or principles applicable to all kinds of film but, on the contrary, a structure rigorously determined by the content. *It is solely through the action, through its epic, dramatic or psychological movement that its supporting rhythm may be perceived as rhythm.* Otherwise it is unjustifiable, ineffectual form without content.

XV

Sense and Nonsense

Nonsense does not exist in the cinema, unless it is deliberate through the effect of intended irony or anarchy. Playing on the logical meaning of objects, it defines itself as absurd and thereby becomes *sense*.

Nonsense is essentially a verbal construct. It is an effect of language and, before we go any further, we should examine its different aspects and interpretation, either negative – as "devoid of meaning" – or positive – "with a meaning which confounds logic".

A grammaticalised phrase could never be absurd or devoid of logic, contrary to what certain logicians, such as Carnap or linguists such as Chomsky, would have us believe. Indeed grammar guarantees the meaning or the legitimacy of the meaning through the simple syntactical organisation of words according to relationships defined by rules. Syntax is independent of meaning, but meaning is not independent of syntax. What is independent is the "meaning of meaning", its exactness, its non-contradiction. Syntax guarantees the fact of having meaning, but not the validity of that meaning.

For Carnap, however, a grammatically correct phrase such as: *The horse is a six-legged beetle* is absurd. Now, although it contradicts the accepted interpretation of the word *horse* to describe a quadruped belonging to the mammalian class, the phrase is not illogical. If the term were universally accepted to mean a cockchafer beetle, the proposition would be equally true. Thus, the error has to do with the choice of words. It cannot be said that this proposition is meaningless because the signifier/signified relationship is inaccurate. It is *not true*; it is not absurd.

On the other hand, propositions such as: *There are horses which are not horses; this dog is both sick and fit* are absurd because they are contradictory, suggesting facts which are materially impossible. Even more absurd is the phrase: *My courage weighs five kilos*, because it is neither true nor false; weight cannot be attributed to a quality any more than activity can be ascribed to inert objects, as in: *Peter is practised by tennis* – which is a simple reversal of subject and object. Yet all these phrases are incorrect, inconsistent with the rules of syntactical formation[1].

According to Chomsky:

> The notion *'grammatical'* cannot be identified with *'mean-ingful'*... in any semantic sense. Sentences (1) and (2) are equally nonsensical, but... only the former is grammatical.
> (1) *Colourless green ideas sleep furiously.*
> (2) *Furiously sleep ideas green colourless*[2].

This much is obvious. The first sentence is clearly correctly constructed but it is self-contradictory in what it states. Ideas cannot be both green and colourless. For the rest, *green ideas sleep furiously* is nonsensical at the level of the concrete denoted but, in the context of poetry, may have a certain metaphorical meaning. In the second sentence (and there is no need for us to pile syntax on top of semantics) the nonsense is the consequence of a syntag-matic deficiency. The elements are not organised relative to each other. And yet, an incomplete grammatical structure does not necessarily result in nonsense. For instance: *You understanding French?* is immediately decipherable (as childish babble or "pidgin") because, though the grammar is wrong, the syntagmatic structure is consistent.

We will not go into formless or distorted words like *sltcieux*, *fortacomble*, *scrumique*, nor similarly constructed utterances like *bdragsomerighphytzvring*, none of which have any meaning other than onomatopoeic. At the level of the *signified* the nonsense is created by variations in the utterances rather than by lexical or semantic variations. Such is the case with the (critical or ironic) confusion/identification between word and object in Chrysippus's remark: "When you say something, it passes through your mouth. You say 'chariot', therefore a chariot passes through your mouth"[3] and other logical developments from illogical premises or faulty reasoning. As, for instance, the syllogism of the pigeon in *Alice's Adventures in Wonderland*: "Serpents eat eggs. Little girls eat eggs. Therefore little girls are serpents" [translator's note: Mitry paraphrases and abbreviates Lewis Carroll. The original syllogism is rather more extended: "I have tasted eggs, certainly," said

Alice, who was a very truthful child; "but little girls eat eggs quite as much as serpents do, you know." "I don't believe it," said the Pigeon; "but if they do, why then they're a kind of serpent, that's all I can say."][4]

At the level of the *signifiers*, wherever an inconsistent element is found within a word, wherever an unusual phonological structure upsets the normal functions of the linguistic constituents established and coded so they may be verbally *communicated*, wherever a nonsense points up the unambiguous quality of the meanings, there lie combinations of what is grammatical and what is not – which is to say puns and portmanteau words. With the exception of alliterations which cannot avoid the categorisation of syntax.

As Michel Butor reminds us, "Alliteration is the perfect poetic process, since it consists of making language stretch towards an ideal of absolute coherence within which sound and meaning become solidly linked by rules". Yet, as in a poem, alliteration is based on syllables rather than words. All it takes is a sequence of alliterations to follow each other more or less systematically for the meaning to be buried under the verbal sound-patterns, ending up as nonsense or a play on words. For instance:

Par les mots d'amis déments / ma mie des mots / les mots mis à l'envers des momies / le maniement des mots / les monuments démis / par le chamois qui chatoie / dans l'Artois qui larmoie / Sois Toi[5]..., etc.

Or:

L'Amant dort / L'âme endort la mandore / qui, seule amante, se lamente. / La menue à l'âme nue / donnant au soudard deux sous d'art / sous les bois saoule et boit[6]..., etc.

Even more significant at the level of verbal nonsense are portmanteau words. Lewis Carroll writes:

Take, for instance, the two words *fuming* and *furious*. Imagine that you wish to pronounce them together... If your thoughts incline ever so slightly towards fuming, you will say *fuming-furious*; if they turn, even by a hair's-breadth, towards furious, you will say *furious-fuming*; but if you are endowed with that rarest of gifts, a perfectly balanced mind, you will say *fru-mieux*... [translator's note. the above is translated from the French, since the equivalent passage does not appear in Lewis Carroll; what follows, however, is directly quoted from *Through the Looking Glass*:

Which echoes Humpty-Dumpty's remarks: "slithy" means "lithe and slimey." "Lithe" is the same as "active". You see it's like a portmanteau – there are two meanings packed up into one word.]

So we have: *fourmidable* (fourmi [ant] + formidable); *famillion-naire* (familier [familiar] + millionnaire). Cléopatra and Léopold are so closely united that they become one: *Cléopold*.

Jean Paris writes:

Why would absurdity be so amusing were it not for the fact that its intrusion upsets the oppressive order of habit, the fixed logic of the adult world is replaced with the free associations of child-hood?[7]

And Freud points out that:

The mind seems nonsensical when it adopts ways of thinking accepted by the *unconscious* but rejected by *consciousness*, that is, when it employs faulty reasoning[8].

Even though, according to Lacan, the unconscious idea is incap-able of altering an acquired meaning unless the unconscious is already *language*. In which case one could argue that the uncon-scious is a good deal less unconscious than psychoanalysis would have us believe, closer to the subconscious than the preconscious.

It remains true, however, that if fuming and furious become *frumious* rather than *furming* and William and Richard become *Rilchiam* rather than *Wilchiard*, it is certainly not because of any rule, but because of a choice determined by speech. There is no limit to these combinations, unless it is the difficulty of pronoun-cing them, phonetic assimilations.

Apart from portmanteau ideas, we should also note the "esoteric words" (as Deleuze describes them) which form the essence of

Jabberwocky and compress still further signifiers that are already compressed:

> 'Twas brillig, and the slithy toves
>   Did gyre and gimble in the wabe;
> All mimsy were the borogoves,
>   And the mome raths outgrabe[9],

Be this as it may, we should note that whatever the sense – or nonsense – of the words used in this poem, the sentence structure is consistent with the rules of syntax. The general effect therefore is as if charged with *meaning that has been induced*. The nonsensical vocabulary opens onto intuitive connotations, onto "the expressed of the inexpressible".

Such is the case with James Joyce's *Finnegan's Wake*. This is a book full of verbal entities whose meaning is not to be found in the object but in the term describing the object and where "every name describing an object may itself become the object of a new name designating its meaning"[10] (Frege's paradox). Thus, in *Through the Looking Glass*: the name of the song is what the name is called but the song is something else; it is not its name. And yet, because it has a name, it must be designated by some other name. Now, what it is *in reality* is not the name designating the name which designates it, etc. [translator's note: the following is quoted directly from Lewis Carroll (p.103): "That's what the name is *called*. The name really is '*The Aged Aged Man*'." "Then I ought to have said "That's what the *song* is called?" Alice corrected herself. "No, you oughtn't: that's another thing. The *song* is called '*Ways and Means*'; but that's only what it's *called*, you know!" "Well, what is the song, then?" said Alice, who was by this time completely bewildered. "I was coming to that," the Knight said. "The song really is '*A-sitting On a Gate*': and the tune's my own invention. . ."]

If, as the Stoic philosophers would have it, sense is *what is expressed in a proposition*, nonsense would be where it is missing or where there is too much of it. Unless it is the expression itself which challenges what it expresses.

We prefer to accept Deleuze's definition, for whom "nonsense consists both of what has no meaning and what, as such, demonstrates the presence of meaning, because it offers meaning" – a meaning which is clearly always distorted.

Film nonsense

In the cinema, because the signifying structures are not provided through rules, it is not possible to "start with structures and arrive at meaning". Rather it is the other way round. As we have previously stated, it is because there is a signified that there are signifiers.

Physical, biological or psychological structures do not exist *a priori*. They are less determinative than already determined and, as Piaget says, they are "constructed according to an active regulating system, an 'autoregulation', forming a 'functioning centre'."

Such is the case – more or less – with the cinema. Shots are organised into structures by virtue of the concrete elements which make them up. The signifying process, constantly in the process of being built, is what generates the structures.

Film nonsense does not affect the being-itself, the object-itself, but the manner of being, the way it acts or reacts in the world, the way things are in a given situation. Whereas verbal nonsense has no concrete referent and refers only to concepts or fictions, film nonsense refers to its constant potential relationship with a true reality.

Film logic, at the level of the denoted facts, is the simple logic of actual reality: that much is obvious. There can be no mistake in categorisation, since categories are used for discussion *with* rather than *about* them. Absurd propositions always directly demonstrate their absurdity or hide it, as with the language of words. Nonsense provides a direct and inexhaustible supply of material for slapstick films. But, in this instance, it is an *absurdity of the world*, not of words – something which shocked a great many people at the time of Mack Sennett's first films. The word dog does not bite, and it certainly does not fly. It was possible to talk about a flying dog, as it was the Cat-with-a-Grin or the Grin-without-a-Cat in *Alice's Adventures in Wonderland*; it was just a fantastic and absurd concept. What was unacceptable, however, in that it *threw reality into doubt,* was the real dog flying through the air like a bird, or the hunter shooting a fish, or the swimmer swimming through a snowfield. "It's silly," people said at the time, without stopping to wonder why.

However, though the logic of facts is instantly apparent, though it requires at least that events should be credible, the logic of asso-

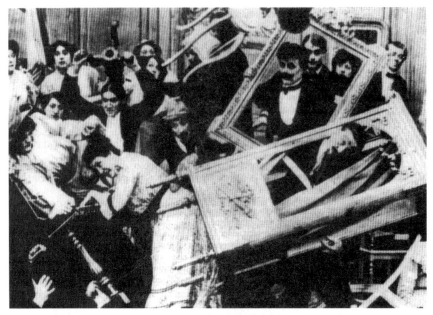

Destruction out of control in a slapstick film from 1911: Jean Durand's
Le Rembrandt de la rue Lepic.

The "broken mirror" effect in a slapstick film from 1913: *Kiki domestique,*
by Ovaro (Italy).

ciations deriving from the relationship of facts or objects within a temporal continuity is quite difficult to define. Associations are worth what such relationships are logically worth as a result of what they suggest to the mind. Connotations must therefore be directed by the meaning of what is denoted, in such a way that their lack of precision should be exploited precisely (but only to a limited extent).

Chaplin's method of story-telling

It merely requires the connoted to be thrown off-balance relative to the logic of the referent for the relationship to seem absurd or for the denoted reality to become absurd.

Which explains the effect in Chaplin's films of inanimate objects rebelling – achieving its highest expression in *One a.m.* The entire film is a constant battle between Charlie and the objects he constantly comes up against. He can't open the taxi door, he can't find his key, he puts his foot into the fish-bowl as he climbs through the window, he finds the key again, returns by the same route to open the door and then, because he is drunk, finds he can't fit the key in the lock... He trips over the rug, his leg is caught in the tiger-skin, he can't hold onto the water-jug, he walks round the table and finds it turning with him... As he climbs the rickety stairs, he doesn't seem to get any higher as he slips on the rug dragging behind him. He doesn't give up and eventually reaches the top as though it were Everest with all the equipment of the perfect climber... But then he is hit by the pendulum weight of the clock, and is crushed by the folding bed. Every single object seems off-course, out-of-kilter, rebellious and vengeful in a kind of waking nightmare where absurdities, constantly springing from every object and every action, assume the disturbing proportions of a surreal hallucination. The diabolical power of inanimate objects is released with the ironic automatism of a destiny which has assembled, at the same time and place, every single improbable chance happening with telepathic, determined and deliberate blindness.

Yet the inanimate object does not always play the part of an unwelcome and mischievous adversary. Frequently it becomes a useful "ally" helping Charlie out of a difficulty and enabling him to turn the changing circumstances to his own advantage. Simply

"By associating the objects he uses with those suggested by his actions":
Chaplin's *Payday*, 1921.

speaking, *objects only become useful to him to the extent that he uses them in the wrong way or ways which are not their own*. Objects then become elements in a strange kind of story-telling through which the universe starts to shake around the central character.

Through accidental analogy, real objects are eclipsed by "fictions" whose practical purposes become substituted for their own. By associating the objects he uses with *those suggested by his actions*, Charlie changes the world in which he moves. He therefore succeeds in removing himself from the reality which hurts him by substituting for it a fiction which he is able to control because it comes from him. He creates a universe in which he is the master and which he can handle in his own way to defend himself or withdraw from the world outside. In other words, he is able to escape from reality only by *denying* it in some way.

Logic decrees that we act with objects by associating them with their category. When an object belongs to a familiar category and we act with it as if it belonged to another category altogether, when we associate it with an order to which it could never belong, this transfer from one class to another and the absence of judgment it implies create a comic shock effect which is the cine-

The Floorwalker, Chaplin, 1916.

matic equivalent of the qui proquo in the logic of discourse. And the comic effect is the greater when it is a commonplace, everyday object, the action turning it upside down and making it unusual.

In *The Fireman*, when Charlie turns on the milk and coffee taps for his breakfast he uses the fire-engine as a percolator (because the American fire-engine circa 1910 resembled a boiler which, with its taps, suggested the idea of a percolator), he accepts what it is while denying it. Through his gesture, the fire-engine *is* and *is not*. He accepts it as an object, then uses it; he denies it as a category, since, for the "fire-engine" category, he substitues the "percolator" category. He denies the object its utility – "destroys" it – by poking fun at this utility. Thus he revenges himself on the object which has enslaved or victimised him.

The idea is essentially poetic, witty in the sense that it is an *idea* and demonstrates the process of wit. Absurd as a *fact*, when taken

literally, with Charlie behaving with the object as though the identification were real instead of being purely imaginary.

Thus there is a dual transposition: on the one hand, from the
object to its use, i.e. to a category different from the one with which
it is associated. On the other, from the idea to the action, presenting
the concept with concrete evidence, objectifying the subjective by
projecting it onto the world, introducing it into an event which it
transforms into its image. The concept thus weighed down with a
reality it could never possess becomes a joke in its own turn.
Charlie ridicules it as he endorses it, as he "realises" it.

Yet this "skewed" usage always attaches a precise purpose to the
object. In effect, when Charlie uses a stethoscope on an alarm-
clock, like a doctor sounding a patient's chest, when he opens it
with a tin-opener and examines its clockwork like a clockmaker;
removing the mainspring as though he were taking out a tooth and
measuring the spring by imitating a cloth-salesman (*The
Pawnshop*), he makes us forget the alarm-clock by eclipsing it
behind various different "fictions". Yet he associates it less with
categories alien to the ideas suggested by his actions: all alarm-
clocks suggest the ticking of a beating heart. Therefore I act with
the alarm-clock as though it were a patient. I use a stethoscope on
it because, *at that particular moment*, I need to give myself the
importance, assurance, authority of a doctor, etc.

He endows *this moment*, more than the object, with a gravity,
which is what gives Charlie his importance. But, being incapable
of justifying it other than through this substitute, he immediately
denies his action and replaces it with another which shows the
fiction for what it is. He can only assert himself through successive
negations in a sequence of time created from single moments
which become valid only by continually contradicting each
previous moment.

The "aura" round Keaton

Keaton's comedy is essentially based on *accidental damage* rather
than an inclination to caricature. His is a comedy of reason more
than emotion, based on *slapstick* more than comedy in the primary
sense of the word.

The comedy indeed comes from *destruction* or *damage*. But this
damage always relies on psycho-social motivations.

The Pawnshop, Chaplin, 1917.

Slapstick is often seen as rather crude caricatural clowning. It is certainly not that in the sense we mean it here. By slapstick we mean comedy based not on a moral or social *value* being destroyed but on *logic* being subverted, degraded, disturbed using the very principles of which it is the expression. An obvious contradiction, the logical development of false or impossible data, the inversion of the laws of probability or causality, these are the bases of slapstick, springing essentially from *absurdity*.

Obviously, the end result of contradiction is not always slapstick – or else it goes far beyond slapstick, as in the story of the prisoner being thrown out of gaol by his warders as a punishment for cheating at cards, under the rule that "all cheats have to be thrown out", in spite of the other rule that "all prisoners have to be kept inside". Lucien Fabre quotes Schopenhauer when he writes: "The absurdity of something has less to do with the contradiction of two unequal rules in which the less important is taken as a guide against all rationality than with the irrationality of behaviour which subjects the proper and permanent duty of a gaoler to an ephemeral whim based on an infrequent and even forbidden game".

Charlie provided a similar example when, to help a poor woman, he steals from the grocer's display which he is supposed to be looking after (*Police*). Yet in both cases – particularly the latter – the prime mover of the absurdity is a mental process, a feeling-reflex. It shows a piece of behaviour linking it to social comedy. Slapstick is founded less on the contradiction of ideas or feelings than on the contradiction of facts or actions. It belongs to that area where implausibility is stuck onto truth, unreality stuck onto reality, and illogicality stuck onto logic (to extend Bergson's – rather inadequate – definition of the comic as essentially "the mechanical stuck onto the living"[11].

Keaton's slapstick is not based on what is false or implausible. Whatever happens to him is *possible* (although wildly *improbable...*). There are numerous examples. To quote some of the more significant examples in *The General*: Buster has mounted a gun on a platform, coupled to the footplate of the "Kansas", and has made several vain attempts to shoot at the men who have stolen "The General" less than a kilometer down the track. He loads the gun, lights the fuse and climbs back onto the footplate. However, his foot catches in the hook coupling the flat-bed to the footplate. He manages to release it but, in so doing, he uncouples the wagon. Its momentum continues to carry it forward but the hook catching on the track makes it jolt. So much so that the gun, elevated at 45°, is moved downwards with each jolt and ends up horizontal, pointed directly at the footplate. In his haste Buster has got his foot stuck again, but jumps over the footplate, climbs out of the cabin, and makes his way along the side of the engine to hide behind the cow-catcher where he closes his eyes, sticks his fingers in his ears and waits...

But the locomotive takes a bend and the gun, slowing down, remains several meters behind. Because it has not yet taken the bend, the gun is now trained on the Yankee convoy up ahead. The gun goes off... *By the most extraordinary chance* the shells burst *just behind* their train causing great panic amongst them because they think they are being followed by a large force.

Towards the end of the film, when he goes to war in the ranks of the Confederacy, Buster takes command of a gun emplacement on top of a hill, facing the Yankee troops ranged on the other side of the river. One of the gunners is shot. He gives orders to another who instantly falls down dead. A third man falls. Buster begins to feel his heroism slip away in the heat of the battle. Indeed, a Yankee soldier, sneaking through the brushwood, has made it across the valley. Hidden behind a bush, ten meters or so below the battery, he "pots" Buster's men one after the other.

Buster encourages the last survivors. With a big and expansive gesture, he draws his sword and shouts: "Fire!" Because his gesture is so violent, the blade detaches itself and flies off and Buster is left holding the hilt in his hand. The shooting stops however. What has happened is that the blade has boomeranged back and *stuck between the shoulder-blades of the enemy sniper!*...

Regaining his courage, Buster takes the place of the gunners. He loads the gun and fires... but his sudden action dislodges the gun which fires the shell vertically up into the air. At the same moment, the Yankee forces charge across the river. The shell returns to earth upstream and lands *right on a ditch* and bursts throwing up a great waterspout which drowns the attackers.

We could go on... So, here we have, as it were, an *inevitability of chance* (which is the equivalent in slapstick of fate in tragedy) for which it acts both as caricature and antithesis, that is, simple statistical exaggeration. It would not take much – two or three extra quirks of fate – to turn *Oedipus Rex* into a slapstick comedy. Tragedy is at the limit of probability. Beyond this, drama becomes ludicrous. Keaton's universe, because it is constantly subject to chance, has therefore no need to be damaged: it *damages* itself. It is not Malec [tr. no idea to whom or what this refers – unless there is a Malec responsible for a law of probability?] who is open to the world (that is, if he pays any attention to it). It is the world constantly opening up under his influence, turning it topsy-turvy but helping it by extending the hand of chance.

A hand which is also very often concealed. As is the case with *Sherlock Junior* (which along with *The General* is without doubt his best film) where Buster finds himself at a particular moment marooned on a coral reef in the middle of the ocean. He wants to dive in to swim to shore. Indeed, he does dive in but when he swims a couple of strokes he finds himself swimming in a desert of sand. He stands up, brushes the sand off his shoes, marches off barefoot only to find himself walking through snow. He quickly puts his shoes back on, swings his arms round his chest to warm himself but hits the trees on either side: he is in the middle of a forest, etc.

The General, Buster Keaton, 1926.

It is true that he is dreaming. Buster, a cinema projectionist, dreams that he is taking part in the action of a film. His "double" enters the world of the screen. But this world rejects and ejects him. Buster triumphs over reality in implausible circumstances but the film fiction has no "true" circumstances to return the compliment. Except when reality and unreality become confused as each "become realised" within the other through a perpetual substitution.

Destruction taken to extremes

Among logical absurdities we might mention certain Laurel and Hardy films. Nonsensicality in their films has nothing to do with the confusion, quiproquo or inversion of objects, actions or circumstances, but more with genuine destruction, demolition extended by the almost mathematical development of an initially harmless effect. The high point of this progressive extension is represented by *The Battle of the Century* (1927) which will remain in the annals of cinema as the masterpiece of slapstick where motivation is eclipsed by consequence, where chaos reigns, physical damage through custard pies taken to a climax never previously reached.

The value of this massive battle (more than 3,000 custard pies and nearly a ton of pastry were used, apparently) is to be found in its rhythm, the precision of its development. First there is one custard pie, then two, then four, then eight. Then suddenly it explodes: twelve, sixteen, twenty-four, thirty-two, forty-eight, etc., but so naturally that absurdity becomes logical, assuming genuine earthquake proportions. And our laughter develops similarly, produced in this logical absurdity by a similarly progressive logic to the point of hysteria and physical pain. "It is the greatest comic film ever shot", Henry Miller writes in *The Golden Age*. In the sense of automatic laughter it certainly is.

Similar to this film, *Two Tars* (1928) is based on deliberate demolition with retaliation becoming more and more extreme.

Renting a Model T Ford in order to take out a couple of pretty girls, Stan and Ollie cause a traffic-jam. They are bumped by the car behind, which causes an argument. The angry driver punches a hole in one of the Ford's headlamps. Ollie pulls a wing off the Buick. The other man drags the door off its hinges. The dispute becomes worse. One after another, the drivers behind them, overcome with destructive rage, start to demolish each other's cars. The road becomes strewn with heaps of metal. A hundred cars without headlamps, wings, doors, windscreens, bump their way down the road, following Stan and Ollie back in their Ford. Then without realising it, the whole procession leaves the road and enters a railway tunnel. A hundred broken cars reverse out backwards. And finally Stan and Ollie's, squashed by the train-engine into the shape of an accordion.

We could also quote five or six equally remarkable films, such as *The Second Hundred Years* (1927), *You're Darn Tootin'* (1928), *The Finishing Touch* (1928).

What is important, however, what makes these films original, apart from their systematised progressive development, is, as we have said, not just the slowness of the acting, but beyond this slowness, *a thinking time* which betrays an intention all the more absurd for the fact that it has been thought about, *calmly* executed with the composure of a ritual. For it is the stupidity of such *considered actions* which gives the events which develop the apocalyptic dimensions of transcendental absurdity. But, though systematisation is an important tool in progressive development based on *automatic behaviour*, it has a damaging effect when it comes to normal behaviour patterns. And it is in the direction of behavioural comedy that Laurel and Hardy's comedy veered at the start of the talkies.

Once the large scale with its large cast is reduced to the two characters, they find themselves confronted by an act of stupidity – or clumsiness – *which is theirs and theirs alone*. From then on all that matters is their actions. Reduced to themselves, these actions are scarcely funny. Now that they are not extended by other characters, all they can do is *repeat themselves*. Once again, while the mechanisation of facts or collective actions ends up as epic absurdity because it involves a *statistical truth*, the mechanisation of gesture and behaviour is irrelevant because it calls into question a *psychological truth* which it denies[12].

Accidental absurdity

Nonsense is clearly not exclusive to comic films – matching errors (which were widespread at one time) have become quite rare. They were scattered throughout certain silent films when there was no such technical grade as script supervisor or specialised editor: a man comes into a set wearing a fedora and leaves with a straw boater. A woman changes her dress instantly she moves from the drawing-room to the dining-room.

However, in films where the action occurs in everyday reality, nonsense – when it exists – is at the level of the signified rather than within the signifiers. It exists in the truth, the credibility of the story or situations and returns us once again to the distinction between the effect of the reality of the filmed objects and the impression of reality which uses this to make improbable events or impossible situations appear true. Which is the thinking behind the crazy rule which, even in the most realistic circumstances, turns the heroine into the incarnation of a mythical ideal. A rule obeyed by films as recently as twenty years ago.

Tay Garnett's version of *The Postman Always Rings Twice* would be a consistently good film were not the first part spoiled by Lana Turner twirling all day long in the filthy garage in a snowy white dress as though she were a homecoming queen. One or two well-intentioned critics have claimed that this whiteness "symbolises the original purity of young womenhood". Even if this were so, which is most unlikely, the artifice destroys any credibility the film might have had.

With her spangled dress, wasp waist and frills and furbelows, Marilyn Monroe is wonderful in the bar-room scenes at the start of *The River of No Return*. But then we see her with some trappers, rafting downstream through various rapids. The journey is supposed to take several weeks. In spite of the rain, wind, spray and the other rough weather she is constantly exposed to on the open raft, her hair remains immaculately curled, as though, at every bend in this river in the Far West, there was some skilful hairdresser to reset her hair! We might think we were dreaming. We are indeed dreaming. Yet the supposed "realism" is dealt a death blow...

The same thing in *Zu neuen Ufern* [*Life Begins Anew*]. In Douglas Sirk's melodrama, Zarah Leander is sentenced to hard labour. All the woman who share this sad fate are more or less dirty, with their clothes in tatters. Not her. Her outfit is spotless and her perfect make-up with pencilled in eyebrows suggests the make-up artist is not far away!.

Dreams and fiction

We frequently accept the most arbitrary situations if they are presented with the merest factual verisimilitude. Superficial verisimilitude, of course, but which has the effect of turning the arbitrariness of the situation into a dreamscape – as was the case with *Susan Lennox*.

The absurdity of dreams is difficult to represent. Although dreams are not "absurd as a rule", we dream with objects (of objects...), which our mental images present to us pretty much consistently with the way they are "in reality". The incoherence of dreams has less to do with the forms of the imagistic data than with narrative relationships. Any subsequent "nonsensicality" depends on editing but it is questionable to what extent this is intelligible. If it is, it is because it is associated with logical constants as in slapstick nonsense, in which case its dreamlike qualities are entirely hypothetical.

Because they are basically subjective, dreams are incommunicable. The images of *my* dream are of interest only to me, are comprehensible only by me. On the other hand, in images transmitted by film, it is not I who is dreaming but *someone else*. I see what that person is dreaming or *what he is dreaming about*. Yet what, for him, is an organisation of the unconscious, is, for me in the audience, merely undecipherable formlessness.

On the other hand, the cinema is quite capable of telling dreamlike stories, developing scenes linked together "like" a dream, and at the same time be perfectly comprehensible. There are numerous examples: for a start, the extraordinary films of the Polish director Wojciech Has, *Saragossa Manuscript* (1964) and *The Hour-Glass Sanatorium* (1973).

Moreover, it is questionable whether the spectator sitting in front of the screen is or is not in the attitude of the dream through the conditions of perception and identification which are involved. Roger Odin writes:

> Christian Metz has proved how mainstream cinema has created a spectator who sits by himself, motionless and silent, in a frame of mind somewhere between daydreaming and dreaming and predisposed to create that all-absorbing fictional construct: diegesis[13].

This is certainly true. Metz reinforces the point:

> Jean Mitry was right to point out that, whenever the "film state" is explained in terms of hypnosis, mimicry, or other purely passive processes, it does not take into account the identification of the spectator with the film, merely the circumstances which make this impossible: the spectator is "disconnected" from the real world, it is true; but he has to be connected to something in order to make a *transfer of reality*, involving an entire emotional, perceptual, intellective *activity* accessible to the spectator only by assembling those of the real world. Thus, in attempting to explain a powerful phenomenon like the impression of reality in the cinema, we fall back on the

need to take account of positive factors: specifically the elements of reality contained in the film itself, the most important of which is the reality of movement[14].

For Michel Colin:

The interest of Jean Mitry's attitude to this lies in the fact that, while concentrating on the imaginary dimensions of the audience's relationship with the film, he is persuaded to reject the concept of identification. "Whereas a confusion between 'self' and 'other' might be inevitable in the case of audience-identification, in the cinema all that happens is a simple correlation of behaviour in a given general situation: the beating a hero gives the villain is the one I would like to give a certain enemy of mine except that my sense of propriety – or weakness – prevents me." For Mitry, "identification" is limited to what he calls "projective association". The spectator-subject defined by Mitry is one who is conscious, "free", and predisposed. What psychoanalysis proves is that this notion of the spectator-subject is inadequate. It is certainly not that the functions of the Self are suppressed, merely that its alertness is diminished, "providing an opportunity for narcissistic retreat, a temporary suspension of interest in the world outside, and the power of objects, at least in their real form"[15].

Now, to claim that the functions of the Self are not suppressed is almost word for word what I wrote in *The Aesthetics*, specifically:

For us the audience, the film image serves as a substitute for reality in exactly the same way as the mental image when we dream. That they are less vivid in the cinema, where we never lose the idea of being present, does not mean that the phenomena of participation are any the less pronounced – with this obvious distinction, however, that, in the dream-state, the imaginary is created by me whereas, in the cinema, it is externally induced and imposed on my consciousness.

As a kind of perceived reality, it is presented to me as an objective reality but, since *I know* this reality to be imaginary, I can always choose not to accept it or associate myself with it. In a certain sense, I enjoy greater freedom with it. My participation is only ever the result of an act of will, a voluntary submission on my part.

In any case, audience-identification (which is merely an excessive belief in the film reality) implies a kind of self-renunciation – if only for the duration of film – in order to identify with the "other person"[16].

Thus, it would be difficult to "empower real objects", since films are – as a rule – projected in the dark, for the precise purpose of substituting the image for reality. A condition which has enabled various psychologists to compare film images with phantasms and dreamscapes. Now, reference to phantasm suggests "alienation", which brings us back to the ideas of Jean-Paul Fargier, Jean-Louis Baudry et al. for whom film production and aesthetics are "idealist" because "they make no clear distinction between those processes which are fictional and those which are real"... Now, the first responsibility of film is to conceal anything that might reveal the manipulations hidden behind what the image shows.

What gives these theoreticians greatest satisfaction is when sound is used a-syncronously, demonstrating its artificiality; when photography is substandard, proving it is an image and not reality; when actors' performances are so wooden that they show they are acting and not real characters, etc. In brief, the work must not be hidden, but be turned into a creative condition. Which is all well and good when the work becomes the *subject*, as with a film about the shooting of a film; but absurd in any other context. If the "transformational business of the work must be shown from the inside so that it may serve as an agent of revelation", to point out that the film is contrived and the story made up is the deny the cinema and destroy everything which makes it interesting.

Jean-Louis Comolli writes: "With direct [cinema], alienation stops being both the basis for the cinema and its function[17]." I would be more inclined to believe the opposite. Actually, in direct cinema presenting itself as an "objective" document there is no misrepresentation at the level of the shot: what it shows is true. Whether or not it is "direct", film always involves the editing of a number of shots into a particular order. And that order is capable of making the images say "something other than what they show", but also the opposite of what they imply.

I have already pointed out – using this example among many others – that Frank Capra's film *Why We Fight*, made as anti-Nazi propaganda, was in large part made up of shots from German newsreels whose purpose was diametrically opposite.

The cinematic and the filmic

To conclude this short survey, we shall endeavour to define what is meant by *film specificity*.

"What on earth does the word *cinematic* mean?" a certain critic writes ingenuously, who, if he does not know the answer, ought to change his profession. He is obviously poking fun at those facile comments, as pointless as they are peremptory, which state: "That's cinematic" or "That's not cinematic". However, it is perhaps more useful to try and give an explanation.

By definition, anything recorded on film and projected onto a screen has to do with cinema, in the same way that anything printed has to do with writing. But, anything to do with writing is not necessarily the expression and signification created by a certain way of using words. Thus, to describe a film as "not being cinematic" means that what is expressed in it is not solely due to the means or interaction of means – images, speeches and sounds – which make the cinema what it is: a composite art.

It must be said that the term "cinema" is ambiguous: we "go to the cinema" (auditorium where the film is projected); we "create cinema" (make films) using the "tools of cinema" (camera, sound).

Cohen-Séat makes a shrewd distinction between the *cinematic* and the *filmic*: the simple recording of something in motion, whatever it may be, is a cinematic effect. The filmic consists of being expressive. Apart from the exclusive use of imagery (the organisation of which gave the silent screen its "specific identity", passing over the often obtrusive subtitles), whatever depends on only one or these means (imagery excepted) is not part of film expression.

The independence of an art exists in the *production of meaning* and the *signifying forms* created with the means *specific* to it alone. The resulting signified is also specific to it. When all the film does is record ideas expressed or conceptualised through significations alien to it, it becomes nothing more than a vehicle. Which means that whatever is "carried by this vehicle" is nothing more than a verbal message transmitted through audiovisual means.

It is possible to write books about a painting, analyse it from a pictorial, symbolic or metaphysical point of view, but no text could ever express what it expresses. No film, no image could ever translate a verbal expression. And vice versa. All a translation or an adaptation can ever be is an "approximation", not even an equivalent.

When Cézanne painted three apples set out on a white table-cloth, he was using objects with no *a priori* significance. But, through his composition, the interplay of shape and colour, he provided them with a *value* and a *meaning*. Which derive entirely from the pictorial expression given specific form in the painting.

In the same way, the specificity of the cinema consists in giving a metaphorical, symbolic or other significance to objects, actions or facts which have no other meaning than that they are objects or actions, and which find themselves involved in a flow of meaning which suddenly turns them into signifying elements.

We saw how difficult it was for the cinema to express ideas other than through narration – constructed or "deconstructed, continuous or discontinuous" – that is, through a series of reciprocating and self-determining *facts*, through which connotations establish their meanings. Consequently, more than in any other art, content is inseparable from form. If content only assumes meaning through the form which expresses it, form, by way of contrast, only exists by virtue of whatever it provides the form for. It is not a structure existing as such, it is not a matrix; it is merely a *means for the content to exist* – or appear. Thus, to claim that: "Ideology does not exist within the raw material used by art, but in the techniques used to develop that material. Ideology exists within the form" (Tretjakov) or "Form is always ideology" (Eisenstein) seems to me particularly suspect. Of course, ideology does not exist "within the raw material used by art", but nor does it exist in the way it is used. It exists within the *formalised* material, not in "whatever does the formalising". And though whatever does the formalising appears to exist as a *function* of an idea, though it is what gives the content its whole meaning, it is the content which is *sole agent* for that *meaning*.

In fact, "the concrete content is indicative of the manner of its external, perceptible realisation". The content determines the form in which it appears, but the form is perceptible only through the substance of the content. In other words, the form is governed by *an* ideology, but not the *particular* ideology revealed by the content alone.

Any reference to form necessarily involves a reference to content. And vice versa. Formalism consists of concentrating on the latter to the exclusion of any consideration of why or for what it exists. But it also consists of concentrating on the content to the exclusion of the work as a whole, the ideas outside the context of what they are within the story and the purposes of the story.

As we have tried to prove during the course of this study (if proof is possible in respect of aesthetic values), since all any film ever shows are actions and facts, no grammar could ever hope to control the presentation, description, ordering of such actions and facts. Indeed nothing could, as we have said, apart from the simple logic of everyday experience.

As Christian Metz acknowledged at the start of his investigations, *in the cinema there are only rhetorical codes. In other words, anything is possible in the cinema which is justified, i.e. which signifies within a given context.*

XVI

Image, Language and Thought

As I have said, all language, because it is a way of translating the modalities of thought, has of necessity to refer to the mental structures which organise them, that is, the processes of the mind which consist of thinking, judging, reasoning and ordering according to relationships of analogy, consequence or causality[1].

What has yet to be determined is whether language is *innate*, as Chomsky and a number of linguists maintain, whether thoughts do not exist unless they are formulated in words, or whether, on the contrary, thought is not *previous to language*, which allows thought to be expressed but does not create it. This important problem is particularly relevant in that it draws on the most recent research in psychology and neurophysiology, with specific reference to mental representation and, by extension, moving images.

Let us, first of all, reexamine the idea suggested by Eichenbaum that the perception and comprehension of film is indissolubly linked to the formation of an "internal language", without which the cerebration "absent in normal usage where words retrieve and replace other means of expression would be difficult, tiring and would soon make the film incomprehensible[2]..."

This idea was given short shrift. In fact, if we are capable of thinking and judging during a film, this judgment does not require any specific formulation, and an understanding of events, their connections or associations, derives from the simple logic of things, i.e. actual (or cultural) experience, and not from an "internal" language – whether it be articulated or not.

This "understanding" may use words as reference, that much is clear, and does so most of the time. But it is a reflex action, an easy habit, not an obligation.

Concerning "internal language"

If, when I see the image of a chair, the word "chair" comes to mind, it is certainly because, from my childhood, I have learned to name objects at the same time as knowing them. Yet, from the simple fact that I do not speak German, the word "armstuhl" will never occur to me. Supposing, then, that I have no knowledge of any of the languages spoken in the world today, I might be forgiven for wondering into what "internal language" I could translate the image of this chair. Will a deaf-mute represent it through gesture (completely externally) or will he retain, as I do, a mental image of the film image without having to call up some more or less internalised linguistic representation?

Even more recently, Emilio Garroni has taken up this idea, with reference to logical positivism and the Theses of the Prague Circle[3]. It is clear that we think a good deal more than we speak and that language cannot be reduced to a discourse "externally displayed with the competition of an observable semiotic substance", that is, what Garroni (following Eichenbaum) calls "external language". From the fact that we express ourselves with words, we also think with (more or less unformulated) words, but, in addition, with ephemeral mental representations: my cigarette packet is empty. Consequently, I "see" the tobacconist on the nearest corner, I make a vague representation to myself of the route to it and, according to the time available, I put on my overcoat and leave wearing it. That is all. There is no need for me to formulate in my mind an explicit phrase for, though thinking is a mental activity, it is not a linguistic action in the strict sense of the word, as would be the case with "interior monologue". Of course, thinking requires a semiotic support but, as we shall see later on, this substratum does not necessarily have a linguistic characteristic.

If, as Garroni maintains, film expression (metaphor or other) is no more than the "display, in the form of translation or transcription, of a linguistic realisation already institutionalised into a visual realisation", then film is nothing more than the illustration, the "visualisation" of a verbal discourse, i.e everything but the film expression...

Thoughts of a mouse

Before going on, and without calling on Köhler's famous experiments into the intelligence of the higher primates, I would like to quote as a concrete reference the experiments of Henri Laborit into the behavioural habits of a mouse.

The animal is let into a tunnel with two branches each leading to a reward. The mouse takes the right hand branch, but there is a small electric current in its way. It chooses the left-hand path where nothing prevents it from reaching the reward. The next experiment: the mouse spontaneously chooses the left-hand tunnel. After which it tentatively makes its way down the right. Not finding any resistance, it reaches the piece of cheese. The next experiment: the mouse starts down the left, receives an electric shock, stops and goes down the right where it finds the path is clear. The next experiment: the mouse immediately takes the right-hand tunnel, and so on.

The experiment is repeated a number of times, either alternating the obstruction, or repeating it on the same side, or removing it. The consequence is that each time, the mouse starts down the tunnel which previously had no obstruction; then cautiously considers its position before eventually entering the tunnel which shocked it.

The conclusion reached from this is that, not only does the mouse "memorise" the event, but that it brings some sort of judgment to bear on its eventual choice. It is not reacting with a simple sensori-motor reflex. It is plainly exhibiting a "thought-process", however rudimentary – with no need for any internal language to direct its behaviour. Obviously, this "knowledge" operates in a "closed-circuit": unless there is some "mouse language" we do not know about (which seems highly unlikely), it cannot communicate this knowledge with any other mice. . .

Genesis of thought

On a higher level, numerous experiments have been conducted on the behaviour of new-born infants. One of the main criticisms levelled at the Würtzburg School and, in part, at Gestalt, is that the "experimental field" was only applied to adults, that is, it only took into account subjects already formed by a socio-cultural environment – which, of course, distorted all the responses relative to the formation of language and thought[4]. Which is why, in the chapter on the image and *perceived reality*, not having had to trace its origins, I was considering perception from before the age of Man, taking it in its totality. Now, it is clear that, within this context, perception involves sensation and the sensori-motor coordinates which (from earliest infancy) gradually start to organise it – such as the intuitive judgments which complete consciousness, not to mention all those potential complexities added by this perceptual organisation to the basic sensory data.

Since Piaget and his school, important research has been conducted into the new-born, and a large part of this experimentation has revealed that babies develop much earlier than was previously thought. Whether the genesis of intelligence occurs through assimilation of the external world in successive stages, as Piaget maintains or, continuously, as Konrad Lorenz's experiments seem to prove, what is important is the genesis, i.e. the properties *innate or not* (wherein lies the problem) of the psychic apparatus for, long before it becomes language, thought becomes evident in the actions, gestures, sensori-motor reflexes animating the child. The fact that in the first few days he knows how to distinguish sounds or syllables is in no sense a proof that language structures are already conditioned in his mind, for there must not be a confusion between language and the infrastructures which enable it. As Dorothy McCarthy points out, "there is a psychological gulf between the simple emission of the phonetic form and the symbolic or representational use of the word in the appropriate situation[5]." It is the case that, from birth, through his actions which develop and become cognitive, the child at between six to eighteen months learns a certain awareness of objects, the logic of objects: he picks up a toy, fingers it, weighs it in his hand, brings it up to his mouth, turns it round and then throws it down. A moment later, when he wants to throw it further, he has to make a bigger effort. If he lets go of his toy, he falls and does so again in exactly the same way. The little tot draws no conclusion from this regarding weight but he observes it and takes it into account.

According to H. Sinclair de Zwart, "the child becomes capable of acting on an object with another object, then reproducing the same action on other objects, establishing relationships, moving on to crude classifications[6]". Cognitive organisation happens gradually by virtue of the diversity of interactions with the environment and the emotional relationships with the environment, especially with the mother. However, in Barbel Inhelder's view, "though the knowledge of objects develops through manipulation and exploration of those objects, it is only by studying the continuous transformation of the child's activities that it becomes obvious that these lead to the actual processes of thought. In fact, sensori-motor activities not only allow thoughts to be replenished with new contents, they actually lead the thought to be structured[7]". As Piaget writes:

> The structural properties appearing in these activities enable the child to create its own precise representations and form the necessary basis for the acquisition of a more or less defined semantic field. [...] Intelligence precedes language not just ontogenetically, as the example of deaf-mutes proves, but phylogenetically, as is proved, moreover, by the extensive work on the intelligence of the higher primates[8].

"When the monkey opens its eyes, it is already ready to see", writes Torsten Wiesel (following David Hubel's experiments on sight in general[9]). From which he concludes, with Konrad Lorenz, Roger W. Sperry or John C. Eccles, that there is an innateness in neurophysiological structures. Which does not infer an innateness of language presupposing an already structured intelligence.

Moreover, Chomsky recognises that:

> If it were possible to show that these prelinguistic symbolic systems share certain significant properties with natural language, we could then argue that these properties of natural language are acquired by analogy. [...] But since no one has succeeded in showing that the fundamental properties of natural language [...] appear in prelinguistic symbolic systems or any others, the latter problem does not arise. [...] The primary symbolic systems to which he [Goodman] refers are "rudimentary prelinguistic symbolic systems in which gestures and sensory and perceptual occurrences of all sorts function as signs"[10,11].

In other words, though language may not be innate, at least the mental structures on which it is based are, which means that they in turn are directly dependent on cerebral structures.

But Piaget argues that:

> We should follow the hypothesis according to which nervous connections *directly* explain the formation of such and such a

mental structure, as though consciousness were limited to recording the existence of preformed nervous structures in order to translate them into terms of representation or operation. Yet we might presume that the nervous structures *describe the table of possibilities or impossibilities determining the boundaries of the field within which the construction of behaviour will take place*[12].

From thought to language

Thirty or so years ago Logical Positivism[13] reduced mathematics and logic to linguistics, as forming a general syntax and semantic code. This association of thought with language contradicted the Würtzburg school which claimed the opposite. Now, just as thought is not the "mirror of logic", so logic is not the simple mirror of thought. There is no preestablished harmony between perceptual structures and the laws of the physical universe (though there is a kind of isomorphism): whereas formalised logic presumes an abstract construction (which we have no time to examine here) the most elementary perceptual processes involve an implicit logic.

Recalling the extraordinary parallels between the visual perceptual sphere and the tactile-kinesthetic sphere, Piaget sets great store by the reciprocal interaction and influence of these data but, in my view, does not pay sufficient attention to visual perception which, as I see it, is more important in the formation of thought than the sensori-motor signals acting at the level of affectivity and consciousness of self, rather than at the level of a knowledge of the world.

Like the monkey, a child sees from the moment he opens his eyes (or within a few days...). Like the mouse, he remembers (doubtless a good deal more effectively). Thus, he represents objects for himself, mental images with which he intuitively builds relationships of comparison, distinction, size, form, colour, situation, etc. Now, representation involves interpretation, the construction of a pattern in the cerebral structures – which is the same thing as thought organising itself into a system of significations and giving meaning to the perceived objects, even at the elementary stage of a child between six and eighteen months.

From which we may deduce that *we think in images, with images, long before we think with words.* Relationships of images are obviously language in that they express something, but it is preverbal language, incapable of being communicated and involving only the subject doing the thinking – a genuine "internal language". To claim, as Lacan does, that "the unconscious is structured like language" is, to my way of thinking, merely to recognise that – in the adult as in the child – the mental image involves direct associations, an intuitively constructed combining process, and linguistic structures have no part to play in it. Moreover, to claim, as certain linguists do, that "ideas previous to language do not exist, unless they are innate", is to confuse the idea with its expression, the expression of thought with the thought itself, as though this expression were the source of the thought, reduced to a mere system of verbal clichés.

Far from being a return to outdated ideas which could not conceive of thought in images except as a collection of clichés drawn from a fixed state of mind, mental images are, on the contrary, always changing and different, like the world which inspires them. So much so that the images are less important than the relationships between them, which the mind organises with a creativity using material logic as a referent (when it does not soar off into pure imagination). And, in reply to criticisms which are already old-hat, we should remember that the brain is not a "storehouse of images": images are not stored in the brain any more than music is stored on a magnetic tape. The explanation for this is to be found in neurophysiology but, if the brain is no more than an operator, we might well wonder how intelligence is formed.

Gestalt sees the real act of intelligence only in terms of a kind of "direct comprehension" (*insight*) which Köhler explains as a sudden restructuring of the perceptual field.

As though – Piaget objects – intelligence were merely an extension of the perceptual structures, as though the child's activity and other tentative steps leading to an eventual intuition were not already intelligent...

Innate infrastructure, acquired intelligence

For Gestalt, sensations are *structured*, not *structuring*, elements; they comprise a totality, presented as such. Now, though I accept (at least for the most part) the principles of Gestalt, I have never been able to approve of this "a-priorism". Mental structures do not exist "in themselves"; they have a genesis and a relationship with the subject. Indeed, genetic epistemology suggests that sensations are the structuring elements. Yet the question remains as to what this structuring activity bases itself upon, what are its limits, what is its substratum.

I offer the following hypothesis (acknowledging that it has to be verified at the neurophysiological and psychological level): this substratum is no more than *a collection of perceptual thresholds, forming an innate infrastructure and, through its limits, a kind of "framework" which sets out the boundaries of perception and reorganises the perceived into a "form" which includes the representation of objects, the source of all thought.* This, while keeping a constant balance between the visual and tactile-kinesthetic spheres.

If this is so, we might consider sensations as structured elements – but structured through and in terms of the preconscious framework, and not through some imagined innate quality. A framework which, though it is capable of being altered from the inside by the actual perceptual activity, is incapable of transmitting a preformed, intellectually organised pattern from which language might develop, but controls it and enables it to be formed.

"How did the human mind come to acquire the innate structure that we are led to attribute to it?" Chomsky wonders[14]. It seems to me, on the contrary, that it is the innate structure, the sensory infrastructure which enables thought to be formed and be known as thought. What is *innate* is the *framework*, not what has been framed.

It is the case that, while language develops from a partially structured intelligence, there is a reciprocal structuring process: *thought is formed to the extent that it is formulated.* But this formulation is not an exclusive property of verbal language. Whether we do it consciously or not, *we think with images as much as we do with words.* Nevertheless, if we wish to communicate our judgments about the world, we find ourselves unable to mobilise it, reorganise it as we do in our minds. Thus we have to rely on controllable substitutes, words, to describe objects and involve concepts.

This is how it is for the child who, during his first ten or twenty months of life, forms for himself a whole raft of more or less schematic representations but is unable to communicate his "interior world" (though he certainly feels the need – to judge from the

inarticulate sounds through which he reveals it). Now, he gradually learns to speak, to name objects; and we might believe that
this learning process is all the easier for the fact that the child has
already assimilated a number of images corresponding with objects
familiar to him. If he wants to pick up the doll beyond his reach,
from the moment he knows how to speak, the word "doll"
(however halting his pronunciation) is substituted in his mind for
the image which represented it. Which is a justification of Goodman's ideas, for whom the "first-language learning poses no real
problem because, prior to first-language learning, the child has
already acquired the rudiments of a [prelinguistic] symbolic
system in his ordinary dealings with the environment". Of course,
it is not a matter of grammatical structures or the specific properties of language which Chomsky would certainly have expected
(contested by Goodman)[15], but of elementary utterances, words
and not phrases. The child must subsequently learn to replace his
global perceptions with verbal units, to organise these units or
groups of units according to rules governed by the logic of
meaning. Which takes him up to seven or eight, to the age when
he forgets the image of the objects he refers to and retains only the
verbal designations.

In adult language, thought has no need of these images. Or
rather, they are no longer essential to it. Almost unconsciously,
thought becomes language and vice versa; consciousness is
absorbed into speech – which is what we mean by "thinking out
loud". Also, language is not the reflection of objects, but the
consciousness we have of them, the way we think of them. Not a
copy but an interpretation through a system of signs which
imposes on it its own laws.

Concrete fiction

Thus, with the cinema – let us say the moving image – we can
believe and even confirm that, though we are unable to act on the
world, on real objects (or with them) to express our thoughts, we
can at least manipulate their images, arrange them in order, as we
do our mental representations. Such that the structures of thought
are no longer obliged to submit to a system of signs and significations: *they reveal themselves, freely open up* through a continuity
which delivers unexpected connotations. Intuitive thought is

shown to operate free of the domination of words. By formalising in this way a judgment, a view-point, a vision of the world, the film actually becomes like the image of consciousness, the reflection of a thought offered up to the eyes of a third party, the audience – for it to be understood, with no other intermediary than the formalisation itself.

Thus, there is no point in wondering *why* film signifies – any more than in pondering why objects, actions and the effects of everyday life have meaning. Film images, reduced to themselves, are confined to showing and signify no more than what they *show*. On the other hand, by the very fact that we think, we create new relationships – arbitrary, subjective – between what our mental images represent. We give them a specific meaning by organising them according to the signifying intentions we impose on them. Now, with its shooting-script and editing, different shots and angles, film does exactly the same. Whatever the complexities of certain narrative forms, experimenting with time and space, present and past, the here-and-now and memory, film logic develops in the image of actual experience – which is generally understood by most people.

It is said that a single word has different connotations according to the person who hears it. The way it is interpreted depends on socio-cultural habits, and the understanding of a piece of text sometimes varies from one ethnic group to another. Yet the same is true of images. In the cinema, as in other contexts, signification is not absolute. Thus, if what makes the cinema unique is that it creates significations produced using means specific to it alone, there is all the more reason for these to be understood. Which is not to suggest that it must conform to conventions – which, on the contrary, have constantly to be renewed, transformed. The overriding concern is that these new processes should be managed with the necessary associations of an inseparable form and content, the one continually justifying the other. In my opinion, there can be no other rule.

Notes

Preface

1. G. Cohen-Séat, "Le discours filmique", in *Revue de filmologie*, no. 2, P.U.F.
2. In *The Aesthetics and Psychology of the Cinema*, translated by Christopher King, Indiana University Press, 1997; (p. 51–59 of the I.D.H.E.C. roneotyped edition, 1961, not included in the Indiana University Press edition).
3. In *Communications*, no.4, October 1964; reprinted in *Essais sur la signification au cinéma*, Éd. Klincksieck, 1968. A translation of these essays was published under the title *Film Language: a Semiotics of the Cinema*, translated by Michael Taylor, Oxford University Press, 1974.

Preliminaries

1. André Malraux, *Esquisse d'une psychologie du cinéma*, N.R.F., 1940.
2. Cf. Pierre Jenn, *Georges Méliès, cinéaste*, Éd. Albatros, 1984.
3. Jean Epstein, *Le Cinéma vu de l'Etna*, 1926.
4. S.M. Eisenstein, *Film Form*, translated by Jan Leyda, Dennis Dobson, 1961, p.37.
5. Béla Balázs, *L'Esprit du Film*, 1930.
6. Rudolf Arnheim, *Film as Art*, University of California Press, 1967.
7. Articles published in *Les Temps modernes*, 1955–1960.
8. translator's note: in English translations of semiological texts there is considerable divergence as to how to render *signifiant* and *signifié*. Elisabeth Palmer refers to *significans* and *significatum* in her translation of André Martinet's *Elements of General Linguistics*; Michael Taylor gives *signifier* and *significate* in his translation of Christian Metz. I have chosen the simpler version of *signifier* and *signified* used by Wade Baskin in his

translation of Ferdinand de Saussure's *Course in General Linguistics* and by Annette Lavers and Colin Smith in their translation of Roland Barthes's *Elements of Semiology*.

9. Ferdinand de Saussure, a moderniser in the study of linguistics at the beginning of the century (1857–1913).

10. Though I am opposed to Christian Metz' semiology when it delves into linguistics looking for a priori forms and structures, I still hold his work in the highest regard. The more so that it is among his misguided successors that its choking dogmatism is found.

11. Christian Metz, "Propositions méthologiques pour l'analyse du film", in *Essais sur la signification au cinéma*, vol.II, p.98–110.

12. *The Aesthetics and Psychology of the Cinema, op. cit.*, p.373 and p.377.

13. In *Essais sur la signification au cinéma*, vol.1, p.48, c.f. footnote.

14. G. Deledalle, *Théorie et pratique du signe*, Payot, 1979, p.196–197 (a book devoted in essence to Charles Sanders Peirce's work on logic and linguistics). A text published in French in the March 1982 issue of *Jeune Cinéma*.

15. In *Les Cahiers du Cinéma*, no. 352, October 1983. "Interview" with Gilles Deleuze by Pascal Bonitzer and Jean Narboni.

II Signs and signification

1. G. Cohen-Séat, *Essais sur les principes d'une philosophie du cinéma*, Paris, P.U.F. 1945.

2. *The Aesthetics and Psychology of the Cinema, op. cit.*, p.15–16.

3. *Id. ibid.*

4. *The Aesthetics and Psychology of the Cinema, op. cit.*, p.54.

5. Adam Schaff, "Sur la rigueur de l'expression", in *Diogène*, July 1961.

6. n.b. Since all concrete objects imbued with meaning not their own serve as symbols, it follows that signs and symbols – with reference to film – are one and the same thing. It is in this sense – apart from specific exceptions – that the term symbol is used in this book, rather than as the expression of an a priori symbolism from some spurious aesthetic system.

III   The direct sign or the "neutral image"

1. Roger Munier, "L'Image fascinante", in *Contre l'image*, Nrf, 1961.
2. André Bazin, "The Ontology of the photographic image", in *What is Cinema?*, translated by Hugh Gray, University of California Press, 1967, p.13.
3. André Bazin, "The Ontology of the photographic image", in *What is Cinema?*, translated by Hugh Gray, University of California Press, 1967, p.15.

IV   The image and perceived reality

1. This crucial question was posed quite recently at a conference in Washington in September 1984 devoted to the relationship between mind and science, involving physicists, biologists, psychologists and philosophers of all nationalities, chaired by the French physicist Jacques Charron.
2. Pierre Janet, *Traité élémentaire de philosophie*, 1920–31.
3. George Berkeley, *Siris, or a treatise on the virtues of tar-water*, 1744.
4. Edmund Husserl, *Ideas: general introduction to pure phenomenology*, translated by W.R. Boyce Gibson, 1969.
5. Henri Bergson, *Matière et Mémoire*, 1896.
6. Bertrand Russell, *Our Knowledge of the External World*, reprinted by Routledge, 1993, p.129.
7. Both professors at Harvard and Nobel Prize winners for medicine in 1981. Cf. *The Journal of Physiology*, no.160, 1962, and A. Dorozinski, "C'est notre cerveau qui voit", in *Science et Vie*, April 1985.
8. René Zazzo, in *Revue de Filmologie*, no.5, P.U.F., 1948.
9. Phi effect: for instance, when two electric lights ten centimetres apart are lit alternatively, we perceive first one then the other, but when this alternation becomes very quick (over a threshold beyond which there is a kind of short circuit in our cerebral reactions), we stop perceiving two successive points and perceive instead a luminous line which links them according to a continuous to-ing and fro-ing.
10. 25 images instead of 24 for technical reasons, the twenty fifth

of a second corresponding to a single phase in alternating current.

11. D. Michotte Van den Berk, "Le caractère de réalité des projections cinématographiques", in *Revue de Filmologie*, nos.3 and 4., 1948.

12. Marcelin Pleynet, in *Cinéthique*, no.9.

13. J.-L. Comolli and J. Narboni, "Cinéma, idéologie, critique", in *Les Cahiers du cinéma*, nos. 229–32.

14. J.-P. Lebel, *Cinéma et Idéologie*, Éd. sociales, 1971.

15. In *Cinématographe*, no.82.

16. "Just an image", i.e. nothing more than an image. Yet this same image – in respect of what it shows – can only be either just or false. It is better that it should be just. In which case the cinema which "is not a just image" ends up being just a just image... a wonderful tautology! [translator's note: the French pun on the word *juste* does not have an exact equivalent in English, since the adjective *juste* is intended in the sense of *right* or *suitable*. This meaning should be borne in mind during the rest of this chapter].

17. Clément Rosset, *L'Objet singulier*, Éd. de Minuit, 1983.

18. Jacques Petat, in *Cinéma 82*.

V   The shot

1. Pascal Bonitzer, "Voici", in *Les Cahiers du cinéma*, no.273, January 1977. Reprinted in *Le Champ aveugle*, Gallimard, 1982.

2. In *The Aesthetics and Psychology of the Cinema*, *op. cit.*, p.59.

3. *Id., ibid.*

4. Pascal Bonitzer, *op.cit.*

5. Pascal Bonitzer, *op.cit.*

6. Pascal Bonitzer, *op.cit.*

7. Historical data borrowed from Jean Mitry, *op. cit.*, pps. 89–95.

8. For André Malraux, *op. cit.*, the same passage. For Albert Laffay, *Logique du Cinéma*, Paris, 1964, p.11.

9. *Loc. cit.*

10. *Loc. cit.*

11. Christian Metz, "Montage et discours", in *Essais sur la signification au cinéma*, Vol.1, pps. 90–96 (not included in Michael Taylor's selection).

12. Pascal Bonitzer, *Le regard et la voix*, Éd. 10/18, 1976.
13. In several prints, the aircraft is actually seen going down in flames, the French distributor thinking it relevant to insert a piece of actual war footage, which obviously totally destroys the intended effect.
14. Noël Burch, *Praxis du cinéma*, Éd. Gallimard, 1969.
15. Frank Woods, *New York Dramatic Mirror*, 10 July 1909.
16. Marc Vernet, "Le regard à la camera: figures de l'absence", in *Iris*, Vol.2, no.2, Analeph, 1984.
17. "Camera, perspective, profondeur de champ", in *Les Cahiers du cinéma*, nos. 230–234, 1972.
18. To forestall any argument, I should point out that it was created in part by Von Stroheim in *Greed*, his cameraman William Daniels using a 25mm lens stopped wide open. However, orthochromatic film-stock made it possible to light very brightly using arc-lamps, and the optical distortion inherent in short focal-length lenses did not exist. William Wyler did the same in 1942 in *Little Foxes*.
19. Henri Fescourt, *La Foi et les montagnes*, Éd. Paul-Montel, 1959.

VI   Iconic significations

1. Cf. Albert Laffay, *Logique du cinéma*, Éd. Masson, 1950; Barthélemy Amengual, "Le je, le moi, le il au cinema", in *Image et son*, 1950; Mitry, *The Aesthetics and Psychology of the Cinema*, *op. cit.*, p.210.

VII   Indical significations

1. Michel Colin, 'Coréferences dans *The Adventures of Dolly*', in *Griffith*, Éd. L'Harmattan, 1984.

VIII   The inferences of montage

1. These experiments have remained celebrated in the annals of the cinema. Taking from one of Bauer's old films a close-up of Ivan Mozhukhin, looking vague and deliberately without expression, Kuleshov made three prints of it. He spliced onto

the first a shot showing a plate of soup standing on the corner of a table; onto the second a shot of a male corpse lying face down; onto the third a shot of a naked woman lying on a sofa in a provocative and lascivious pose. Then putting the three "object-subject" segments together, he projected them to an unsuspecting audience. Everyone unanimously applauded Mozhukhin's talent in being able to "express wonderfully the successive feelings of hunger, grief and lust".

Because Mozhukhin was expressing nothing, it was therefore proved that the audience was "seeing" something that did not really exist. In other words, by linking together their successive perceptions and relating each detail to an organic "whole", they constructed logically the necessary relationships and attributed to Mozhukhin the expression of what he normally might have expressed. They endowed the actor with the responsibility or equivalence of their own feelings.

2. S.M. Eisenstein, *Film Form*, translated by Jan Leyda, Dennis Dobson, 1961, p.37.
3. S.M. Eisenstein, *Film Form*, translated by Jan Leyda, Dennis Dobson, 1963, p.62.
4. As might be deduced, we are referring to discursive, and not iconic, connotations, as described above, p.91–93.
5. S.M. Eisenstein, "Montage 38", in *Reflexions d'un cinéaste* [*Thoughts of a Film-maker*], p.69. Éd. Étrangères, Moscow, 1958.

IX   Concerning syntagmatics

1. A. Martinet, "Le mot", in *Diogène*, no.51, 1965.
2. Cf. Christian Metz, *Essais sur la signification au cinéma*, vol.1, p.125–146, Éd. Klincksieck, 1968.
3. Christian Metz, in *Langage et Cinéma*, Éd. Larousse, 1971.
4. Dominique Chateau, "De la théorie à la connaissance", in *Hors Cadre*, no.1, 1983.
5. *Id., ibid.*
6. P.P. Pasolini, "Le cinéma comme langue", in *Études cinématographiques*, nos. 112–114, 1977.
7. A. Martinet, *Linguistique synchronique*, 1965.

X   Codes and codifications

1. Christian Metz, *Langage et Cinéma*, p.155–156, Éd. Larousse, 1971.
2. *Id.*, p.146.
3. Mikel Dufrenne, "Comment peut-on aller au cinéma?", in *Revue d'Esthétique*, special issue about the cinema, 1978.
4. Christian Metz, *op. cit.*, p.20.
5. In *Revue d'Esthétique*, special issue on the cinema, April 1973.
6. In *Muriel*, p.239, Éd. Galilee, 1972.
7. In *Sociologie du cinema*, Éd. Aubier, 1978.
8. Christian Metz, "Problèmes de denotation dans le film de fiction", in *Essais sur la signification au cinéma*, vol.1, Éd. Klincksieck, 1968.
9. *Id., ibid.*

XI   Images and speech

1. Cf. *The Aesthetics and Psychology of the Cinema*, *op. cit.*, p.230.
2. Cf. *Histoire du Cinéma*, vol.III, p.254.
3. Published for the first time in French in *Les Cahiers du cinéma*, nos. 220–221, June 1970.
4. "Langage verbal et éléments non verbaux dans le message filmico-télévisuel", in *Revue d'Esthétique*, nos. 2-3-4, April–December 1973.
5. Reading over Eisenstein's essays (*Film Form* and *The Film Sense*), one can see that, in his view, it is the other way round. Eisenstein calls horizontal montage what we are calling vertical montage. This is because, in the U.S.S.R., editing tables operate on the horizontal rather than the vertical plane: sound and image therefore seem to be (vertically) superimposed with the images running horizontally. In France and the United States (Mauritone and Moviola), they operate vertically (like projectors). We think our description to be more accurate in the sense that it relates to the way we normally think of film travelling – in projection and shooting.
6. In Jean-Jacques Bernard's "theatre of silence", where the playwright expresses himself more through what is not said (but implied through the speeches), the silence derives from silent objects rather than from an absence of dialogue or a pause between words.

7. Indeed, all that is ever said of this area of acting is that the actor is forced to project his voice and amplify his movements 'so they can be seen in the gods'. This is obviously somewhat simplistic.

8. Maurice Merleau-Ponty, "Le cinéma et la nouvelle psychologie", in *Signes; Sens et non-sens*, Éd. Nagel, 1948.

9. Michel Chion, *Le Son au cinéma*.

10. Michel Chion, *op. cit.*

XII   Narrative structures

1. Christian Metz, "Problèmes de la sémiologie", in *Essais*, vol.1.

2. In *The Aesthetics and Psychology of the Cinema, op. cit.*, p. 343.

3. Émile Benveniste, *Problèmes de linguistique générale*, Éd. Gallimard, 1966 and 1974.

4. *id., ibid.*

5. Christian Metz, *Cinéma et Langage*, p.210.

6. Roger Odin, in *Théories du film*, Éd. Albatross, 1980.

7. Dominique Chateau, *Le Cinéma comme langage*, unpublished thesis, Paris, 1980.

8. François Jost, "La narratologie cinématographique", in *CinémAction*, no.20, 1983.

9. Roland Barthes, "Introduction à l'analyse structurale des récits", in *Communications*, no.8, 1966.

10. In *The Aesthetics and Psychology of the cinema, op. cit.*, p. 165.

11. "Le récit saisi par le film", in *Hors Cadre*, no.2, 1984.

12. Gérard Genette, *Figures III*, Éd. du Seuil, 1972; Mieke Bal, *Narratologie*, Éd. Klincksieck, 1977.

13. François Jost, "Ocularisation et focalisation", in *Hors Cadre*, no.2. 1984.

14. André Gardies, "Le Vu et le Su", in *Hors Cadre*, no.2, 1984.

15. Michel Colin, "La dislocation", in *Théorie du film*, Éd. Albatros, 1980.

XIII   Symbols and metaphors

1. In one version of the film, if I'm not mistaken, there is only one circle, the concentric.

2. Cf. *Histoire du cinéma*, Vol.II, p. 448–498, and Vol. III, p. 193–223.

3. Roland Barthes, "Sur le cinéma", in *Les Cahiers du cinéma*, no. 147.
4. Roman Jakobson, "Entretien sur le cinéma", in *Cinéma, Théorie, Lectures*, Éd. Klincksieck, 1978.
5. Christian Metz, "Le dire et le dit au cinéma: vers le déclin du vraisemblable", in *Essais sur la signification au cinéma*, vol.1; cf. Michael Taylor's translation "The Saying and the Said: Toward the Decline of a Plausibility in the Cinema", O.U.P., 1974.

XIV   Rhythm

1. Jean Epstein, *Esprit de cinéma*, Éd. Jeheber, 1955.
2. *Les Cahiers du mois*, special issue on the cinema, 1925.
3. *Idem*.
4. *Idem*.
5. *Idem*.
6. *Idem*.
7. Léopold Survage. Born in Moscow on the 12 August 1879 of Scandinavian parents. Educated in France and therefore counted among French painters.
8. The statement is reproduced in its entirety in my *Aesthetics*. There is also a study in depth of rhythm, of which I am able to provide only a short précis here.
9. Gaston Bachelard, *Dialectique de la durée*, Boivin, 1936.
10. Paul Souriau, *Esthétique du mouvement*, Alcan, 1918.
11. Matila Ghyka, *Essai sur le rythme*, N.R.F., 1938.
12. Ludwig Klages, *Vom Wessem des rythmus*, Niels, 1934.
13. Étienne Souriau, *La Correspondance entre les arts*, Flammarion, 1947.
14. Pius Servien, *Les rythmes comme introduction physique à l'esthétique*, Boivin, 1930.
15. René Waltz, *La Création poétique*, Flammarion, 1949.
16. Henri Fescourt and J.-L. Bouquet, "Sensations ou sentiments?", in *Cinéa-Ciné pour tous*, 1926.
17. Émile Vuillermoz, "La Musique des Images", in *L'Art cinématographqiue*, Alcan, 1927.
18. Léon Moussinac, *Naissance du cinéma*, Povolotzky, 1925.
19. We should disregard for the time being the abstract films of Len Lye, Rischinger and MacLaren which, based upon music,

take their justification from it and pose rather different problems.

XV   *Sense and nonsense*

1. Cf. Rudolf Carnap, *La Science et la Métaphysique devant l'analyse logique du langage*, Éd. Hermann, 1934; *La Syntaxe logique du langage*, Éd. Hermann, 1938.
2. Noam Chomsky, *Syntactic Structures*, Mouton, The Hague, 1965.
3. Reported by the Greek Stoic Diogenes Laertius.
4. Lewis Carroll, *Alice's Adventures in Wonderland*, p.45, The Folio Society, 1961.
5. In *L'Avé Vénus*, Éd. Le Préambule (Montréal), Diffédit, Paris, 1980.
6. In *Le Panier à salade*: "La mie des mots", Éd. Le Préambule (Montréal) Belles Lettres, Paris, 1983 (5 and 6): fragments of poems written between 1927 and 1932 (the surrealist period) with the idea of introducing such syncope into the norms of classical poetry.
7. Jean Paris, "L'agonie du signe", in *Change*, Éd. du Seuil, 1972.
8. S. Freud, *Wit and its relation to the unconscious*, Moffat, Yard and Co., New York, 1916.
9. Gilles Deleuze, *Logique du sens*, Éd. de Minuit, 1969, pps. 42–44; *Jabber*: uncontrollable chattering; *wocky*: offshoot; *toves*: badger-lizards, corkscrews; *borogoves*: bird-mops; etc.
10. *Idem.*
11. Translator's note: Henri Bergson's study *Le Rire* establishes dehumanisation as the essential process at work in the creation of the 'comique' by which the individual's behaviour suddenly and involuntarily becomes mechanical (the example of someone slipping on a banana skin). Bergson's formula for this process is 'le mécanique plaqué sur le vivant' – the mechanical stuck onto the living].
12. We choose not to include the Marx Brothers' comedy whose "nonsense" is systematic but based on words rather than images.
13. Roger Odin, "Sémio pragmatique du cinéma", in *Iris*, vol.2. 1984.
14. Christian Metz, "L'impression de réalité", In *Essais*, Vol.1.

(not included in the compendium of essays translated by Michael Taylor).

15. In *The Aesthetics and Psychology of the Cinema, op. cit.*, p. 83–85; Michel Colin's quotation contained in *CinémAction*, no.24, "Théories du cinema", p.121–127.
16. *Ibid.*, p.83.
17. In *Les Cahiers du cinéma*, no.292.

XVI   Image, language and thought

1. Cf. *infra.*
2. *Ditto.*
3. E. Garroni, "Langage verbal et éléments non verbaux dans le message filmico-télévisuel", in *Revue d'Esthétique*, special issue on the cinema, Klincksieck, 1978.
4. We do not mean the origin of language lost in the mist of time which would presuppose some sort of linguistic anthropology, but the formation of the mind and the development of language from notions previous to language.
5. In *Séminaire de recherche sur le premier développement de l'enfant*, Paris, 1960.
6. *Idem.*
7. *Idem.*
8. A. Piaget, *Épistémologie génétique et recherche psychologique*, P.U.F., 1957.
9. See *infra.*
10. N. Chomsky, *Language and Mind*, Harcourt, Brace and World, New York, 1968.
11. Compare the following literal translation of the quotation given by Mitry which does not appear to equate with Chomsky's original: "The fundamental properties of languages (articulated sounds/speech) do not appear in prelinguistic symbolic systems acting like signs (mental images, sensory events, etc.). What appears in these symbolic structures are mental structures and, subsequently, the language structures which proceed from them."
12. Piaget, *op.cit.*, (author's italics).
13. That is, Gestalt, Empiricism and Behaviourism, mainly represented by Köhler, Koffka, Wertheimer (Gestalt), Carnap, Hempel, Neurath (logic) and Bloomfield (linguistics).

14. Chomsky, *op.cit.*
15. Chomsky, *op. cit.*, p.119–120. Cf. Nelson Goodman, *The Epistemological Argument*, Boston, 1966.

Bibliography

Main books quoted:

AGEL Henri, *L'Espace cinématographique*, Delarge, 1978.
AUMONT Jacques et LEUTRAT Jean-Louis, *Théorie du film*, Éd. Albatros, 1980.
AUMONT Jacques, BERGALA Alain, MARIE Michel and VERNET Marc, *Esthétique du film*, Nathan, 1983.
BAZIN André, *Qu'est-ce que le cinéma?*, 4 Vols., Éd. du Cerf, 1958–1959., English translation of selected essays: *What is Cinema?*, translated by Hugh Gray, University of California Press, Los Angeles, 1967.
BONITZER Pascal, *Le Regard et la voix*, Éd. 10/18, 1976.
BONITZER Pascal, *Le Champ aveugle*, Gallimard, 1982.
BURCH Nöel, *Praxis du cinéma*, Gallimard, 1969; translated under the title *Theory of film practice*, by Helen R. Lane, Secker and Warburg, 1973.
COHEN-SÉAT Gilbert, *Essais sur les principes d'une philosophie du cinéma*, P.U.F., 1948.
DELEUZE Gilles, *L'Image-Mouvement*, Éd. de Minuit, 1983.
DELEUZE Gilles, *L'Image-Temps*, Éd. de Minuit, 1985.
EISENSTEIN Sergei Mikhailovitch, *Film Sense*, translated by Jan Leyda, Dennis Dobson, 1961.
EPSTEIN Jean, *Écrits sur le cinéma (1920–1945)*, 2 Vols., Séghers, 1973.
FAURE Élie, *Fonction du cinéma*, Plon, 1953.
GODARD Jean-Luc, "Introduction à une véritable histoire du cinéma", Éd. *Les Cahiers du cinema*, Gallimard, 1982.
JENN Pierre, *Georges Méliès, cinéaste*, Éd. Albatros, 1984.
LAFFAY Albert, *Logique du cinéma*, Masson, 1964.
LEBEL Jean-Patrick, *Cinéma et Idéologie*, Éd. sociales, 1971.
METZ Christian, *Essais sur la signification au cinéma*, Éd. Klincksieck, Vol.I, 1968; Vol.II, 1972; English translation of selected essays: *Film Language, A Semiotics of the Cinema*, translated by Michael Taylor, O.U.P., New York, 1974.
METZ Christian, *Langage et Cinéma*, Larousse, 1971.
METZ Christian, *Le Signifiant Imaginaire*, d. 10/18, 1974.
MICHOTTE Albert, "Le caractère de réalité des projections cinématographiques", in *Revue de filmologie*, nos. 3 and 4, P.U.F., 1948.

MICHOTTE Albert, *Revue d'Esthétique*, special issue on the cinema, Éd. Klincksieck, 1978.

MORIN Edgar, *Le Cinéma ou l'homme imaginaire*, Éd. de Minuit, 1956.

MUNIER Roger, *Contre l'image*, Gallimard, 1961.

PASOLINI Pier Paolo, "Le cinéma comme langue", in *Études cinémato-graphiques*, no. 112.

ROSSET Clement, *L'Objet singulier*, Éd. de Minuit, 1983.

SORLIN Pierre, *Sociologie du cinéma*, Aubier, 1978.

CinémAction, no. 20, "Théories du cinéma", a collection edited by Jöel Magny, L'Harmattan, 1982.

Communications, no. 23, "Psychanalyse et cinéma".

Le Cinéma americain – Analyses de films, 2 vol. collection, Flammarion, 1980.

Revue d'esthétique, issue about the cinema, Éd. S.P.D.G. 1967.

Reference Works

BACHELARD Gaston, *Dialectique de la durée*, Boivin, 1936.

BENVENISTE Émile, *Problèmes de linguistique générale*, Gallimard, Vol.I. 1966 Vol.II, 1974.

CARNAP Rudolf, *Philosophy and Logical Syntax*, AMS Press, New York, 1979.

CHOMSKY Noam, *Syntactic Structures*, Mouton, The Hague, 1965.

DELEDALLE Georges, *Théorie et pratique du signe*, Payot, 1979.

DELEUZE Gilles, *Logique du sens*, Éd. de Minuit, 1969.

GHYKA Matila, *Essai sur le rythme*, Gallimard, 1938.

GREIMAS A.-J., *Sémantique structurale*, Larousse, 1966.

MARTINET André, *Linguistique synchronique*, A. Colin, 1975.

MERLEAU-PONTY Maurice, *Signes*, Nagel, 1948.

JAKOBSON Roman, *Essais de linguistique générale*, 2 Vols., Éd. de Minuit, 1963.

PIAGET Jean, *Le Structuralisme*, Collection "Que sais-je?", P.U.F., 1980.

SOURIAU Étienne, *La Correspondance entre les arts*, Flammarion, 1947.

WALTZ René, *La Création poétique*, Flammarion, 1949.

Index

Martinet (André): 132, 139
Marx (The Brothers): 201
Mary Jane's Mishap: 5
Mauss (Marcel): 170
Mayer (Carl): 152
Méliès (Georges): 2–5, 9, 109, 171
Merleau-Ponty (Maurice): 48, 167
Mesguich (Félix): 2
Metz (Christian): viii, 15–22, 26,
    51, 67, 74–6, 131–150, 170–9,
    206, 242, 247
Meumann (Ernest): 219
Michotte Van den Berk: 50
Midnight Cowboy: 134
Miller (Henry): 239
Modern Times: 197
Monsieur Verdoux: 106
Montgomery (Robert): 98
Mother: 198
Moussinac (Léon): 208, 218
Mozhukhin (Ivan): 111
Munier (Roger): 32
Munsterberg (Hugo): 12
Muriel: 145
Murnau (Friedrich Wilhelm): 72

Nana: 80
Narboni (Jean): 52
Neurath (von): 270
New Year's Eve: 152, 187
Nibelungen (The): 152, 190
Noguez (Dominique): 143, 182
Nosferatu: 152
Nuit américaine (La): 85

October: 118, 176, 186
Odin (Roger): 20, 176, 242
Olivier (Laurence): 161
One a.m.: 231
Opium dreams: 143
Our Town: 178

Pabst (Georg Wilhelm): 144

Païsa: 198
Panofsky (Erwin): 52
Phantom Carriage (The): 144
Point Counter Point: 204
Postman always rings twice (The):
    241
Prisoner of Shark Island (The): 80
Public Opinion: 80
Parents terribles (Les): 161
Paris (Jean): 227
Pasolini (Pier Paolo): 20, 136
Passion of Joan of Arc (The): 68–72
Pawnshop (The): 234
Peirce (Charles Sanders): 102, 140
Perrot (Victor): 24
Petat (Jacques): 56
Piaget (Jean): 229, 251–4
Picabia (Francis): 210
Pick (Lupu): 187
Pierrot le fou: 134
Pingaud (Bernard): 164
Pleynet (Marcelin): 51–4
Police: 236
Porte (Pierre): 98
Porter (Edwin): 5, 74, 171
Promio (Alexander): 2, 72
Proudhon: 200
Providence: 205
Public Opinion: 80
Pudovkin (Vsevolod): 12, 106, 112

Queneau (Raymond): 163

Rail (Le): 152
Ramain (Paul): 98
Ray (Man): 210
Renoir (Jean): 80
Resnais (Alain): 168
Richter (Hans): 210
Rideau cramoisi (Le): 166
Rigadin: 84
River of No Return: 241
Robbe-Grillet (Alain): 137